HELMUT NEWTON
ALICE SPRINGS

us and them

TASCHEN

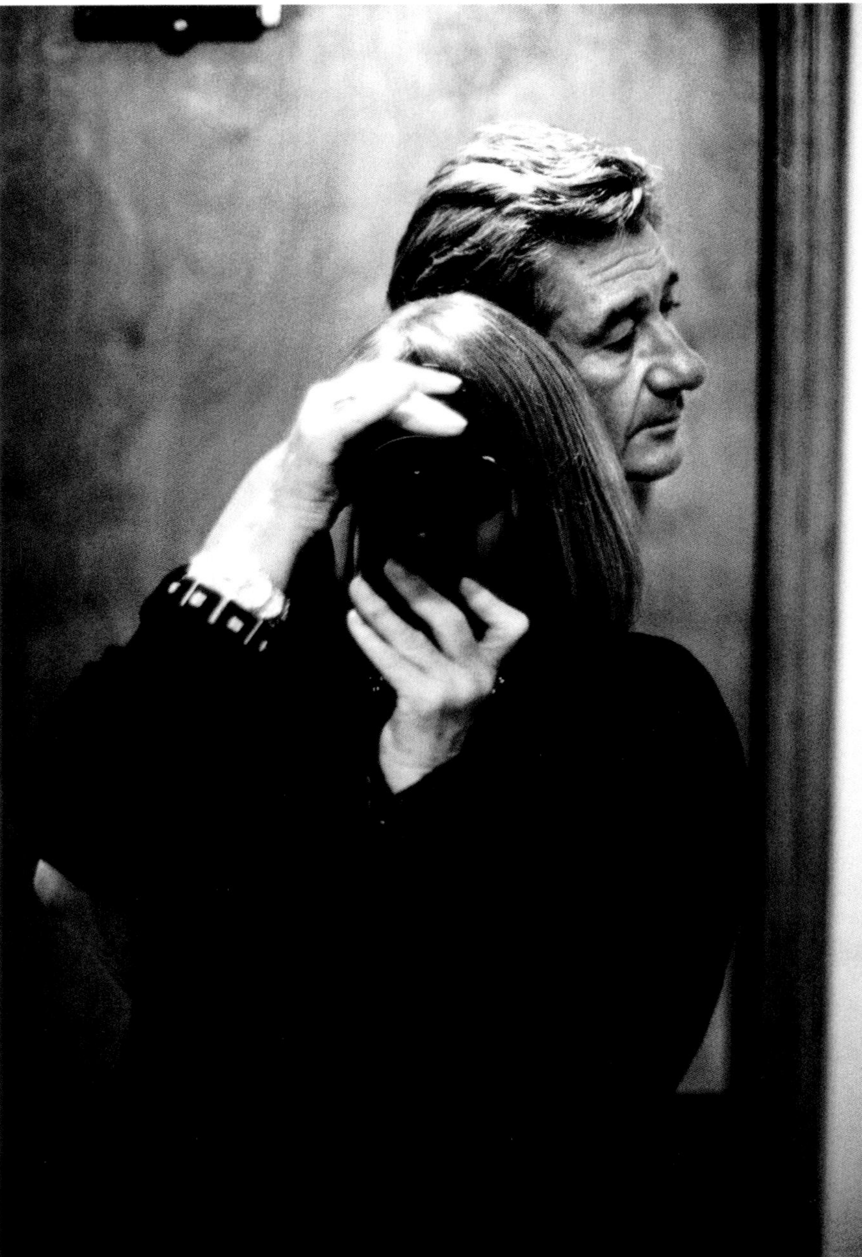

CONTENTS

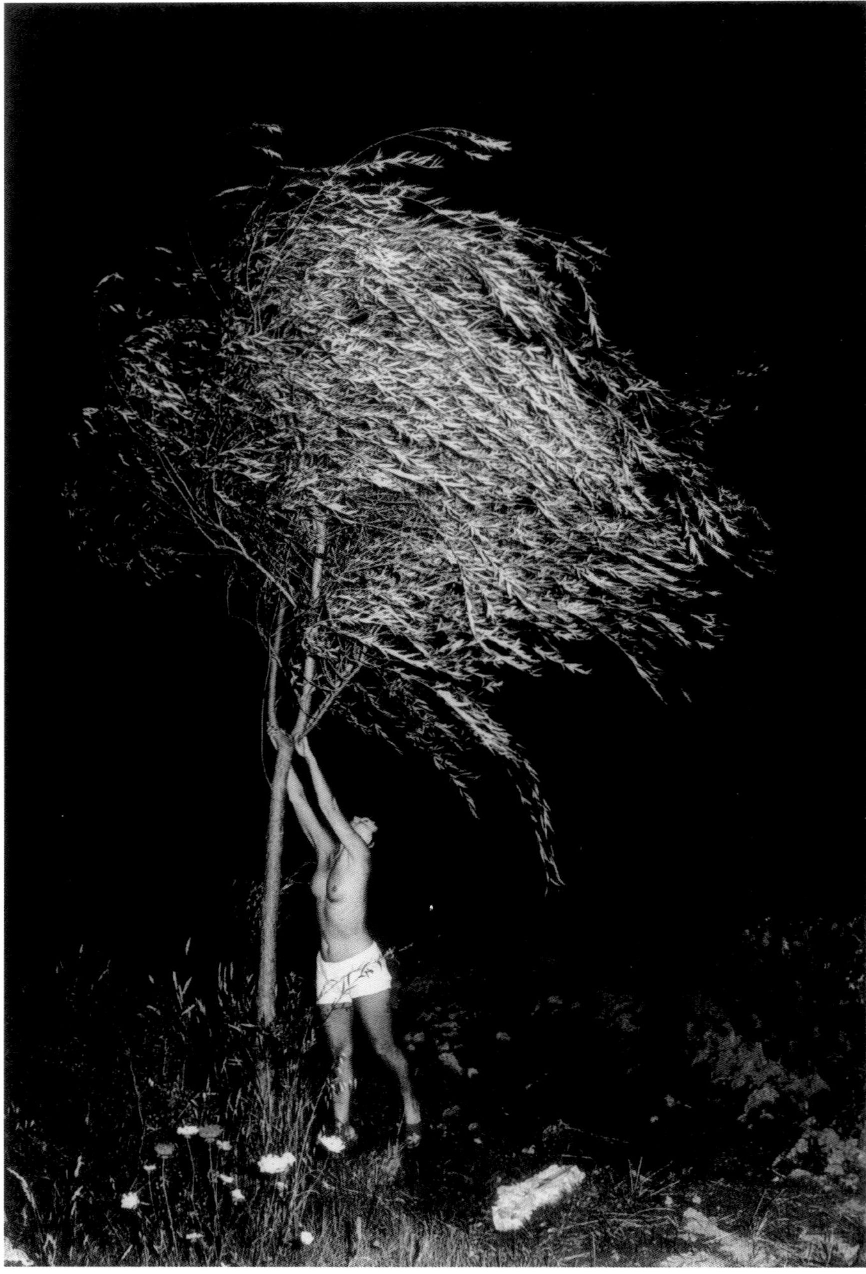

INTRODUCTION

This book shows the work of two photographers: one who has dedicated his whole life to photography, the other who has been an actress and a painter before she has taken up the camera seriously if somewhat sporadically. These two people have lived together for fifty years, and have collaborated closely on exhibitions and book publishing but neither is usually present at the other's photographic sittings. What to me is the interesting aspect of this book is the fact that neither one has in any way influenced the other's way of approaching their subjects. I can see the truth and simplicity in the portraits of Alice Springs. As for myself, I recognise the manipulation and editorialising in my photographs.

Dieses Buch zeigt die Arbeiten eines Fotografen-Paars: Er hat sein ganzes Leben der Fotografie verschrieben, sie war Schauspielerin und Malerin, bevor sie sich ernsthaft, wenngleich eher sporadisch, der Fotografie zuwandte. Sie teilen seit 50 Jahren ihr Leben und arbeiten bei Ausstellungen und Buchprojekten eng zusammen, halten sich jedoch normalerweise aus den Fotoproduktionen des anderen vollkommen heraus. Das Interessante an diesem Bildband ist für mich, dass beide in ihrem fotografischen Ansatz vom anderen völlig unbeeinflusst blieben. In den Porträtaufnahmen von Alice Springs sehe ich Klarheit und Authentizität. Bei meinen eigenen Fotografien dagegen erkenne ich natürlich, wo und wie sie gestellt und bearbeitet sind.

Ce livre est consacré au travail de deux photographes: l'un a voué toute sa vie à la photographie, l'autre a été actrice et peintre avant de se passionner pour la photo, de façon sporadique mais sérieuse. Ces deux personnes vivent ensemble depuis cinquante ans, mènent organisation d'expositions et projets éditoriaux en étroite collaboration, mais se tiennent généralement à l'écart des productions photographiques de l'autre. Ce qui m'intéresse dans ce livre, c'est qu'aucun d'eux n'a été influencé par l'autre dans sa démarche photographique. Dans les portraits d'Alice, je vois de la simplicité et de la vérité. Pour ma part, j'assume les manipulations et distorsions éditoriales appliquées à mes photos.

Helmut Newton, 1999

HELMUT NEWTON

BY ALICE SPRINGS

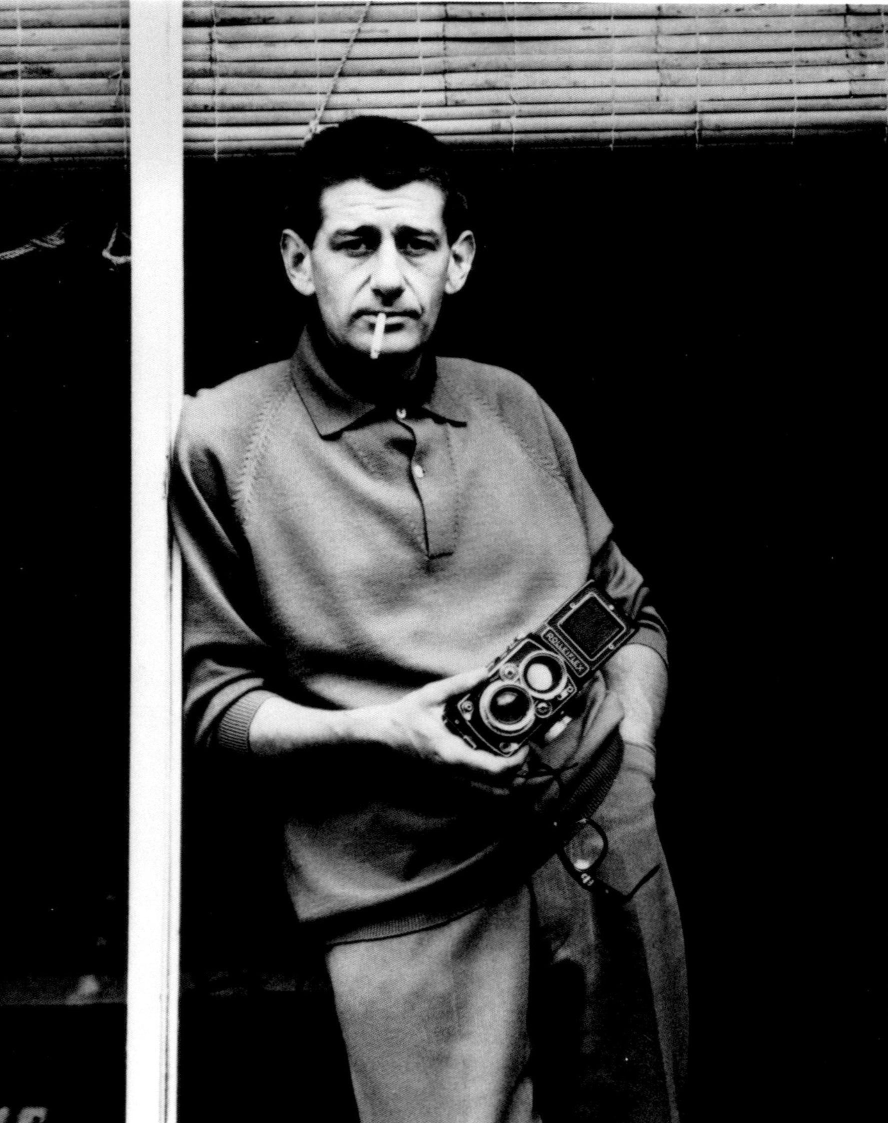

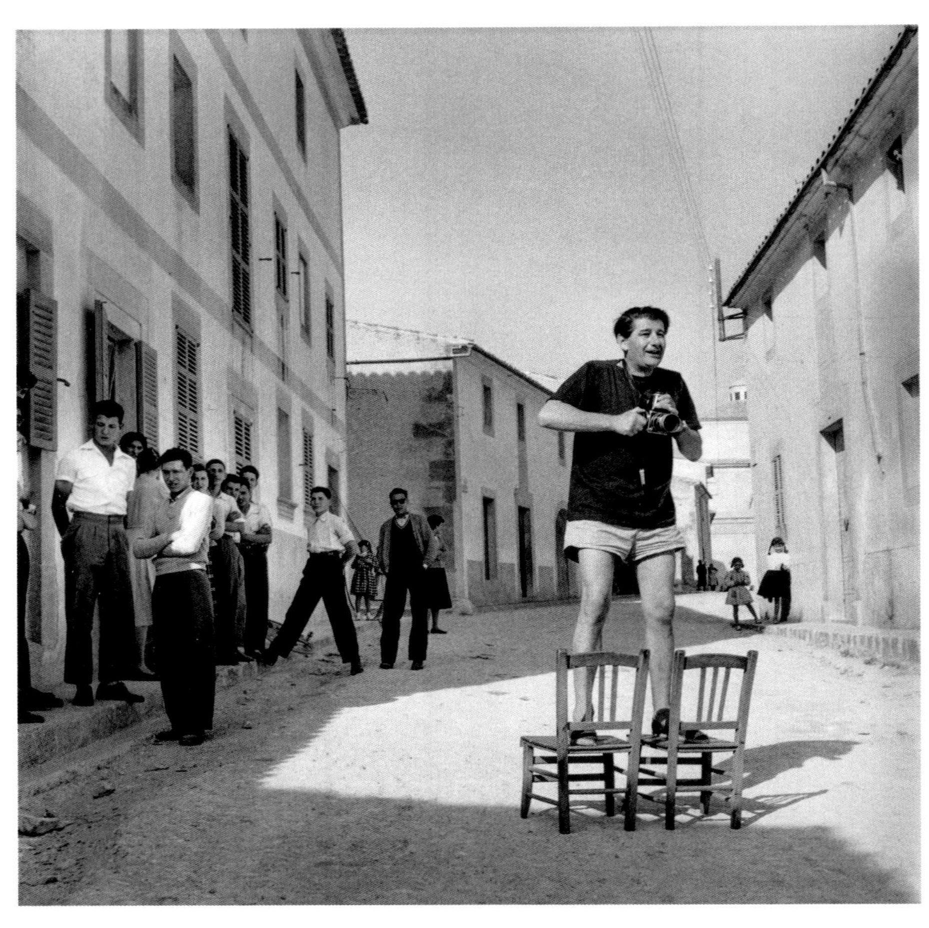

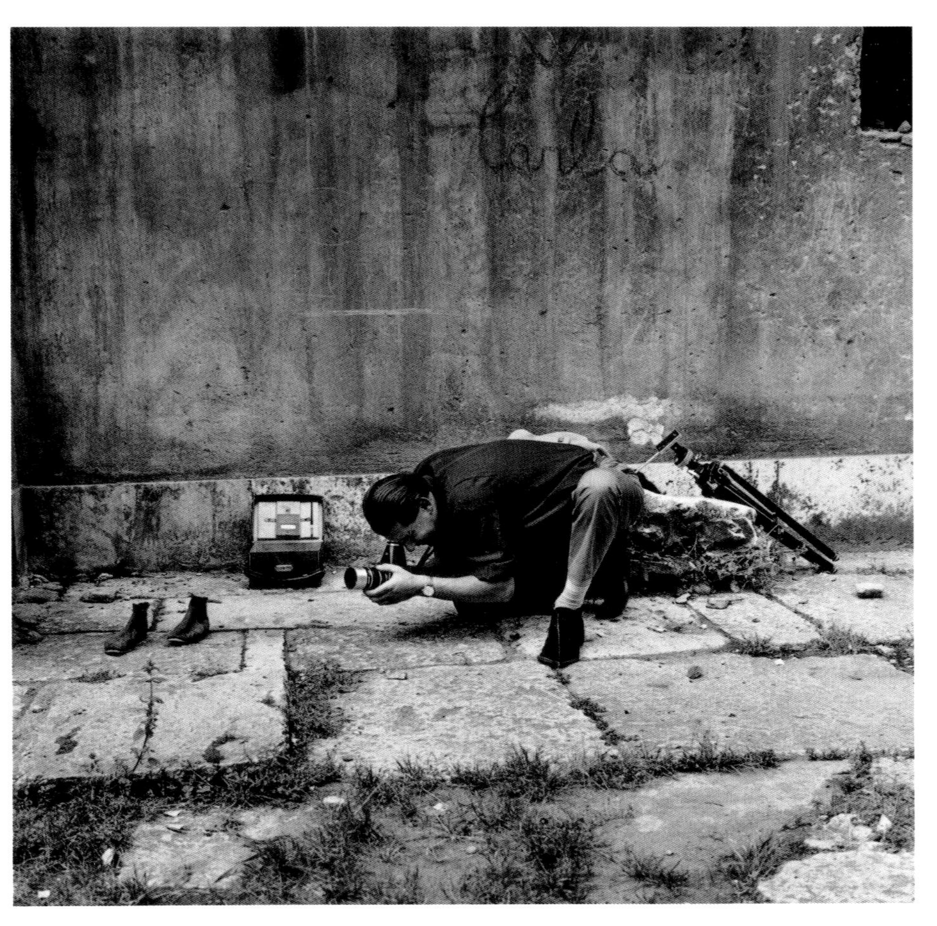

Salzburg, 1956

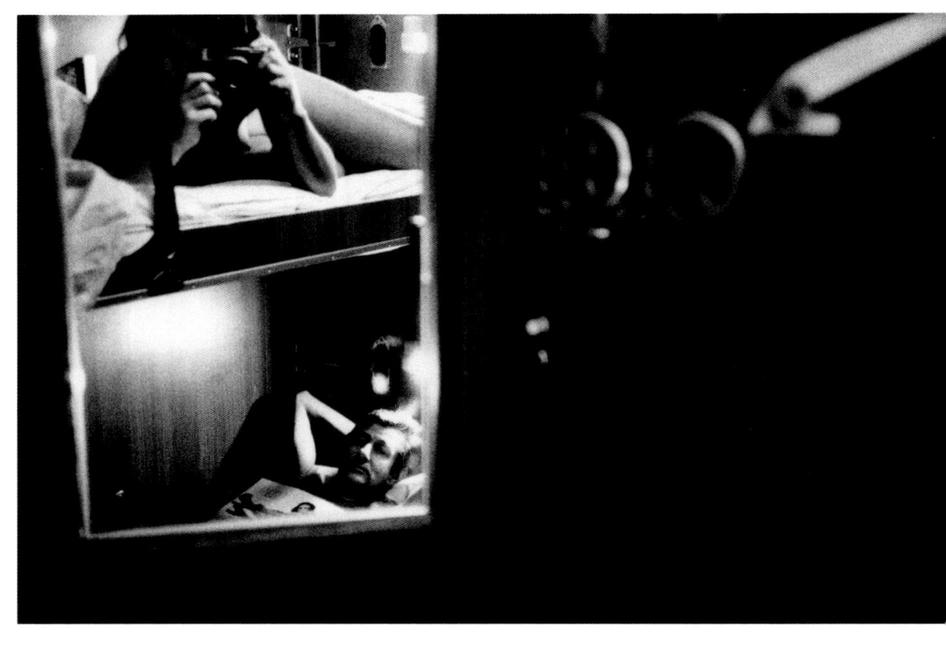

The Golden Arrow from London to Paris, 1957
PAGES 12/13 Rue Aubriot, Paris, 1971   PAGES 14–17 Ramatuelle, 1972

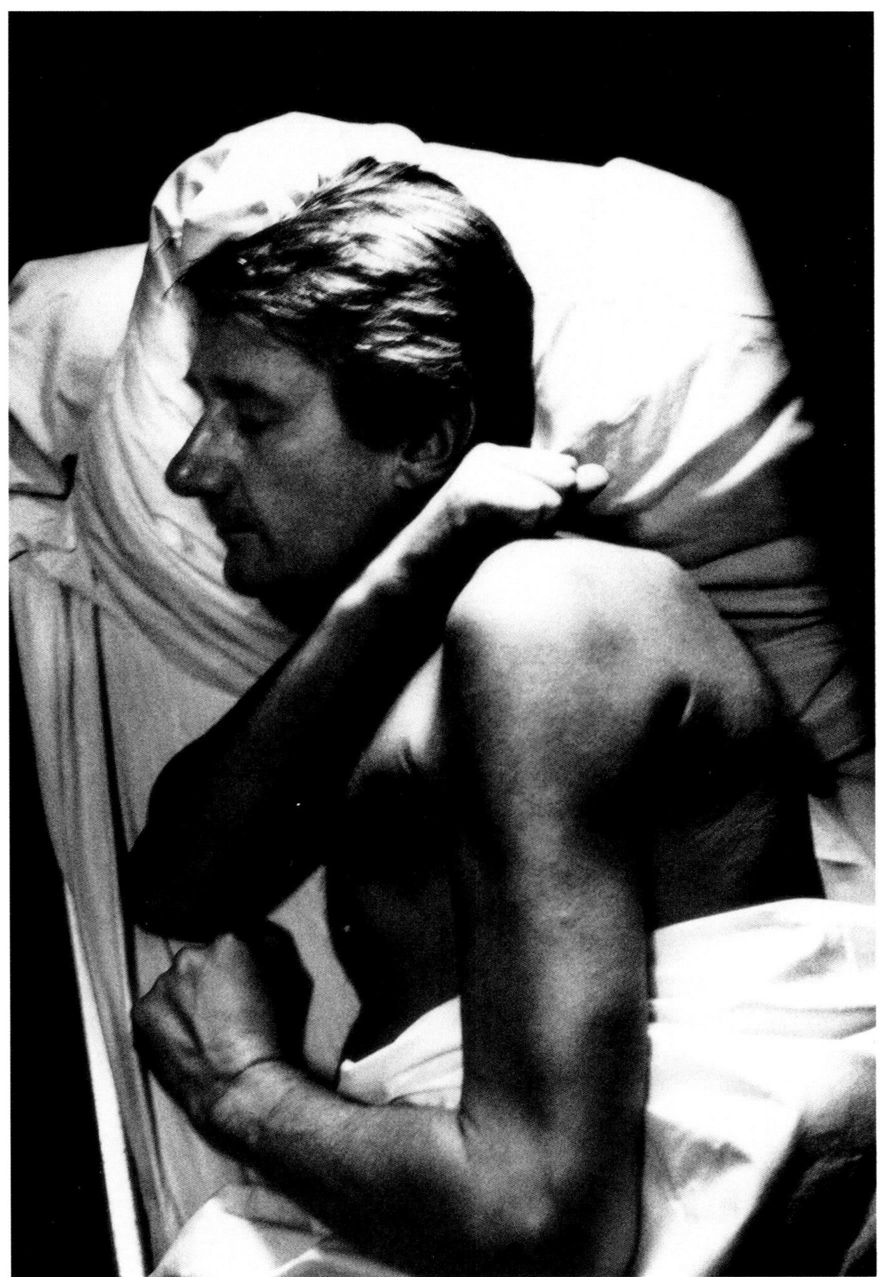

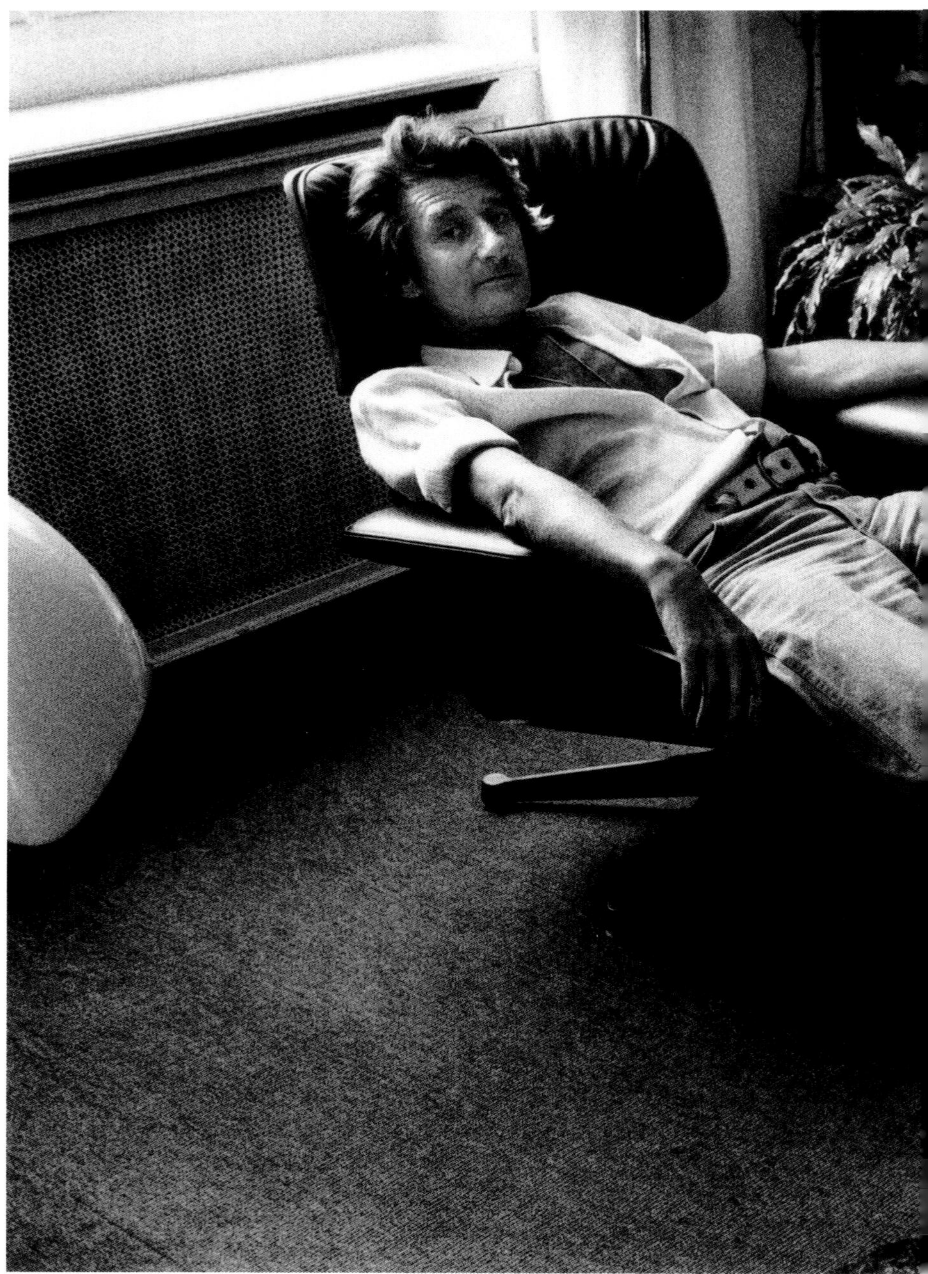

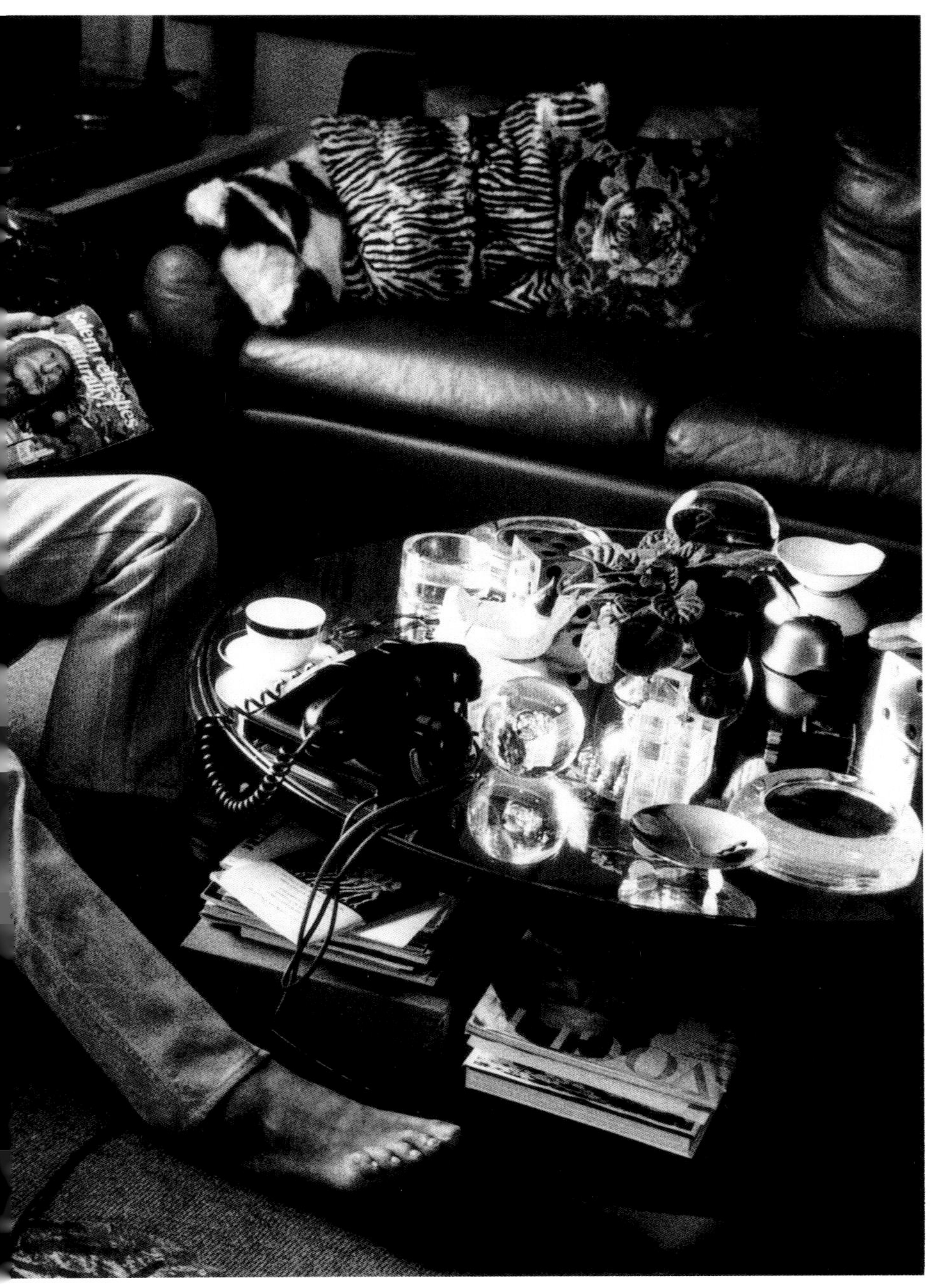

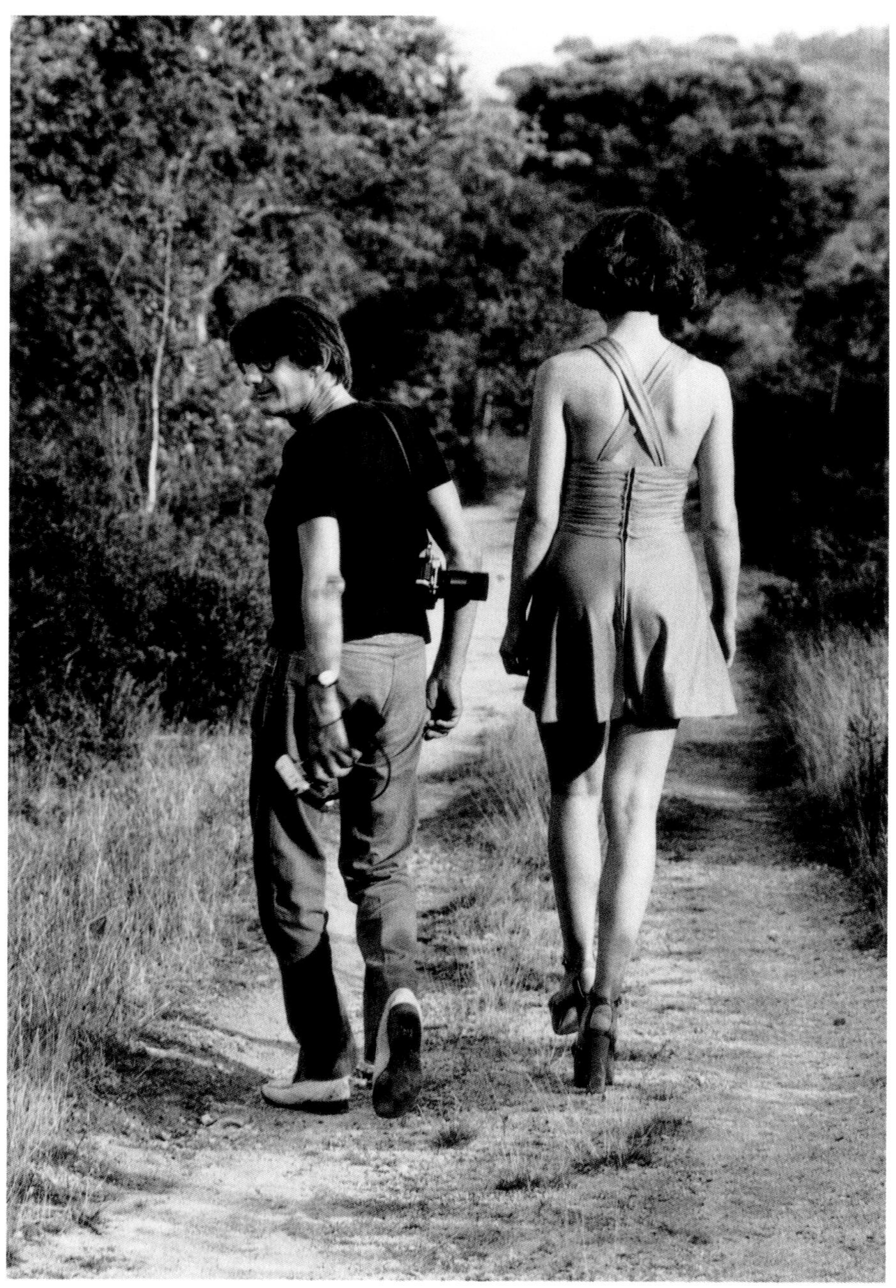

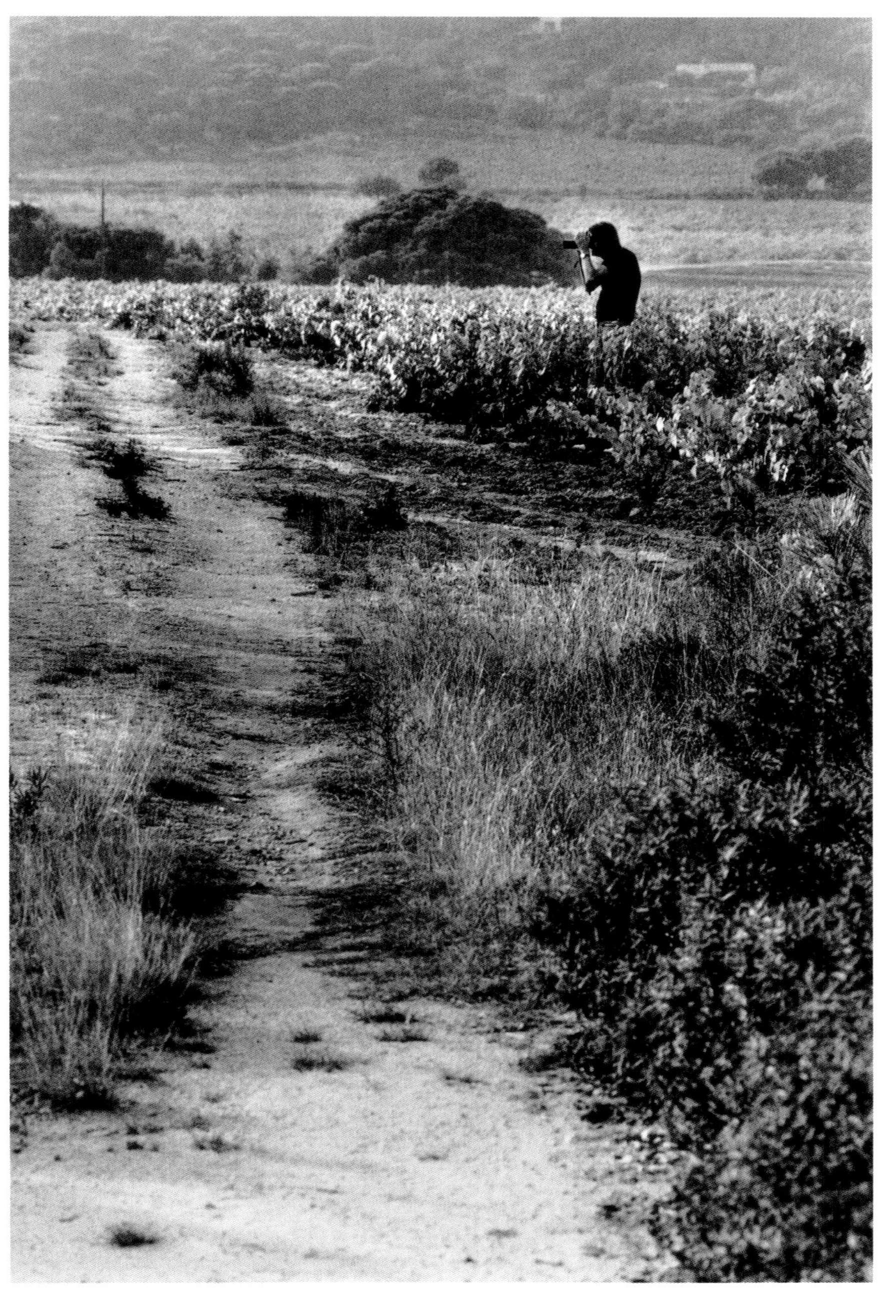

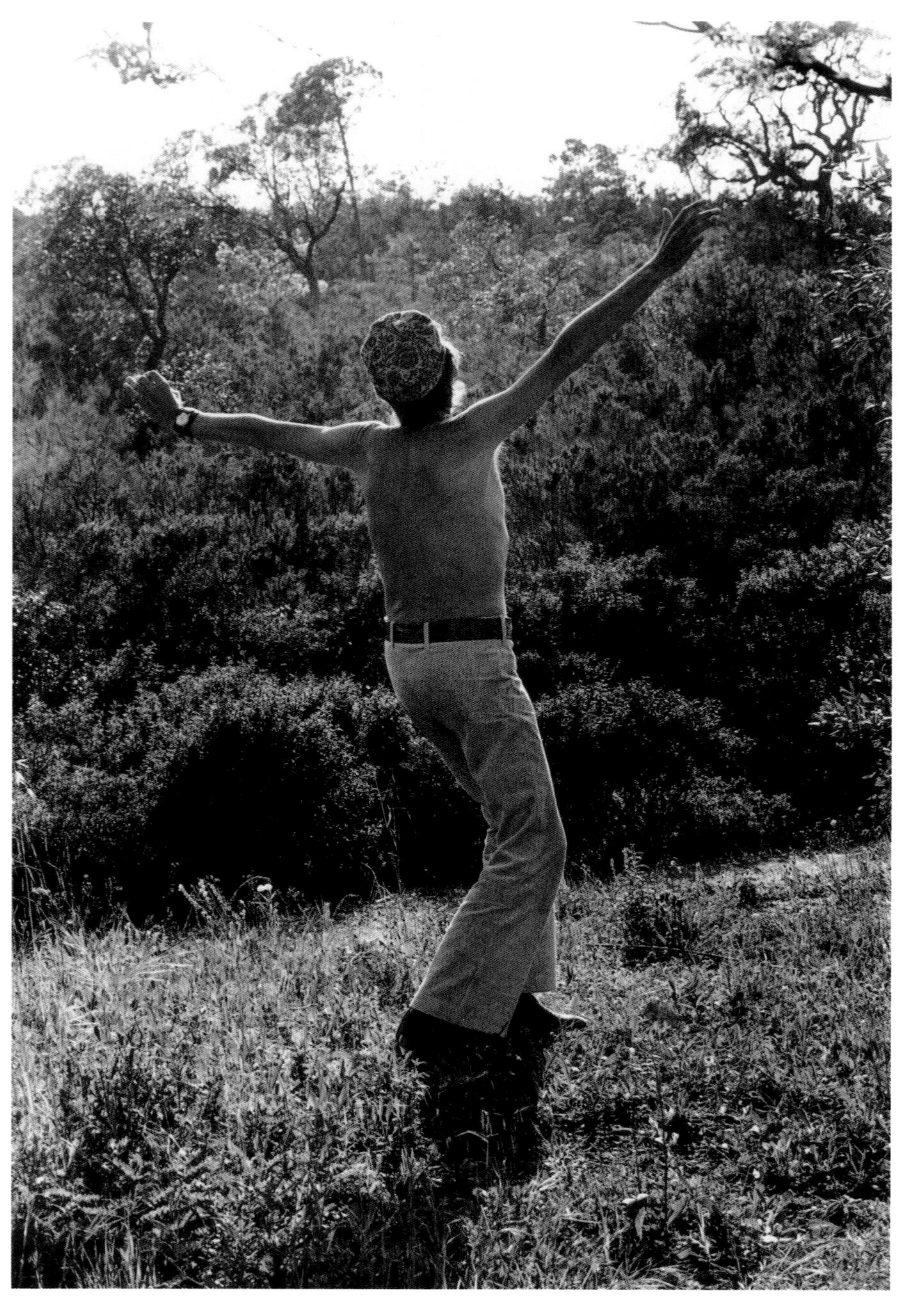

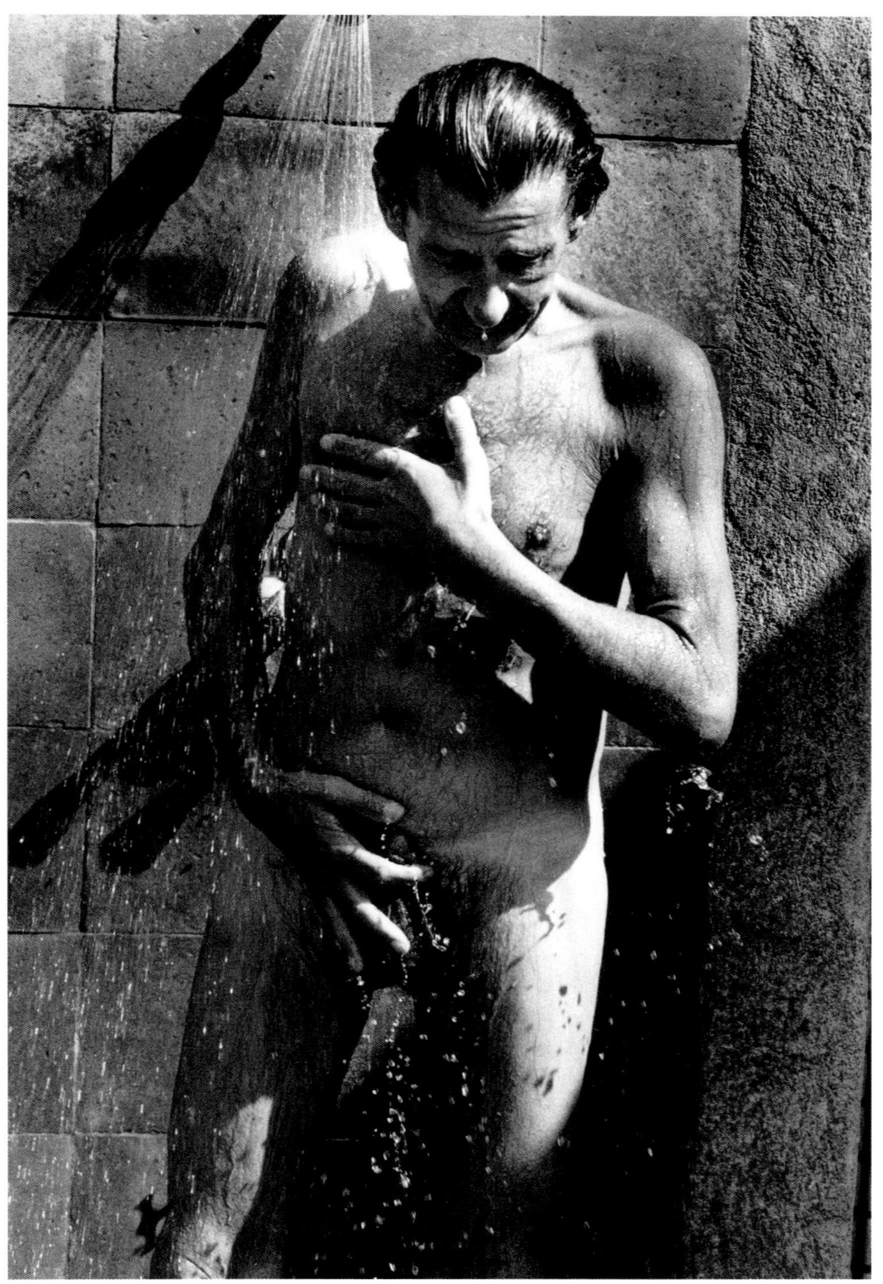

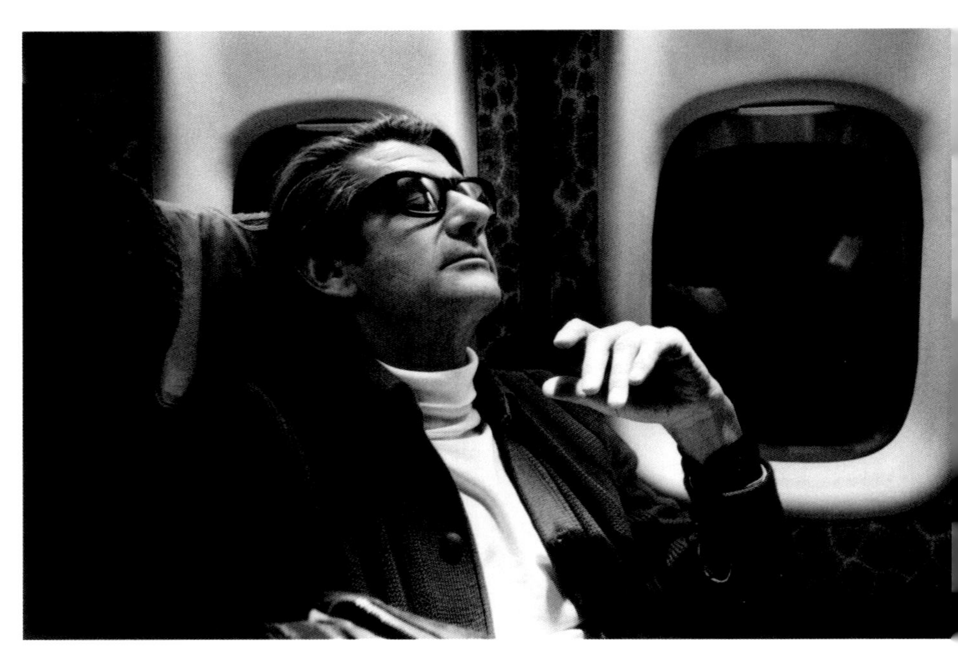

AS: Flying home from New York, 1972

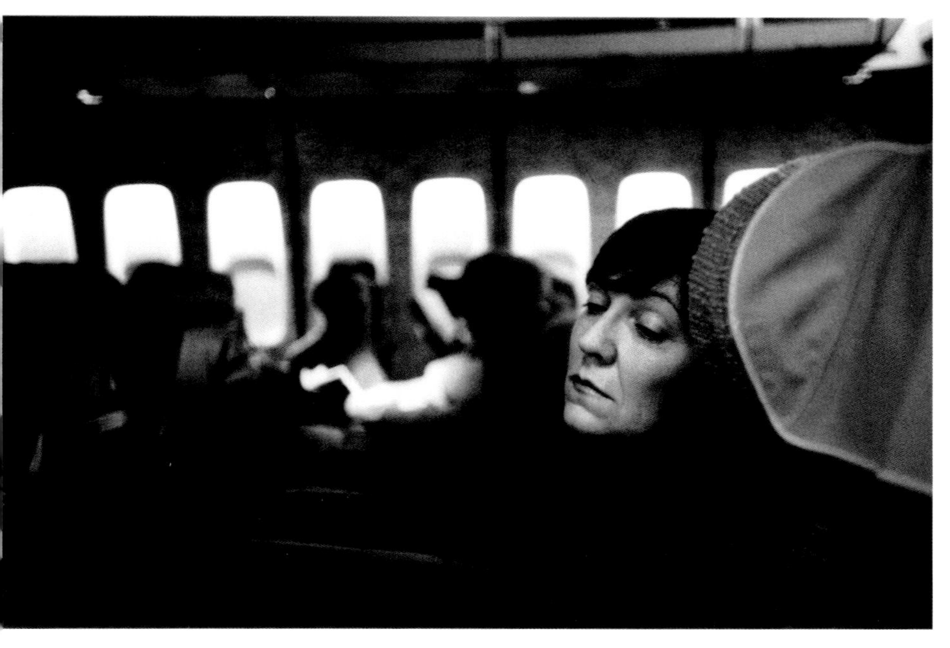

HN: Return to Paris after New York heart attack, 1972
PAGE 20 AS: Nice Airport, 1973   PAGE 21 HN: Nice Airport, 1973

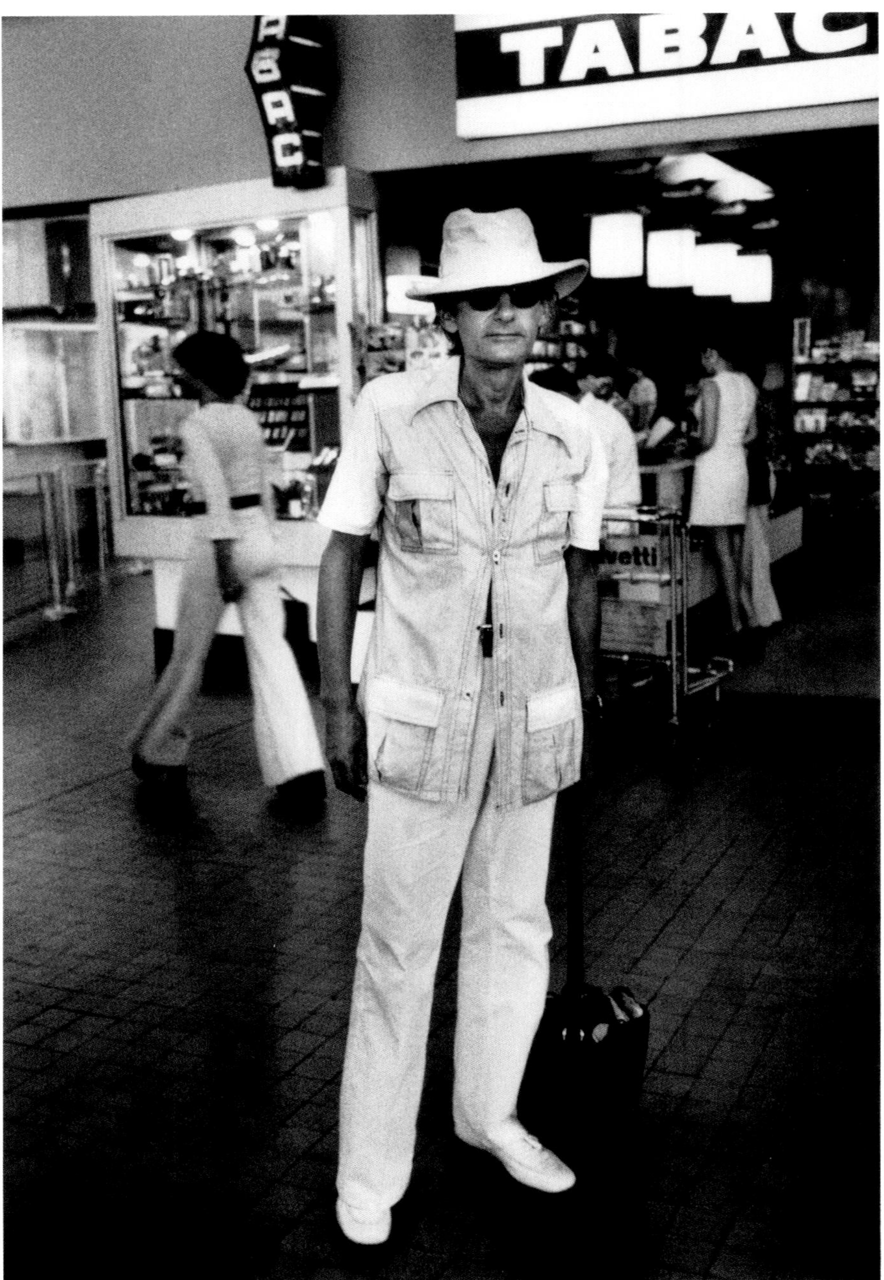

TABAC
TABAC
olivetti

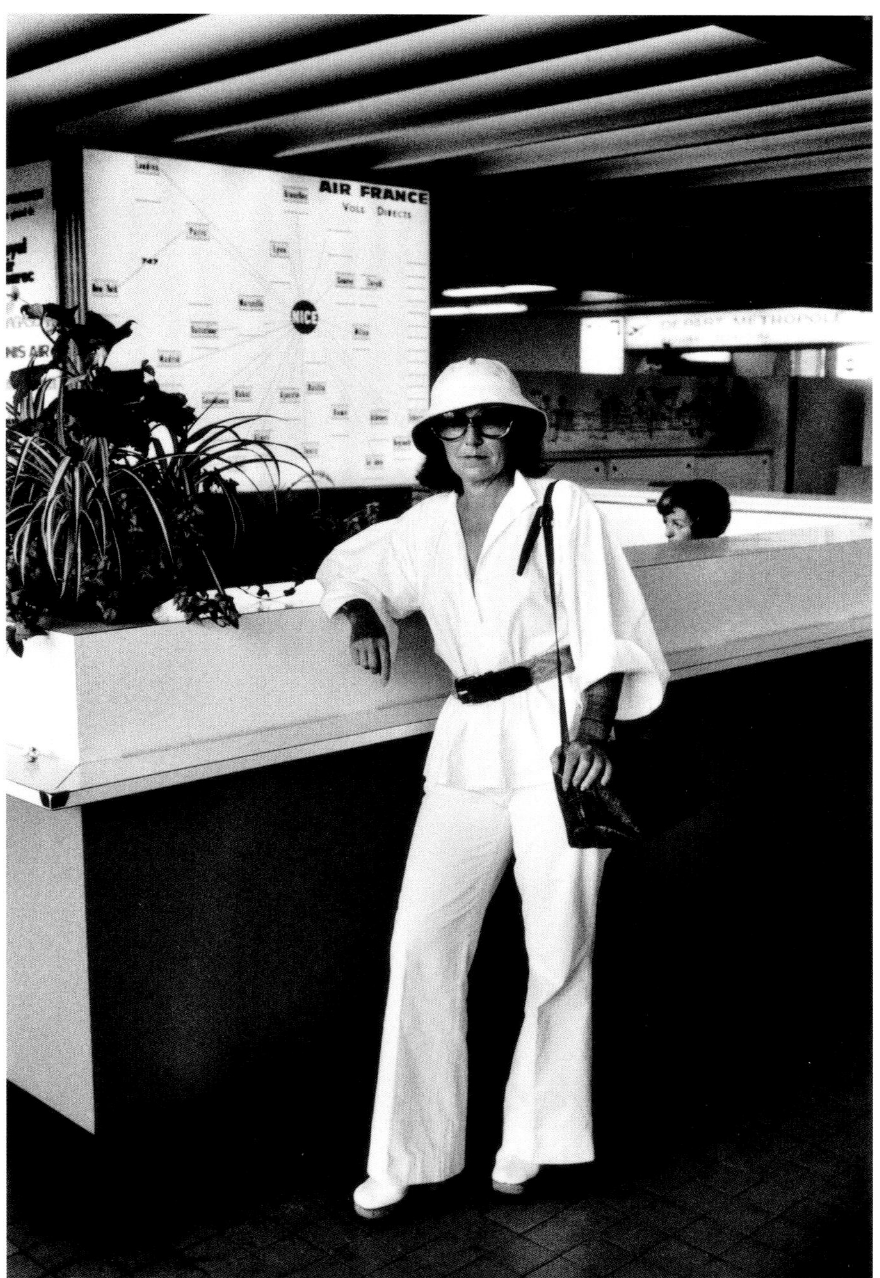

AIR FRANCE
VOLS DIRECTS
NICE

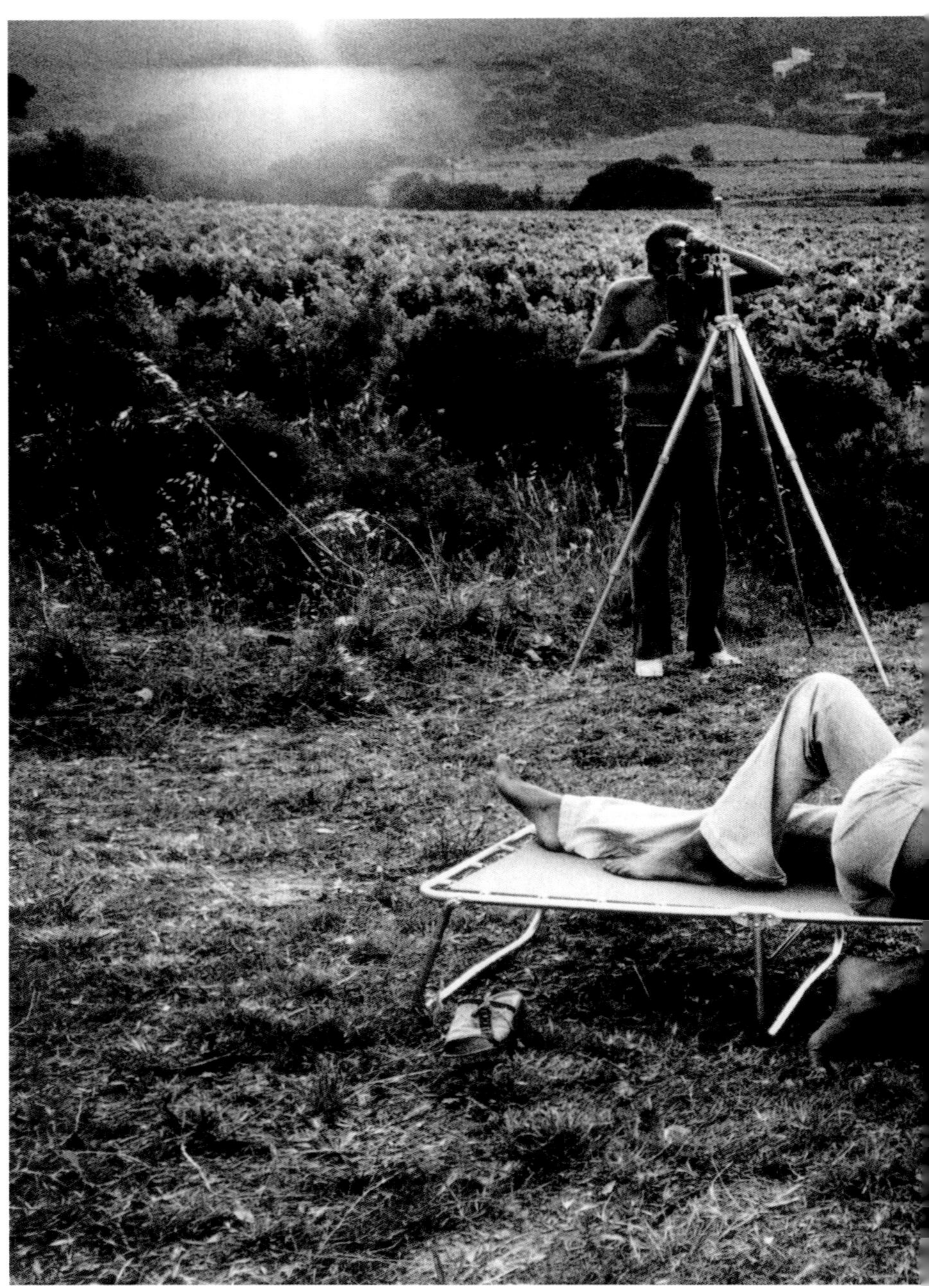

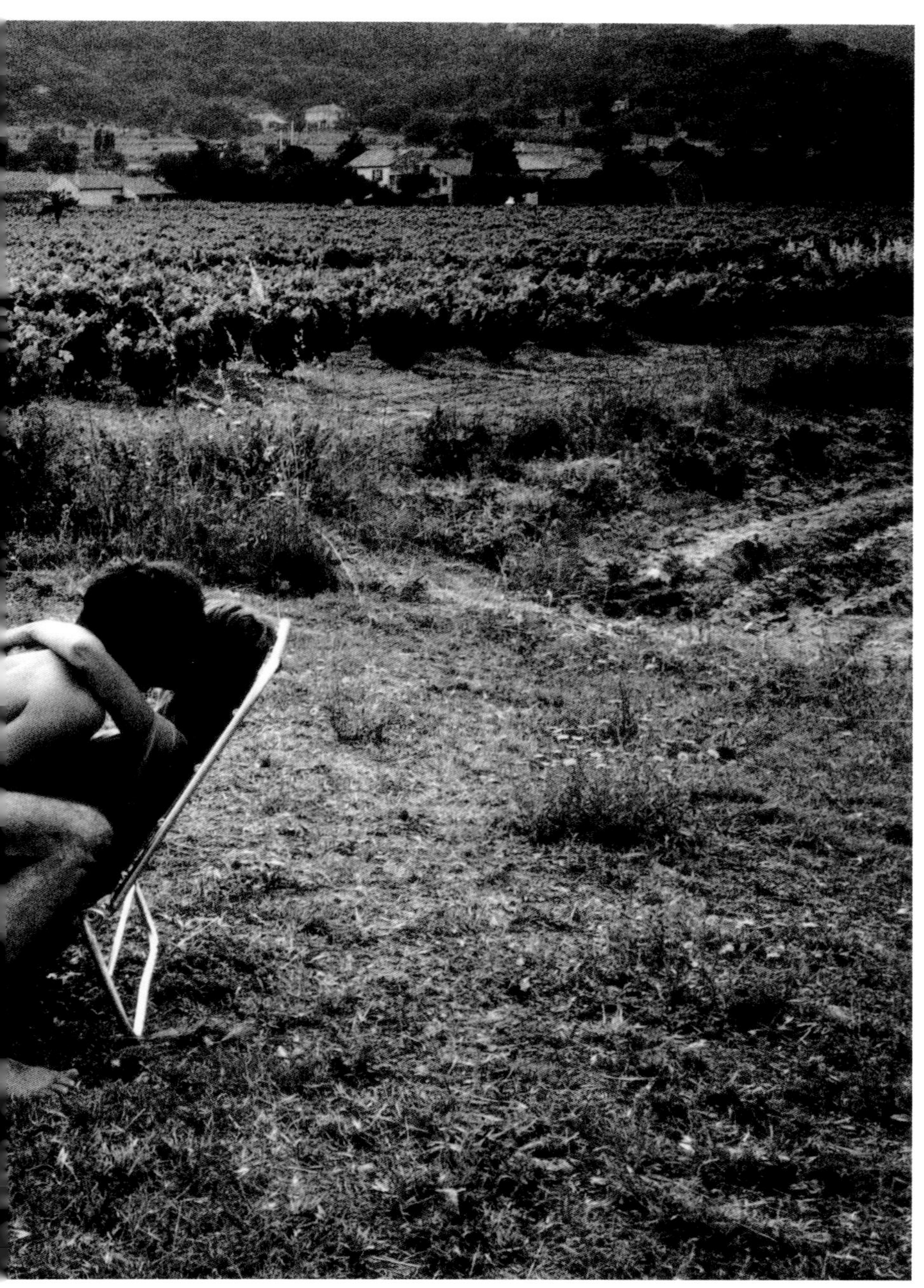

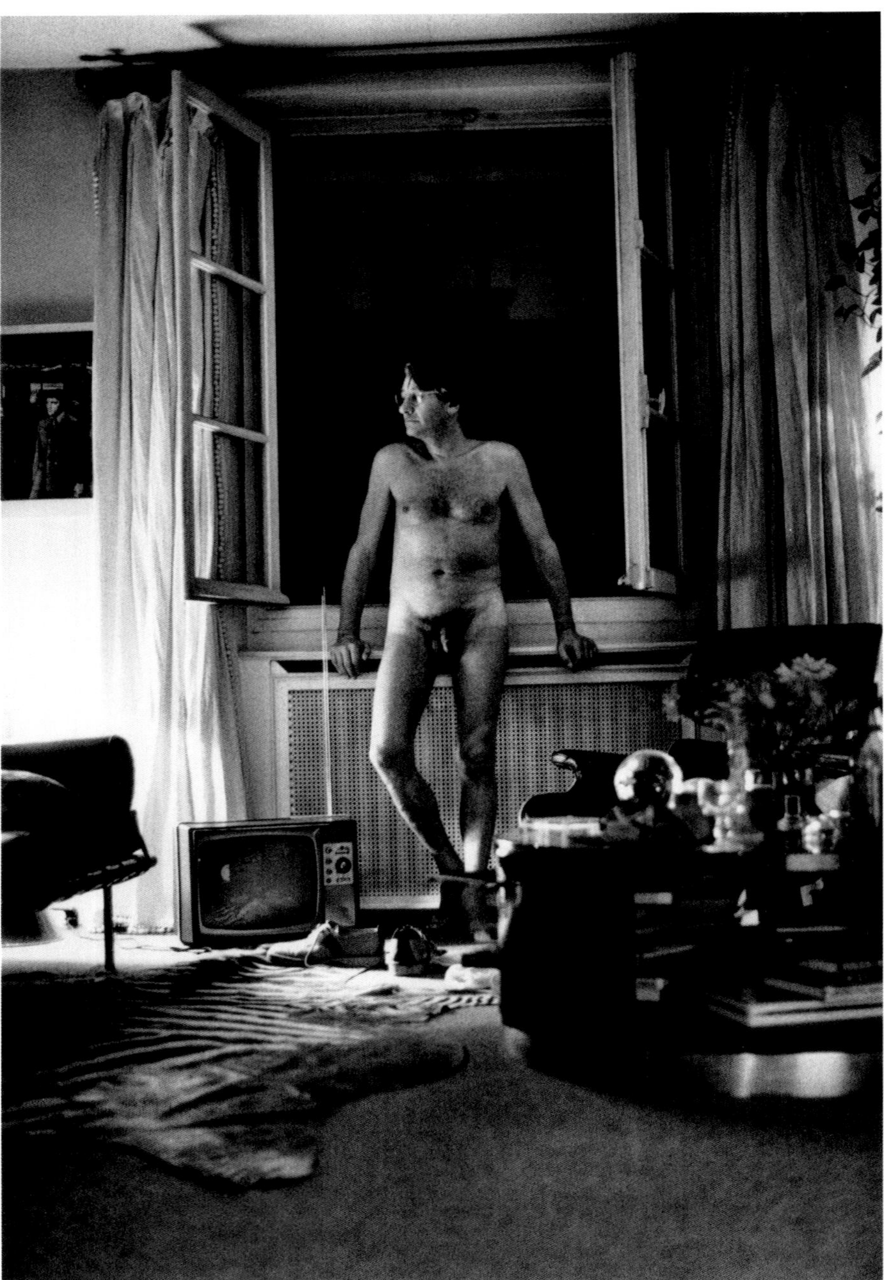

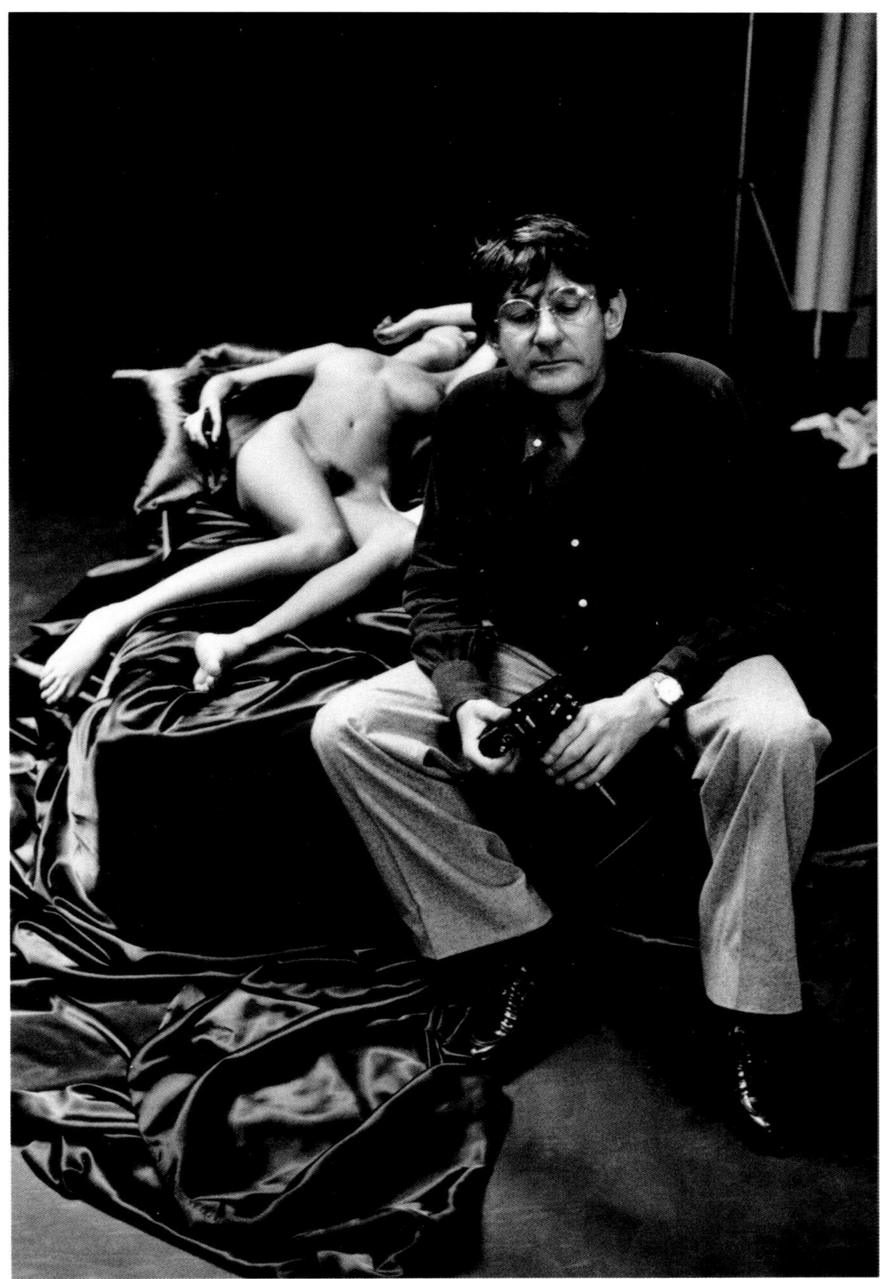

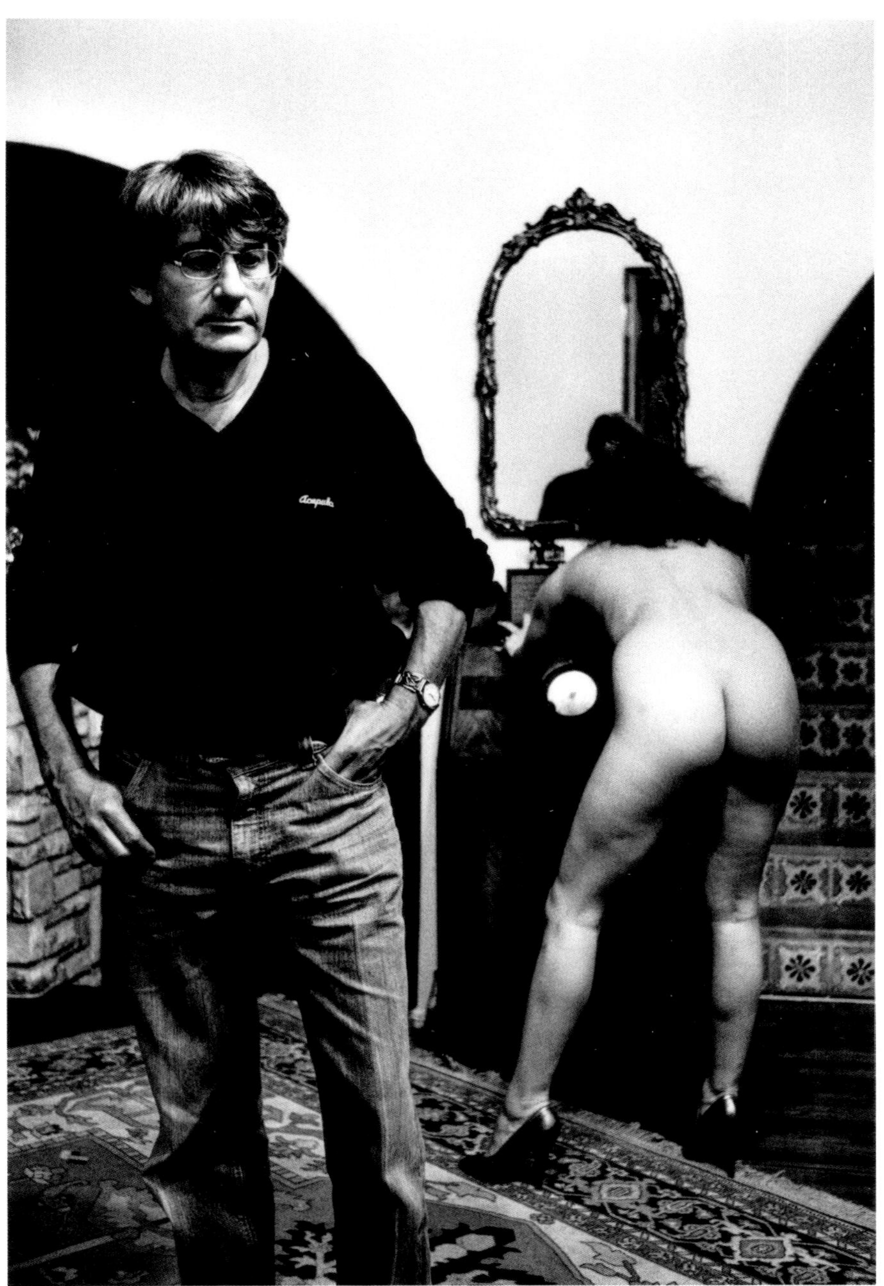

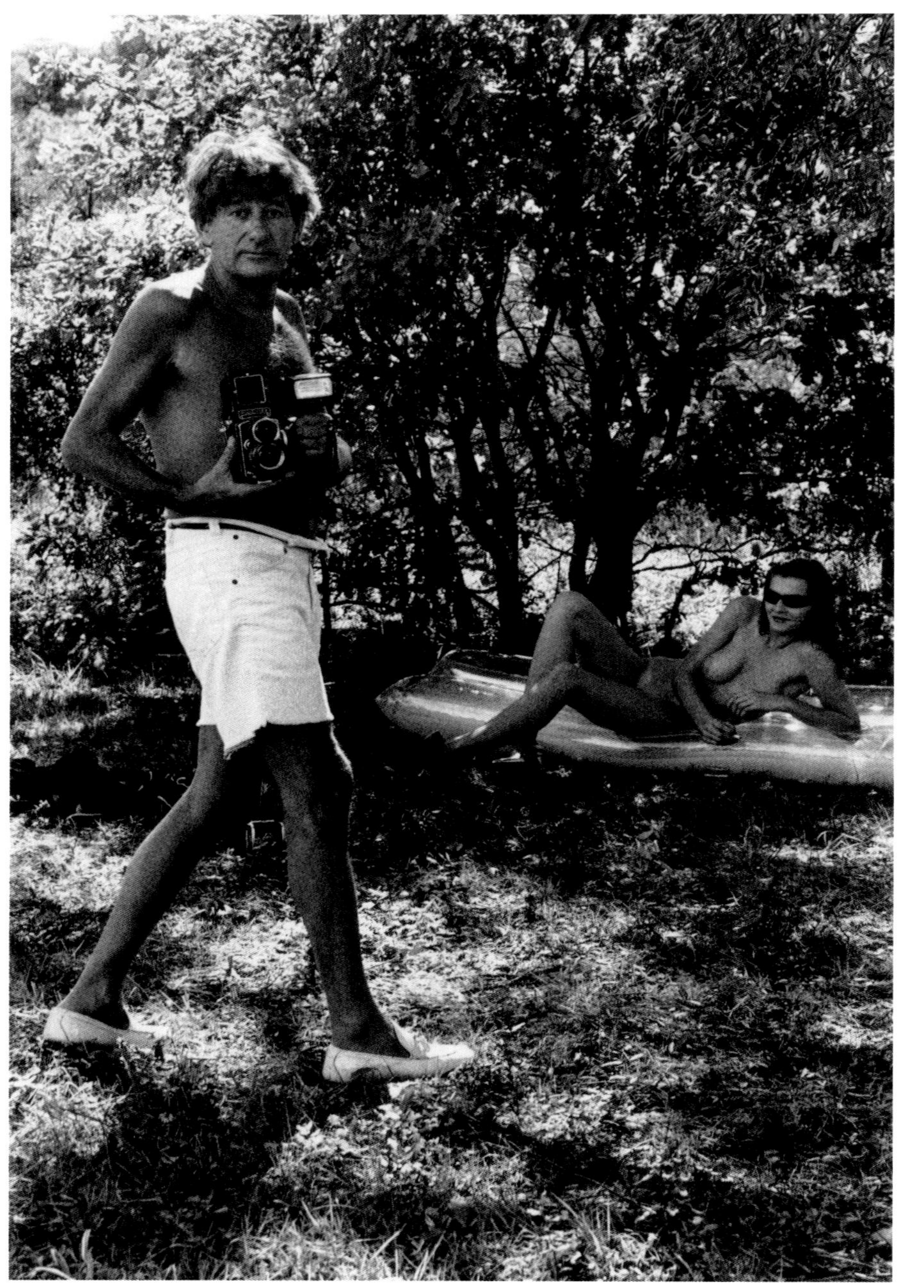

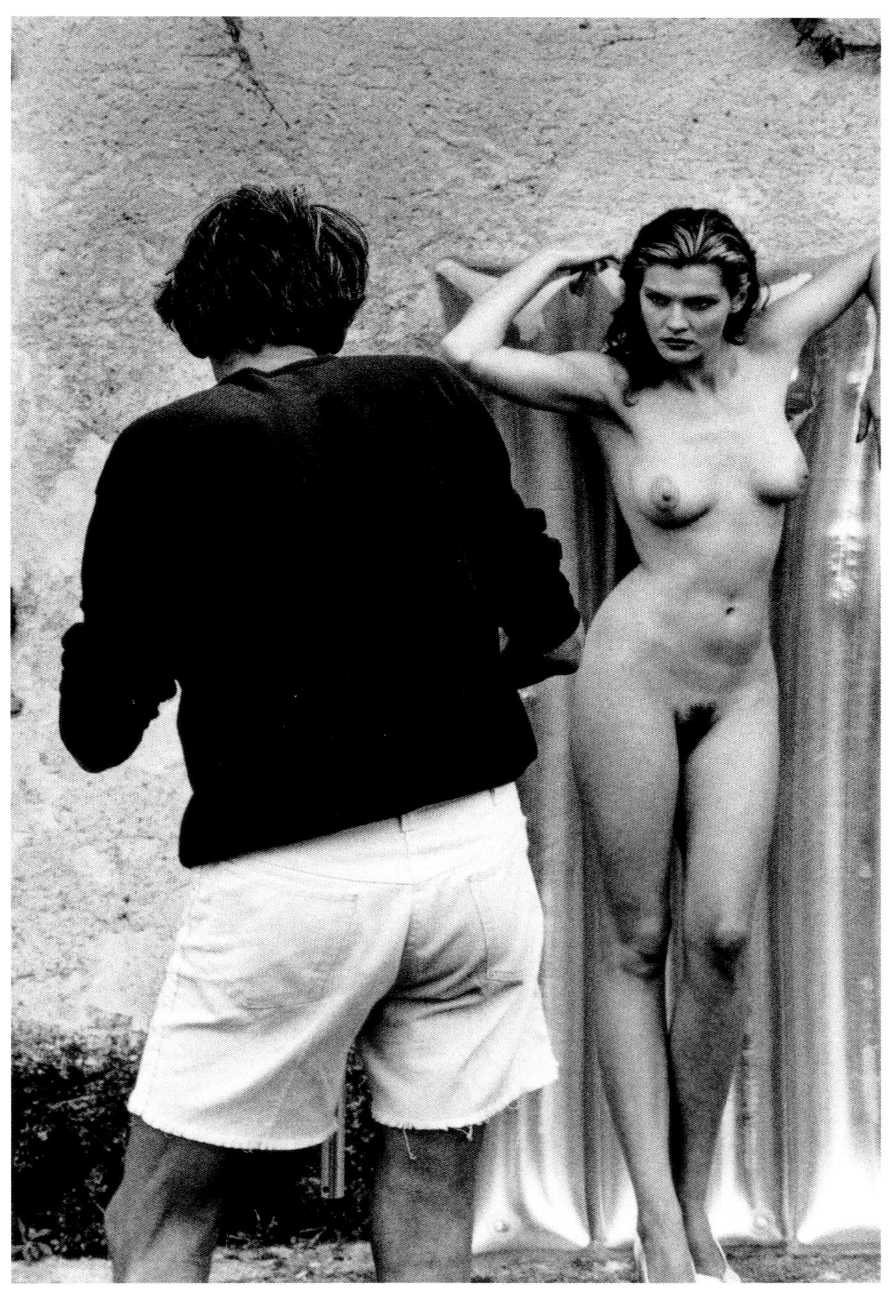

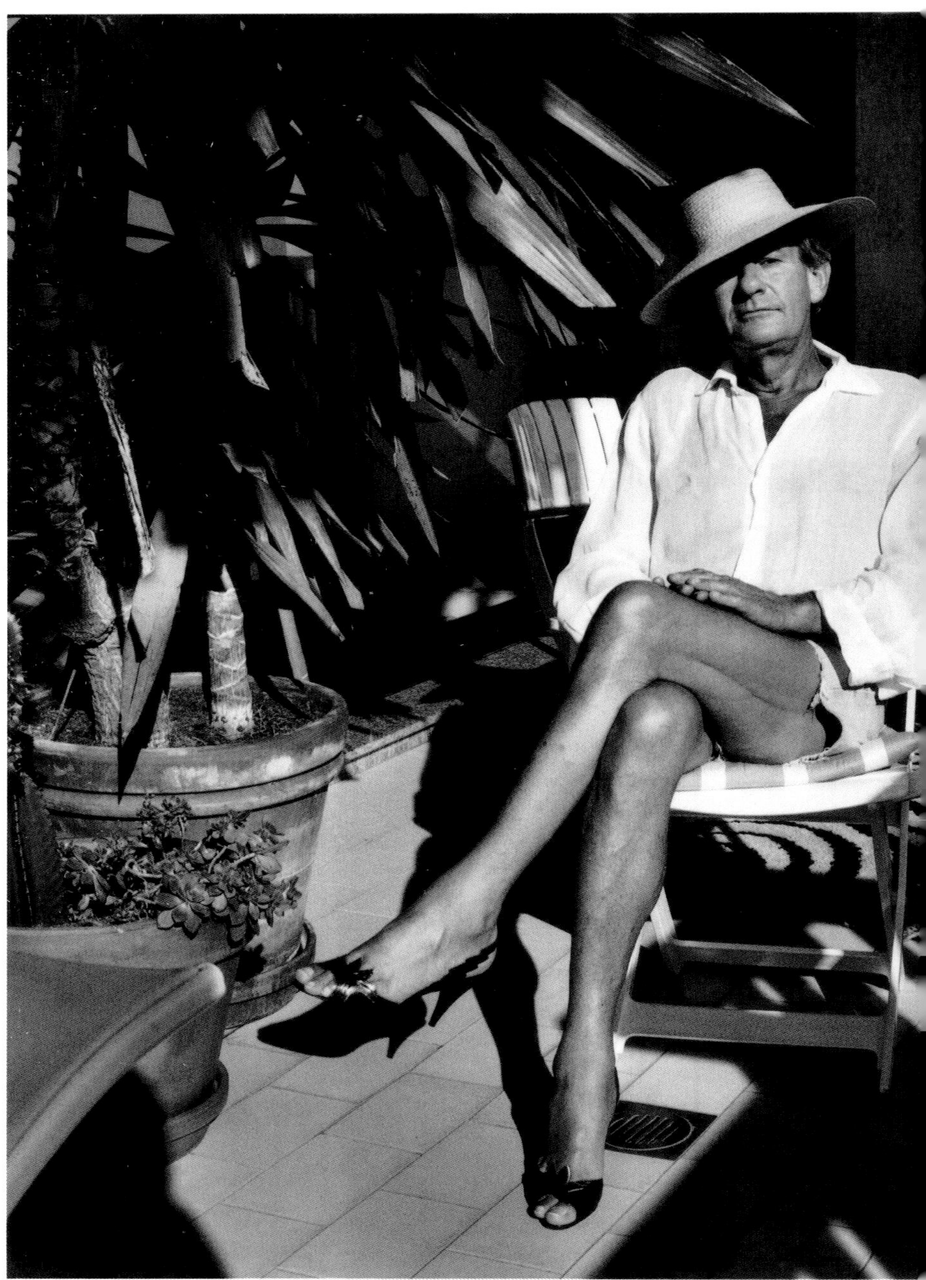

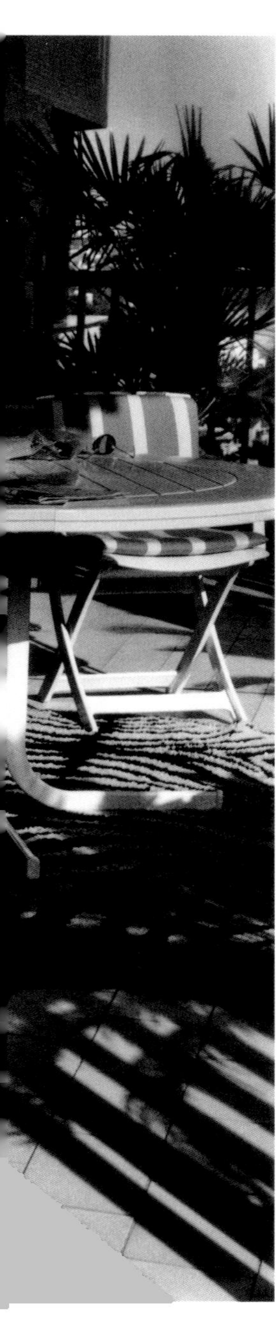

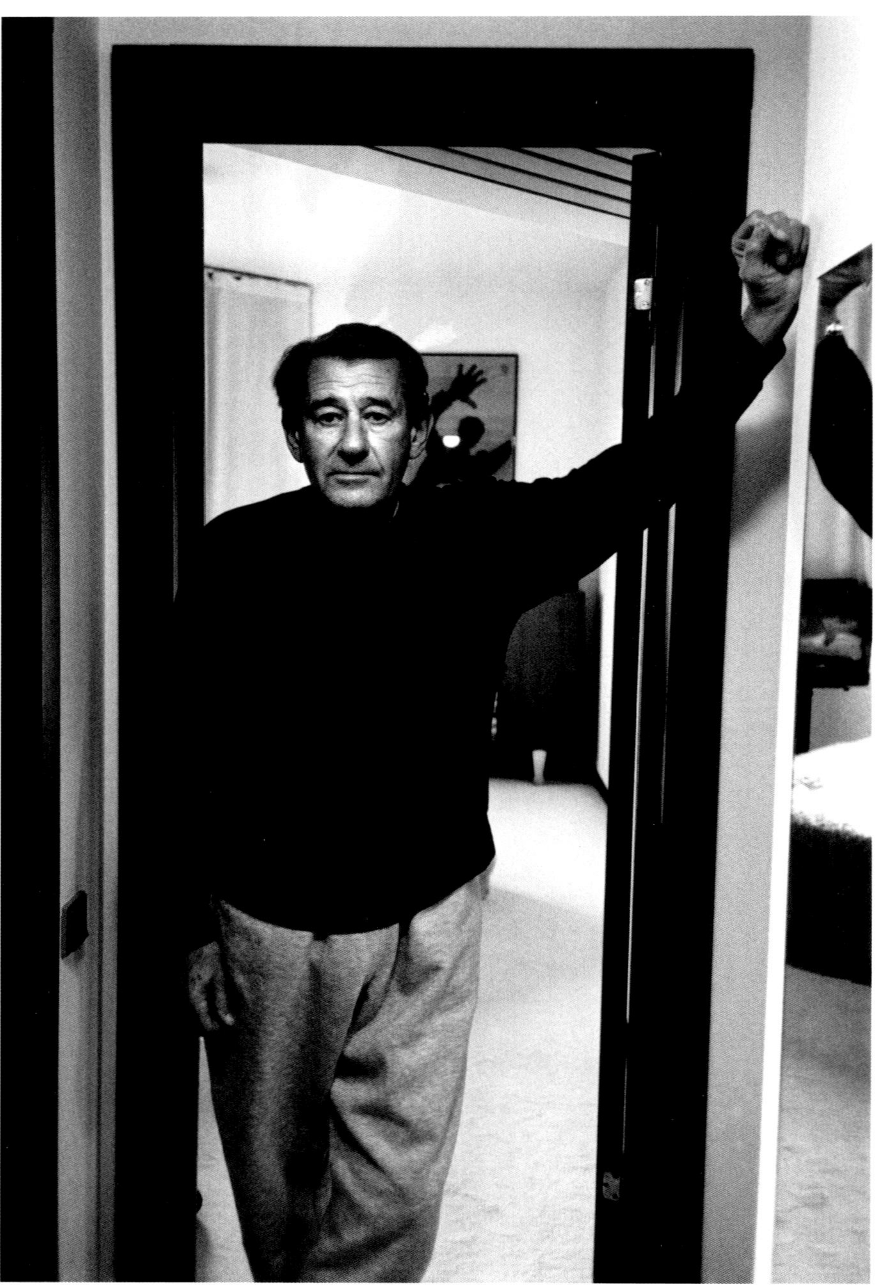

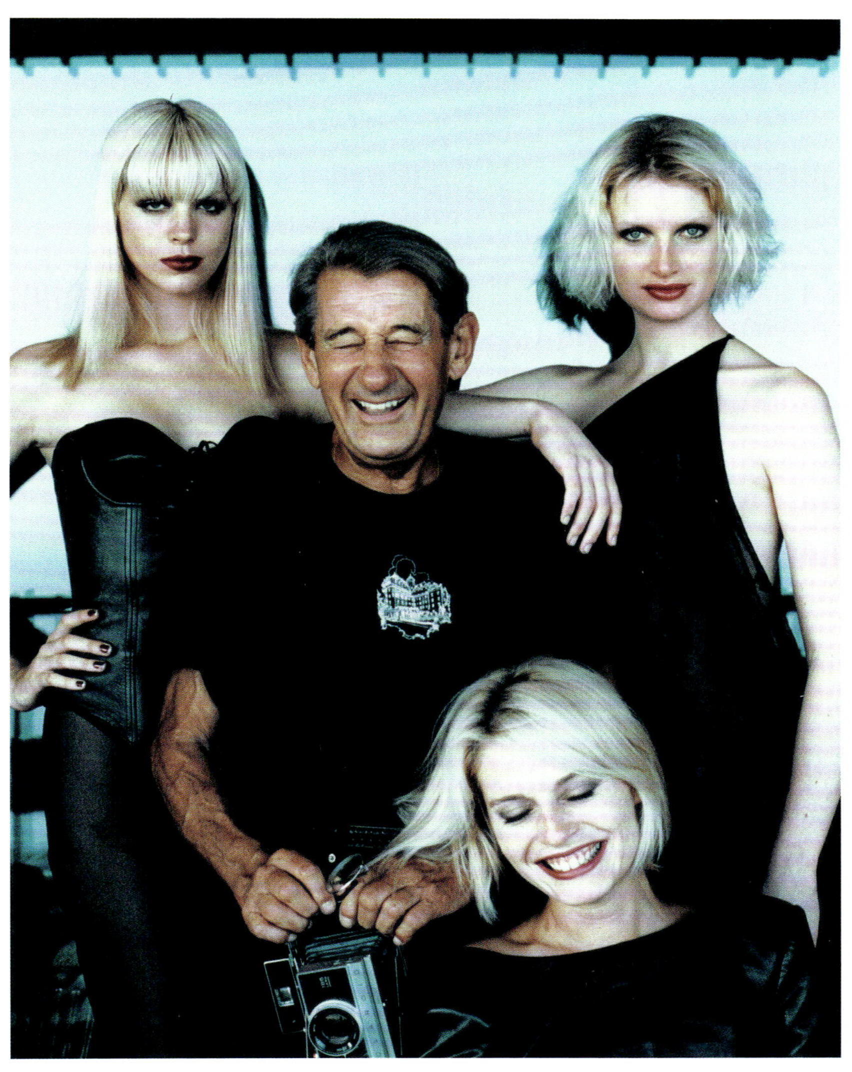

Monte Carlo, 1994
Helmut with models Myka, Nina and Annie, Monte Carlo, August 1997

Miami, 1999

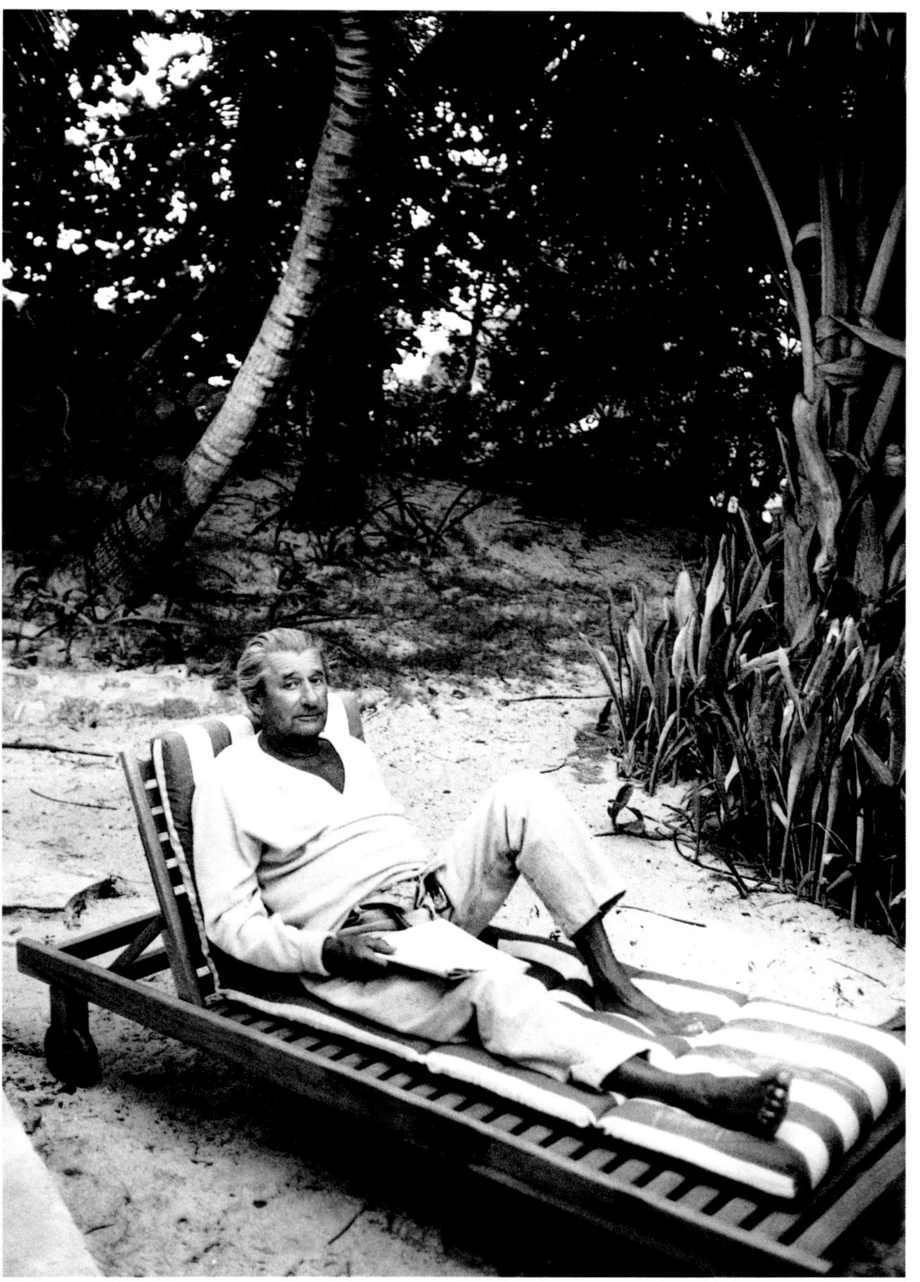

ALICE SPRINGS

SELF-PORTRAITS

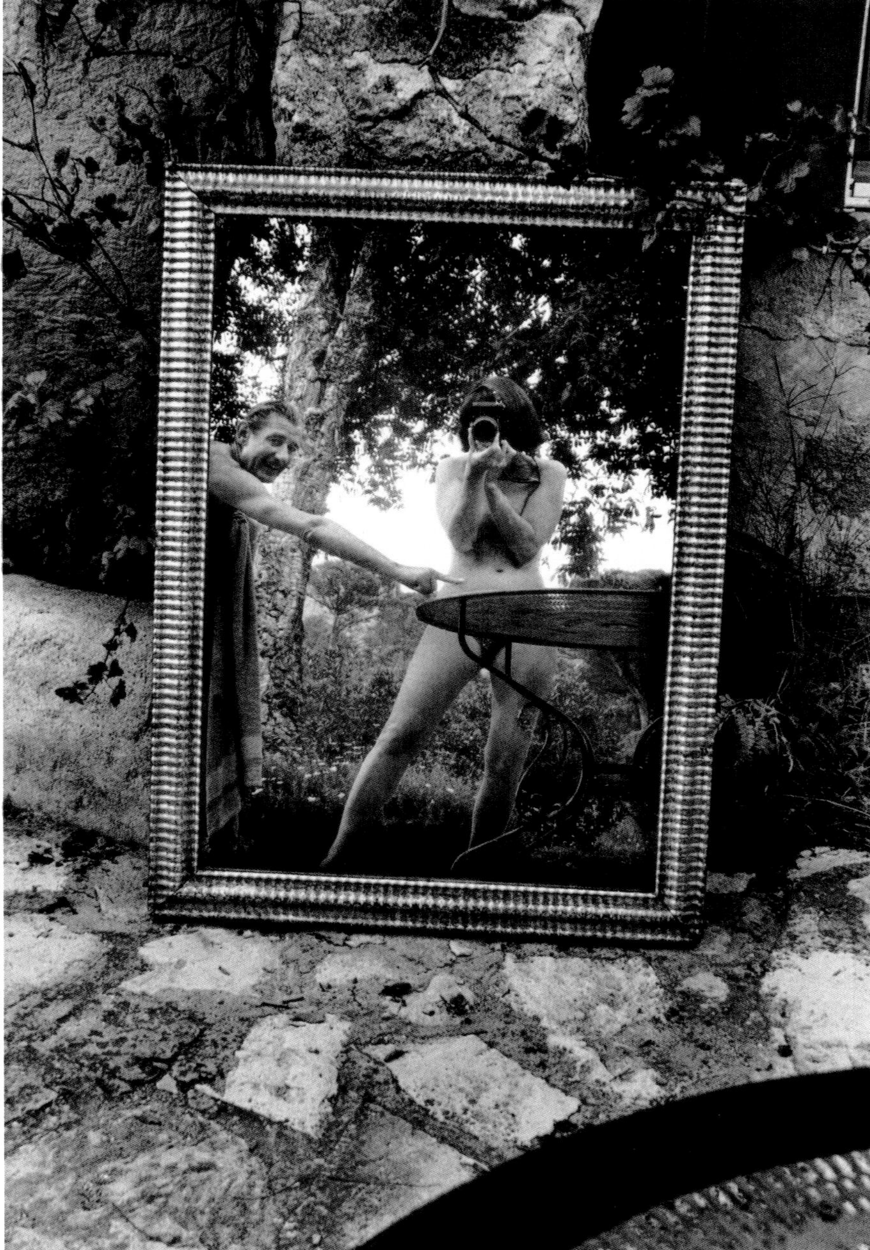

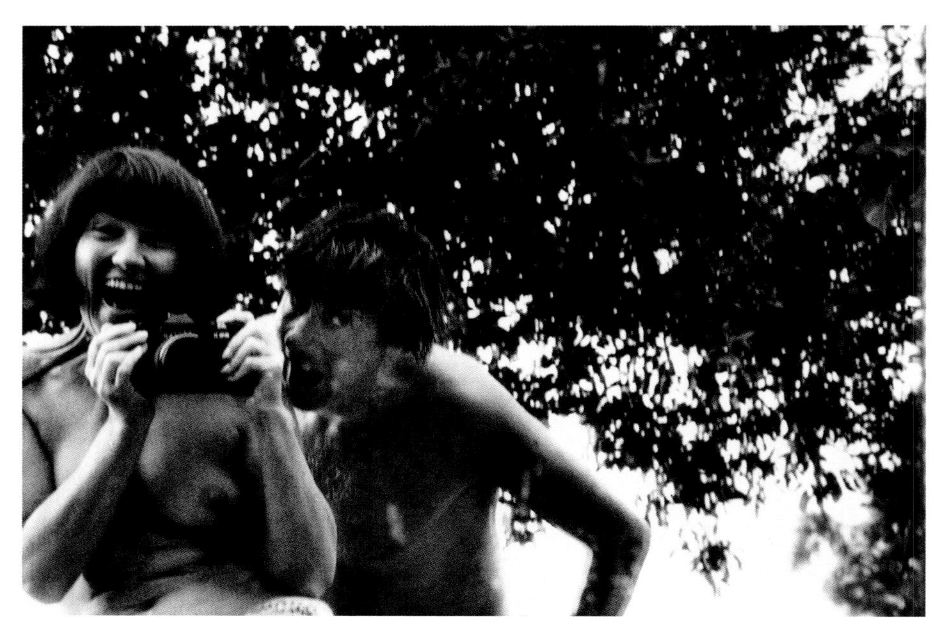

Ramatuelle, France, 1975

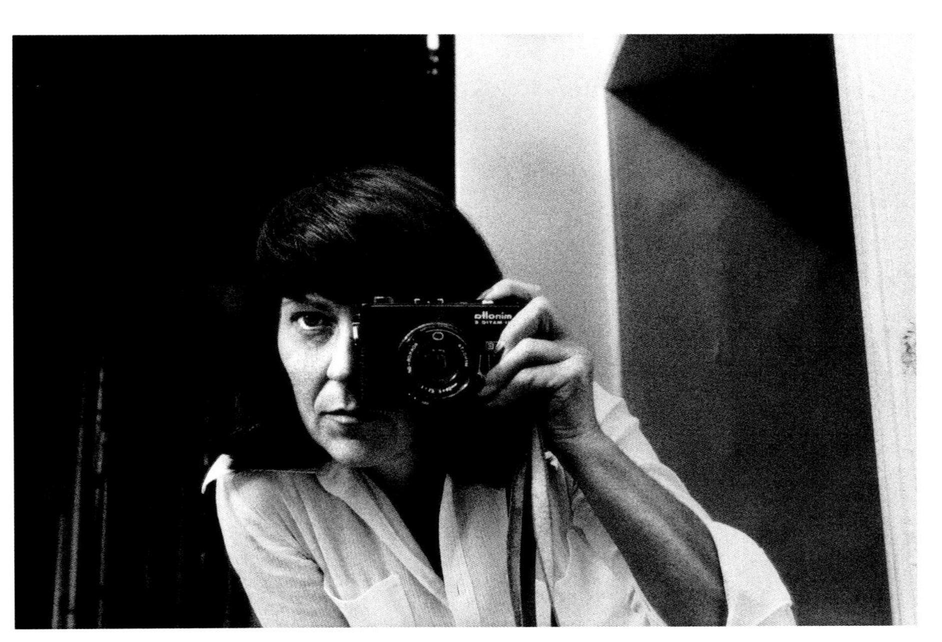

Rue Aubriot, Paris, 1972

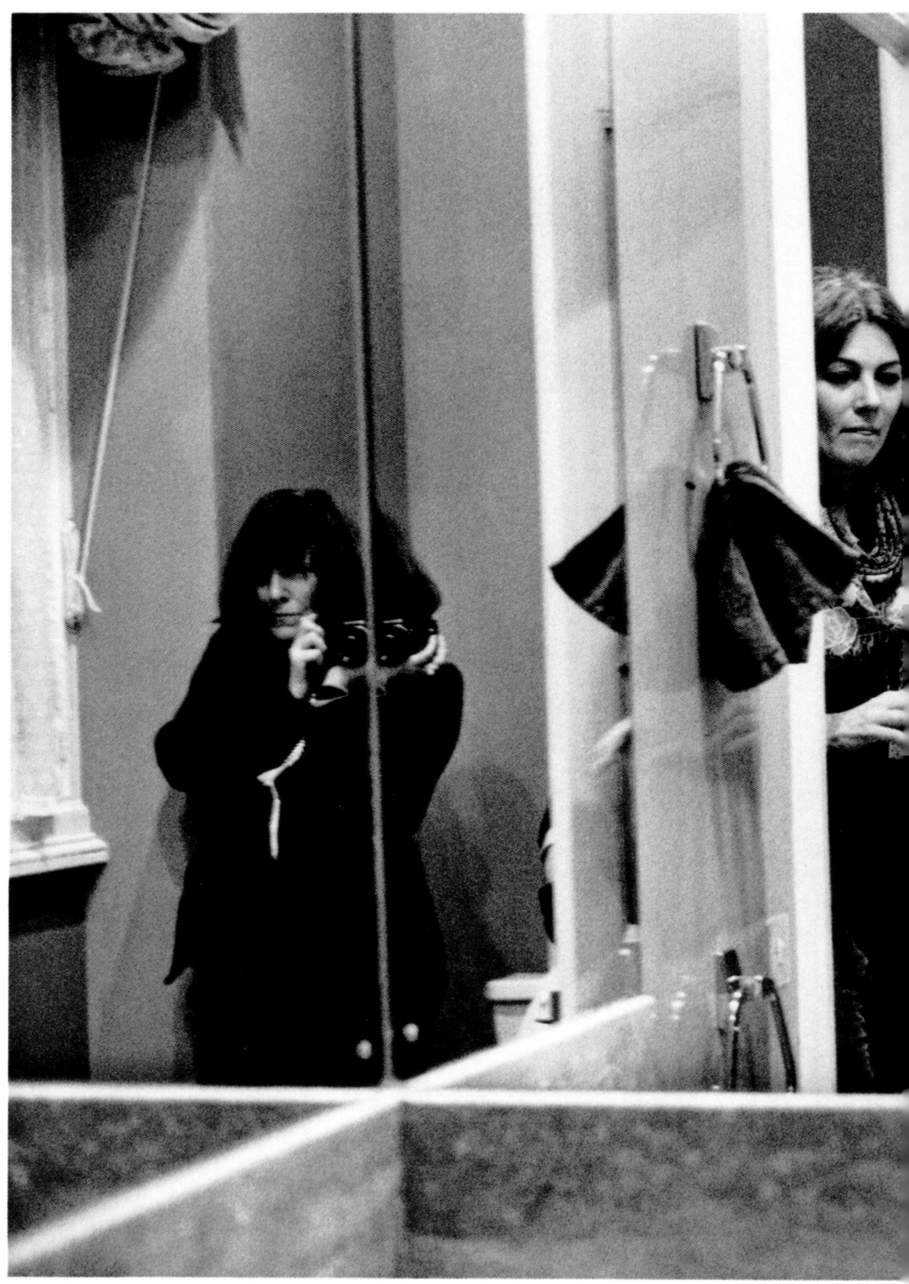

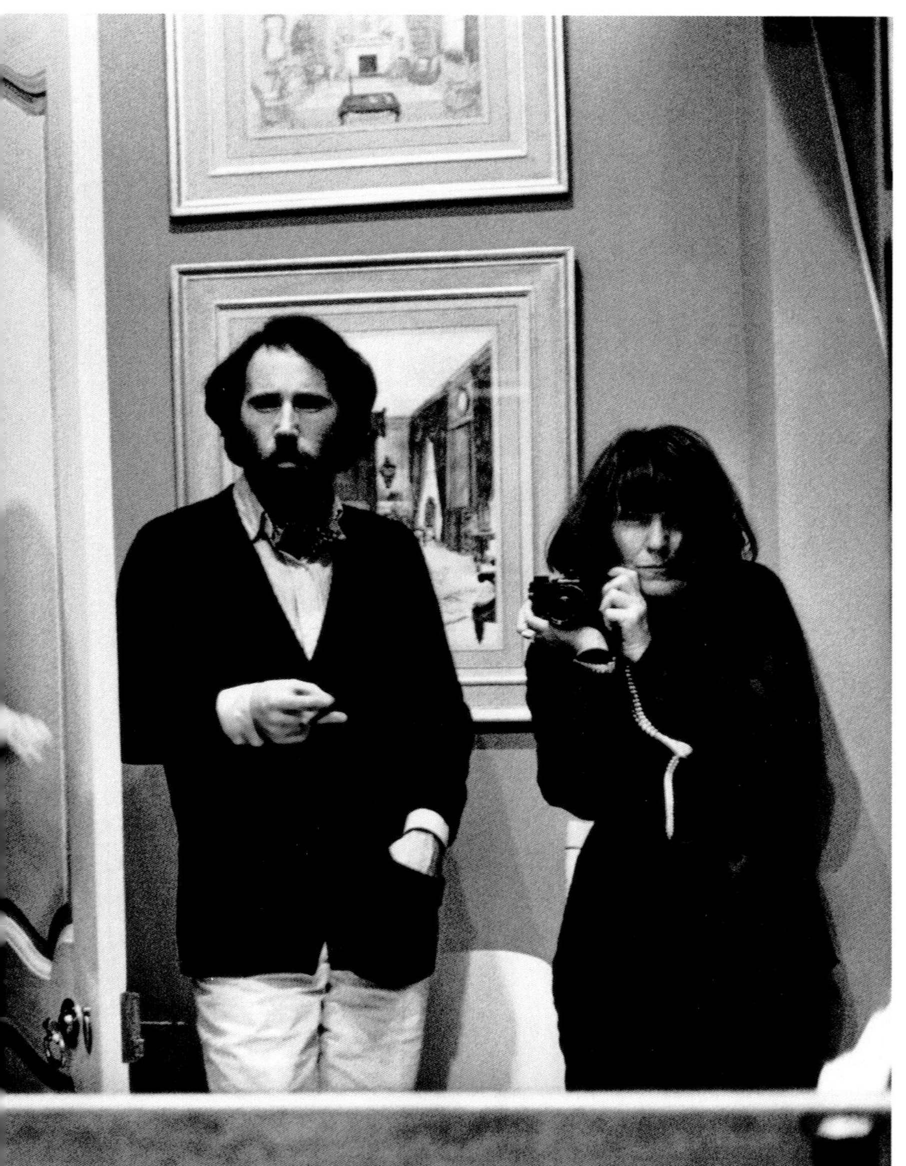

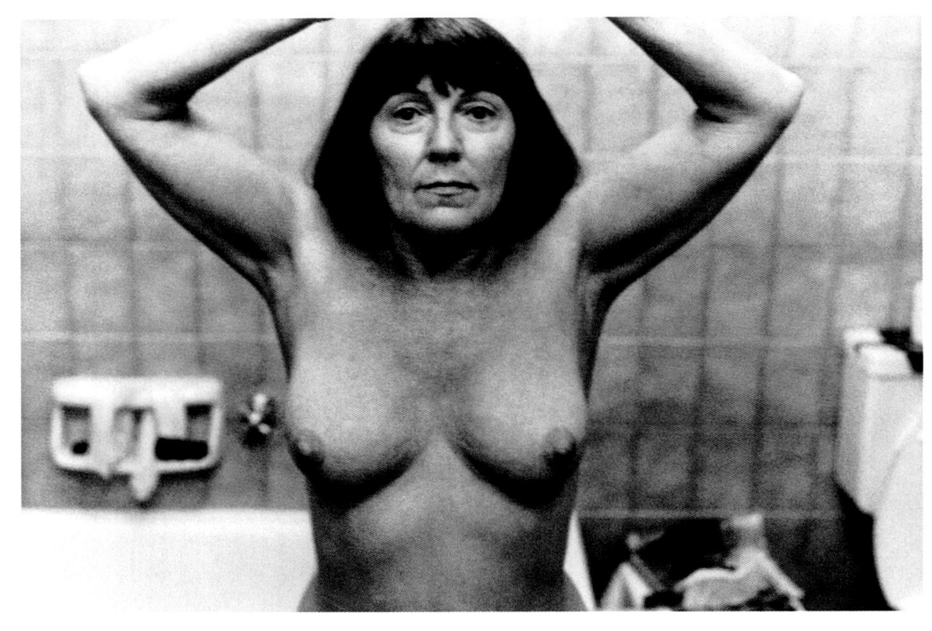

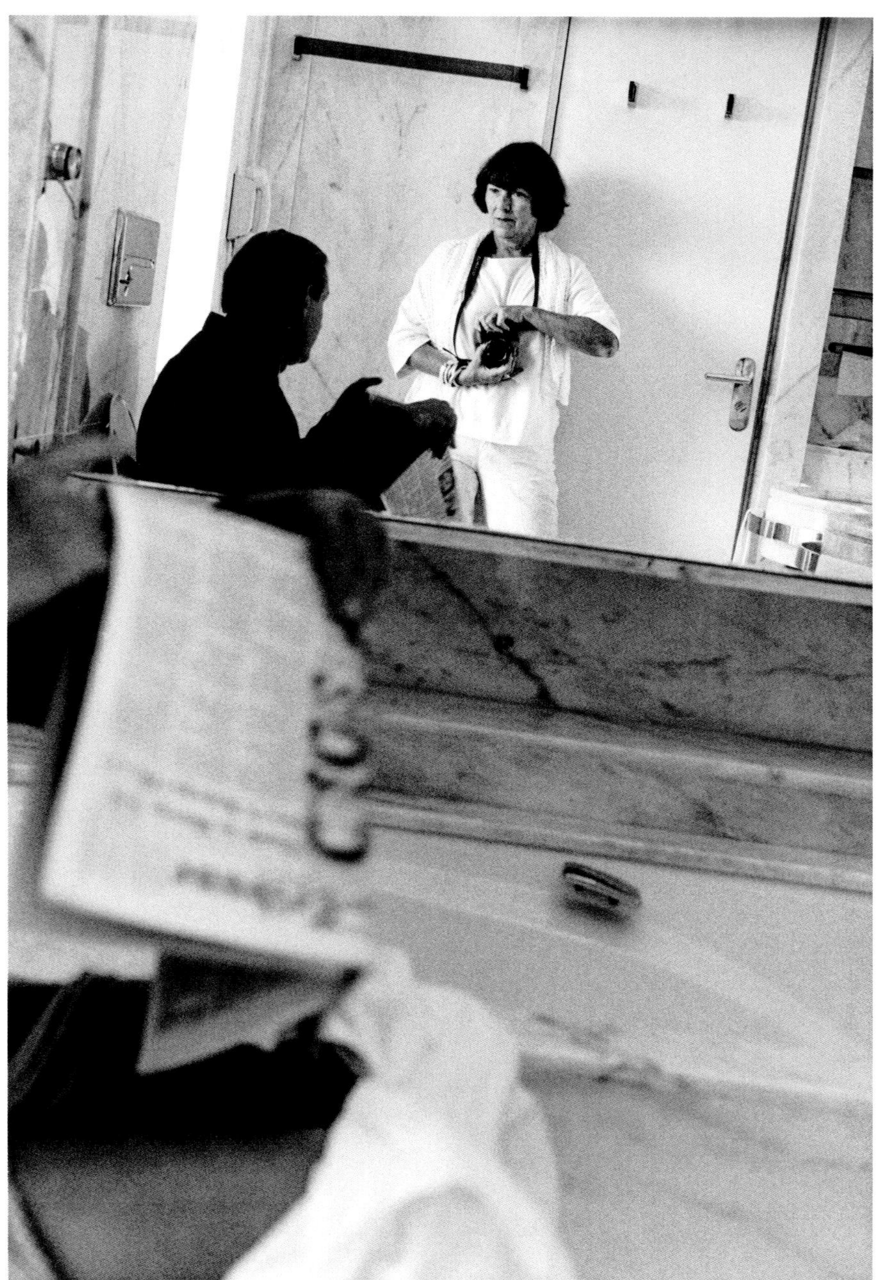

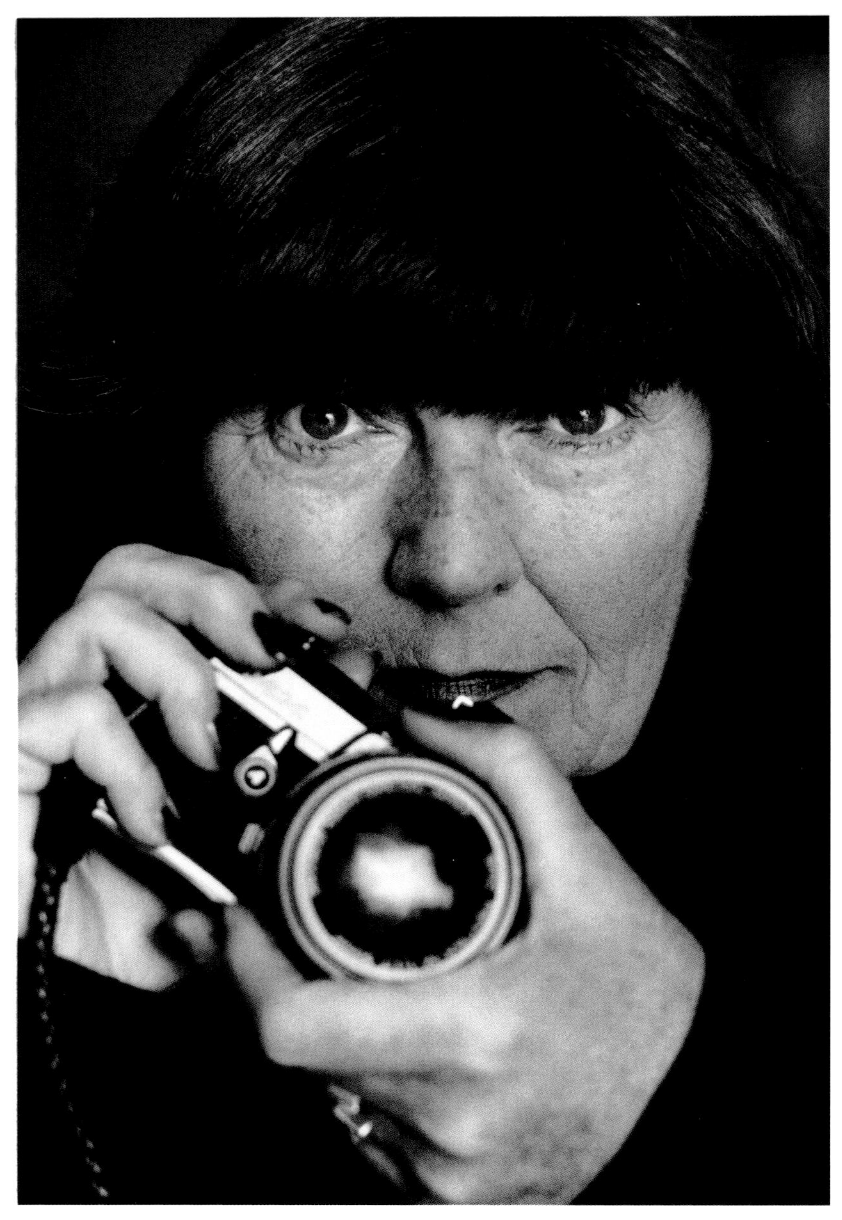

Monte Carlo, 1983

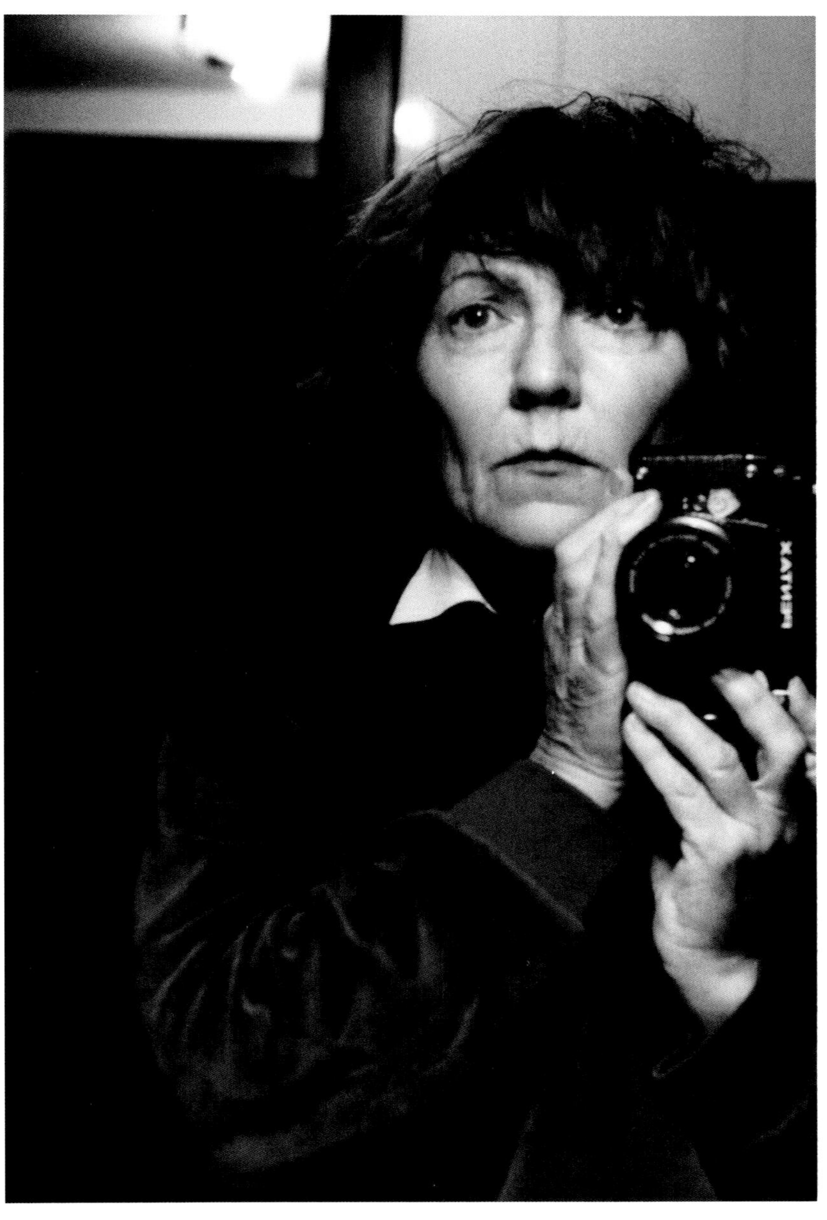

Paris, 1983

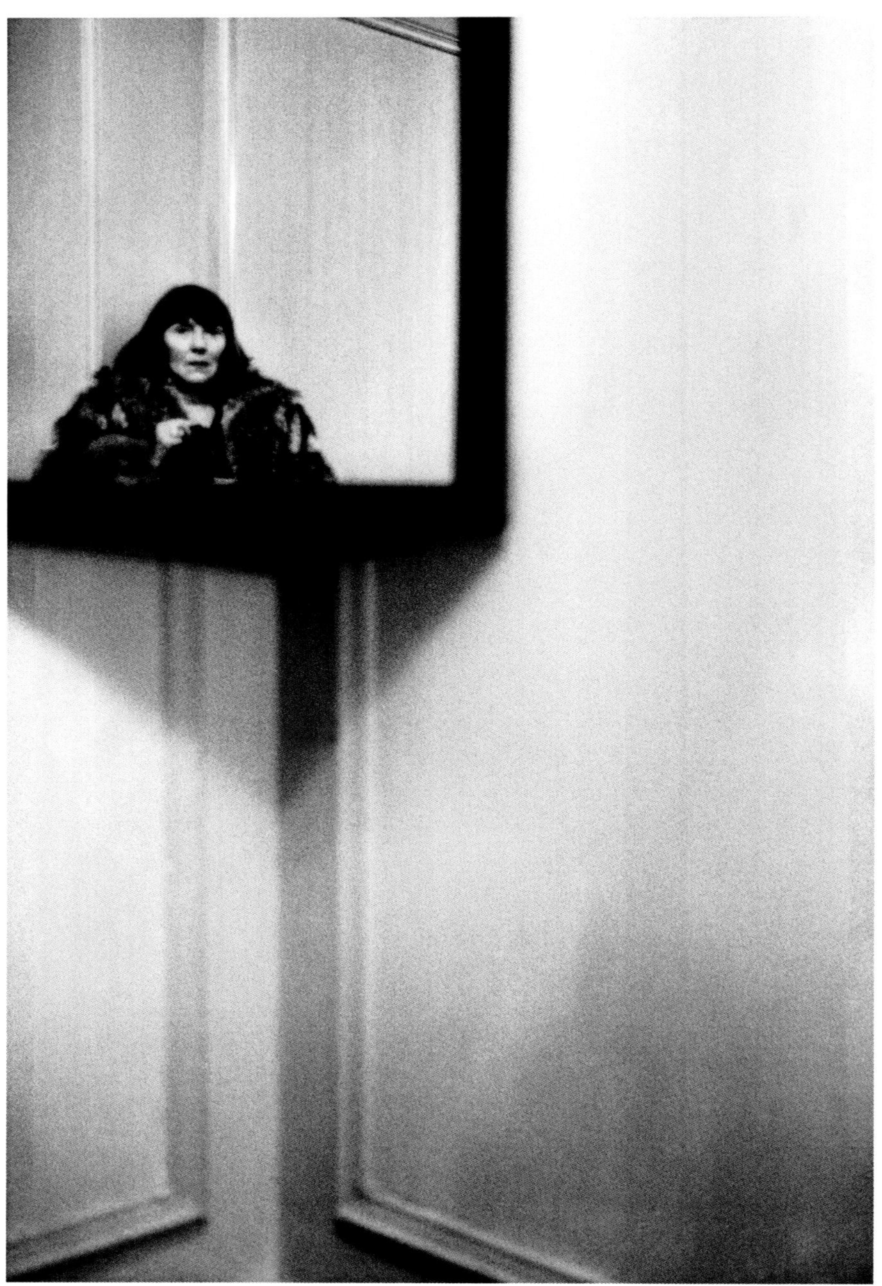

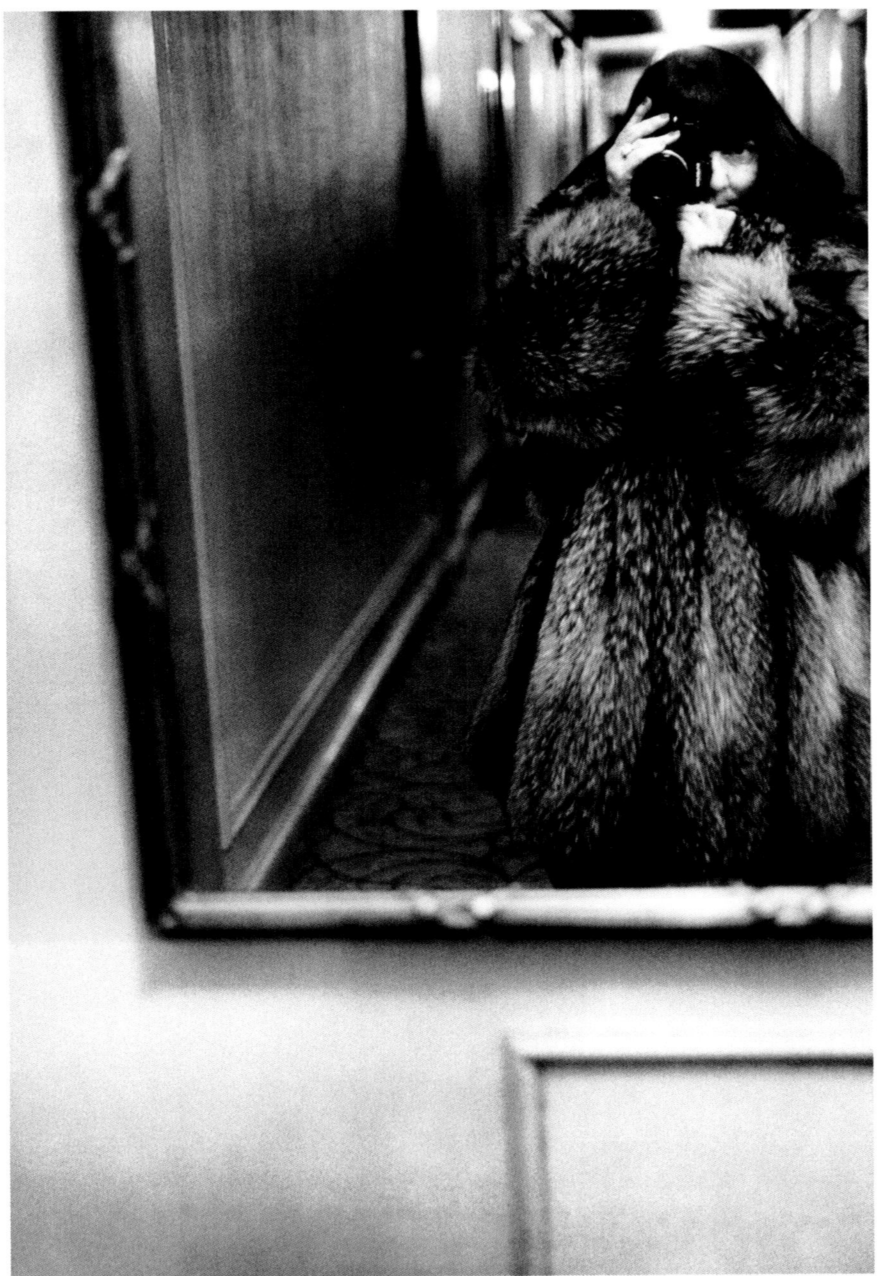

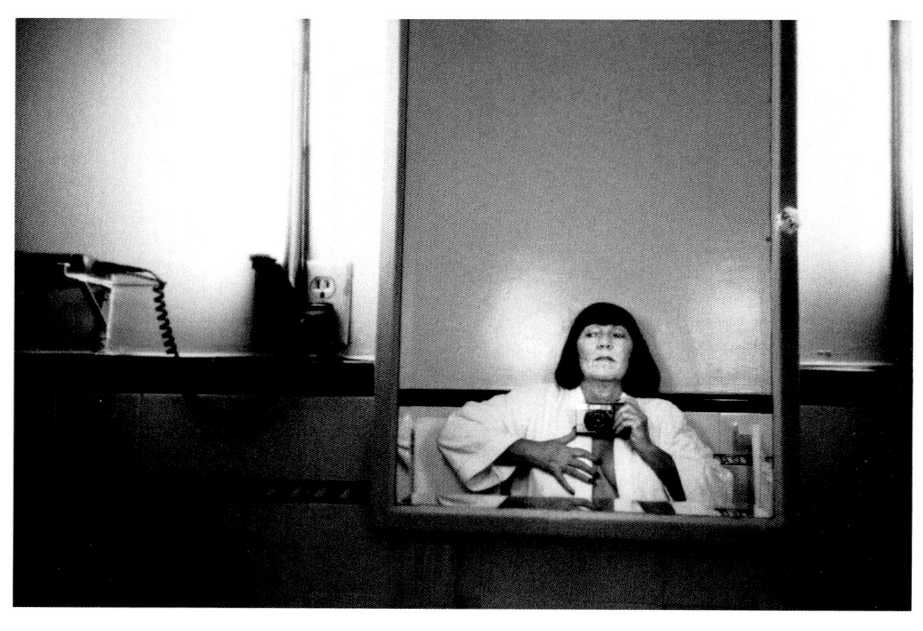

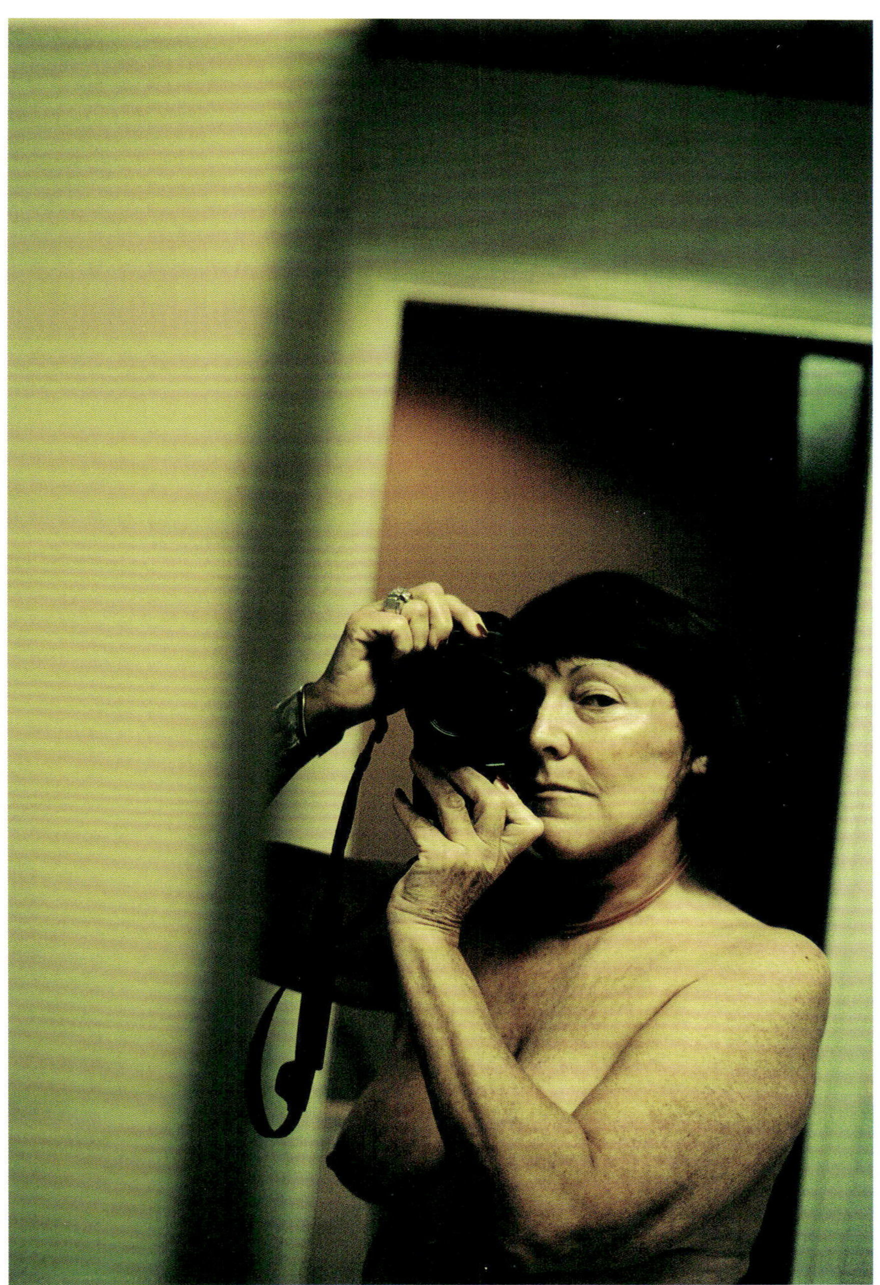

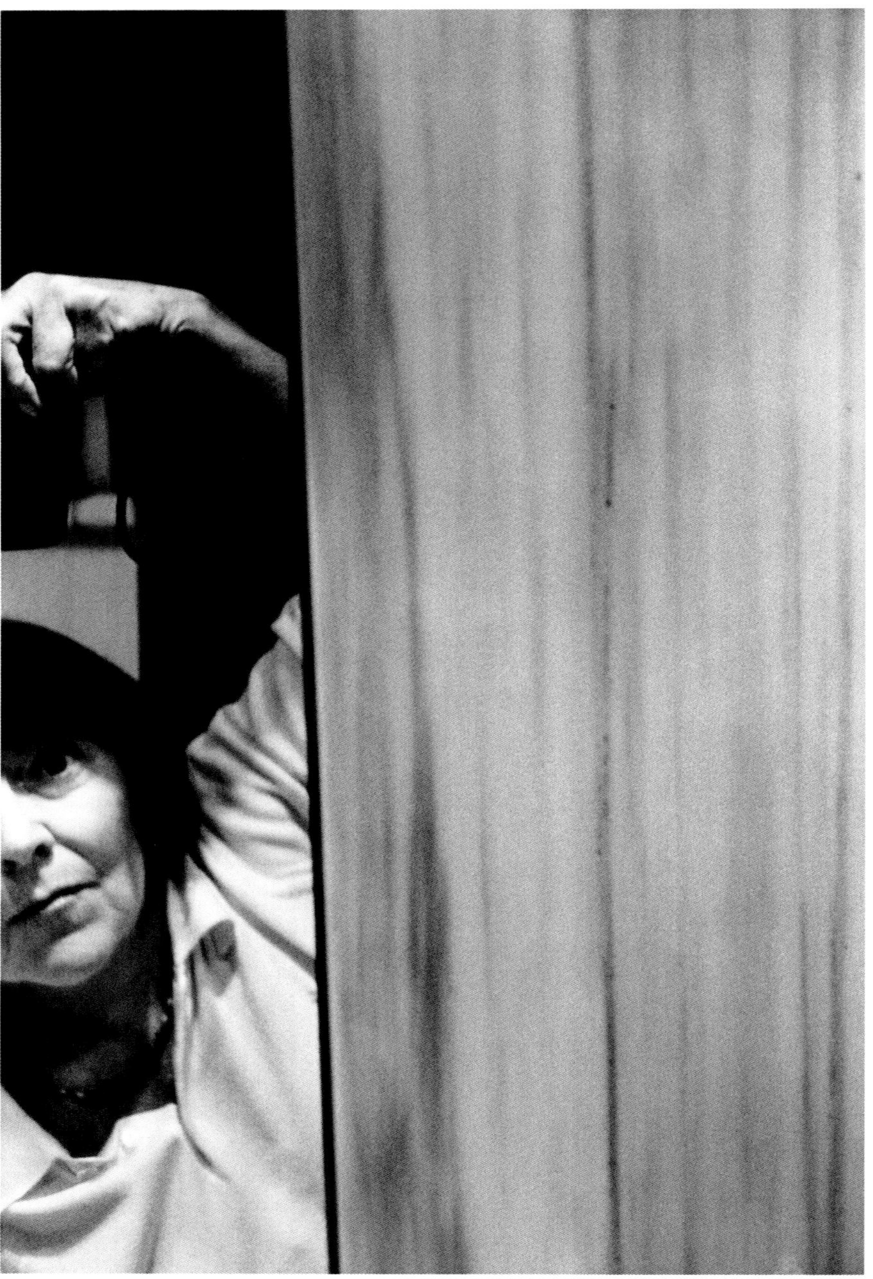

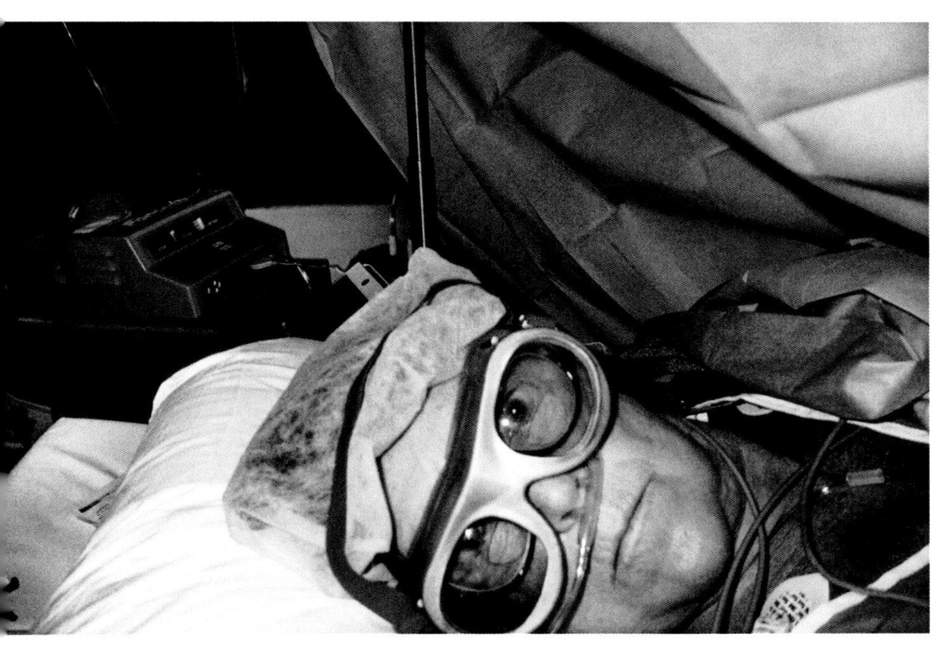

Vail, Colorado, 1996

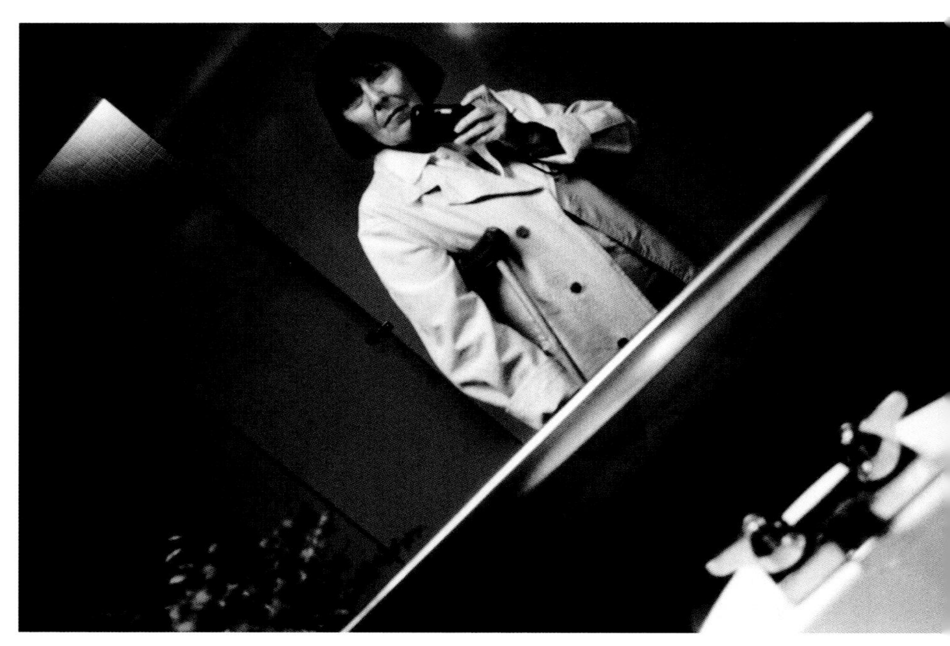

Denver Airport, Colorado, 1996

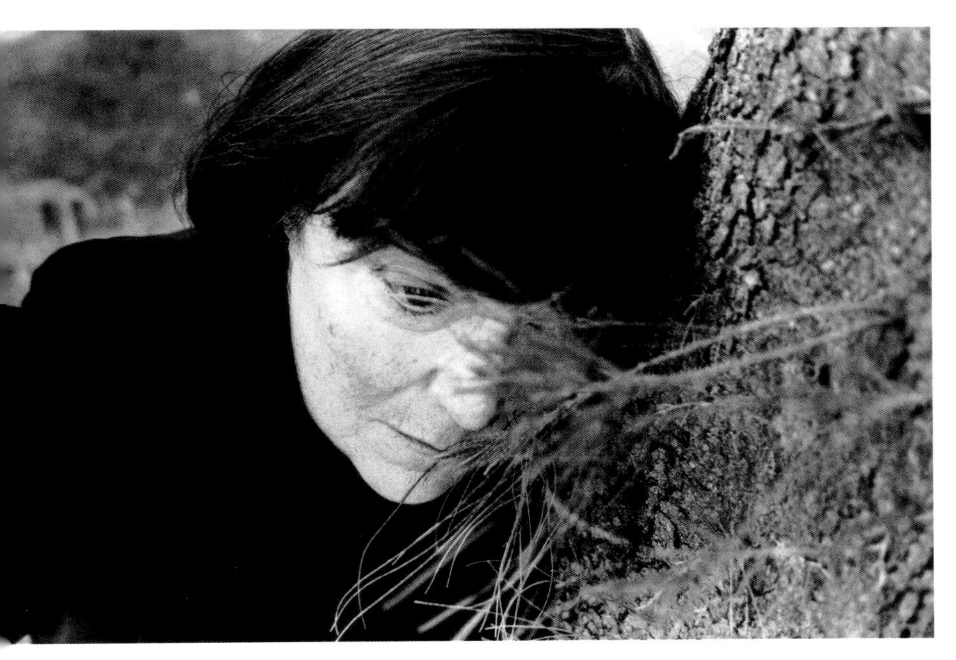

Melbourne, 1997

ALICE SPRINGS
BY HELMUT NEWTON

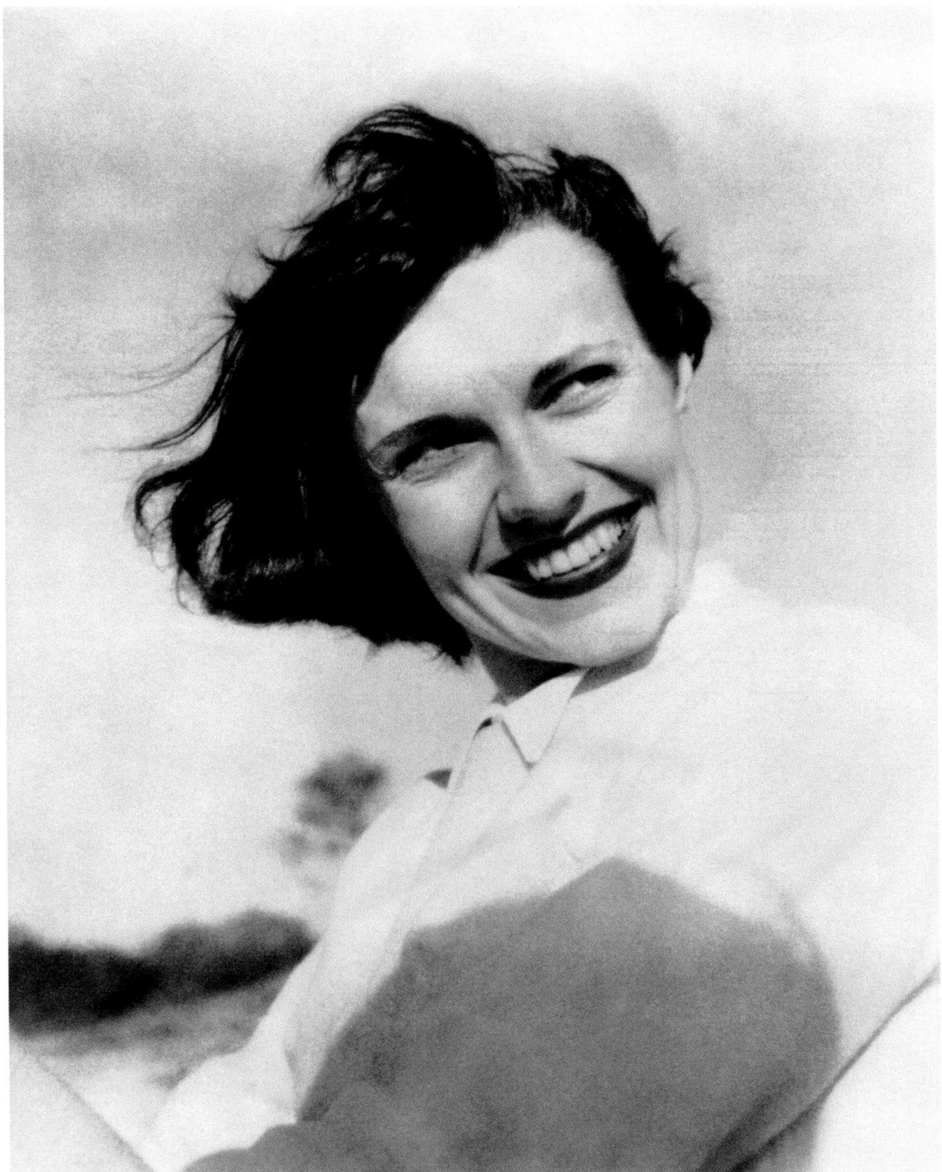

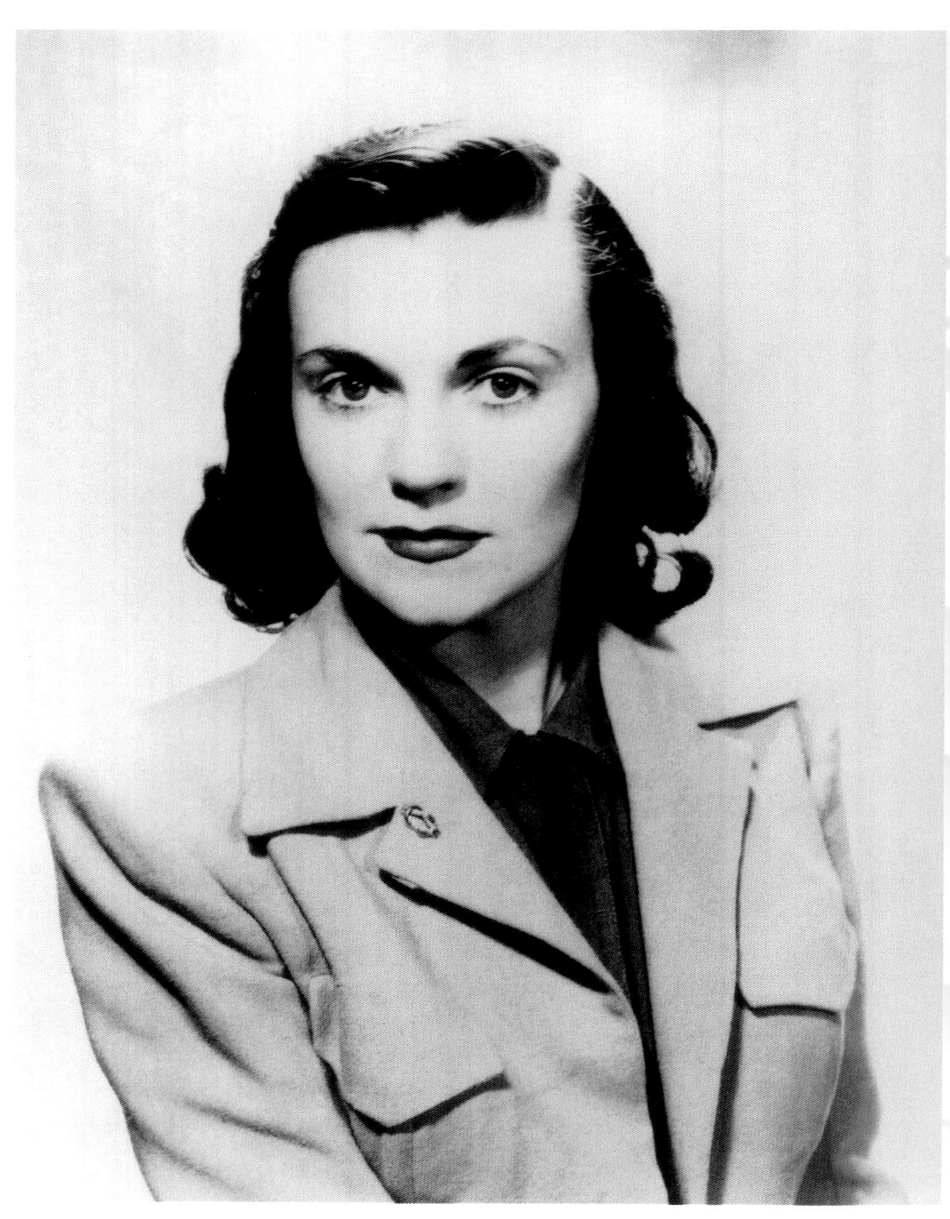

PAGE 55 Metung, Victoria, summer 1947
Melbourne, 1947

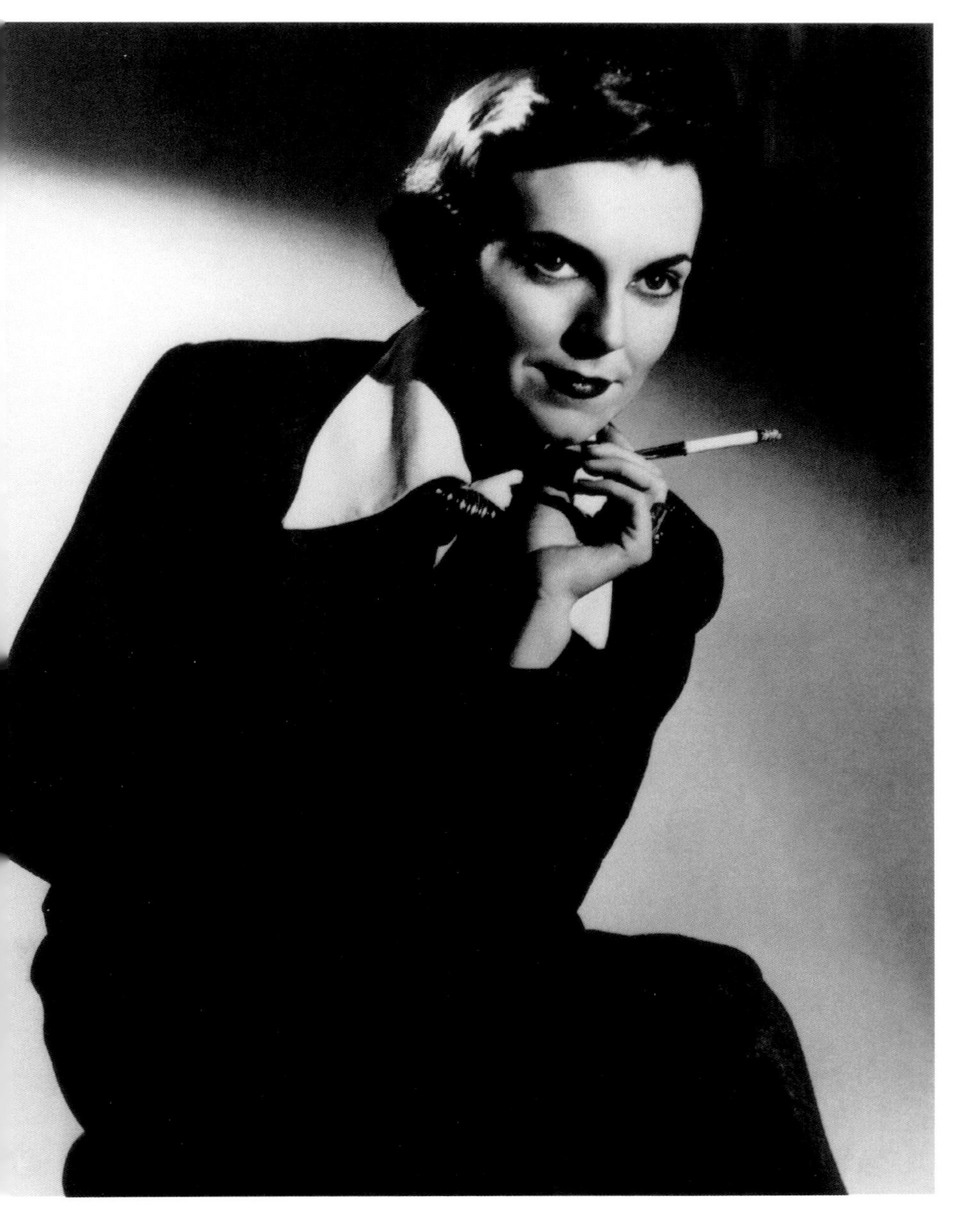

Melbourne, 1949

June as Salome from the play
by Oscar Wilde, Melbourne, 1951

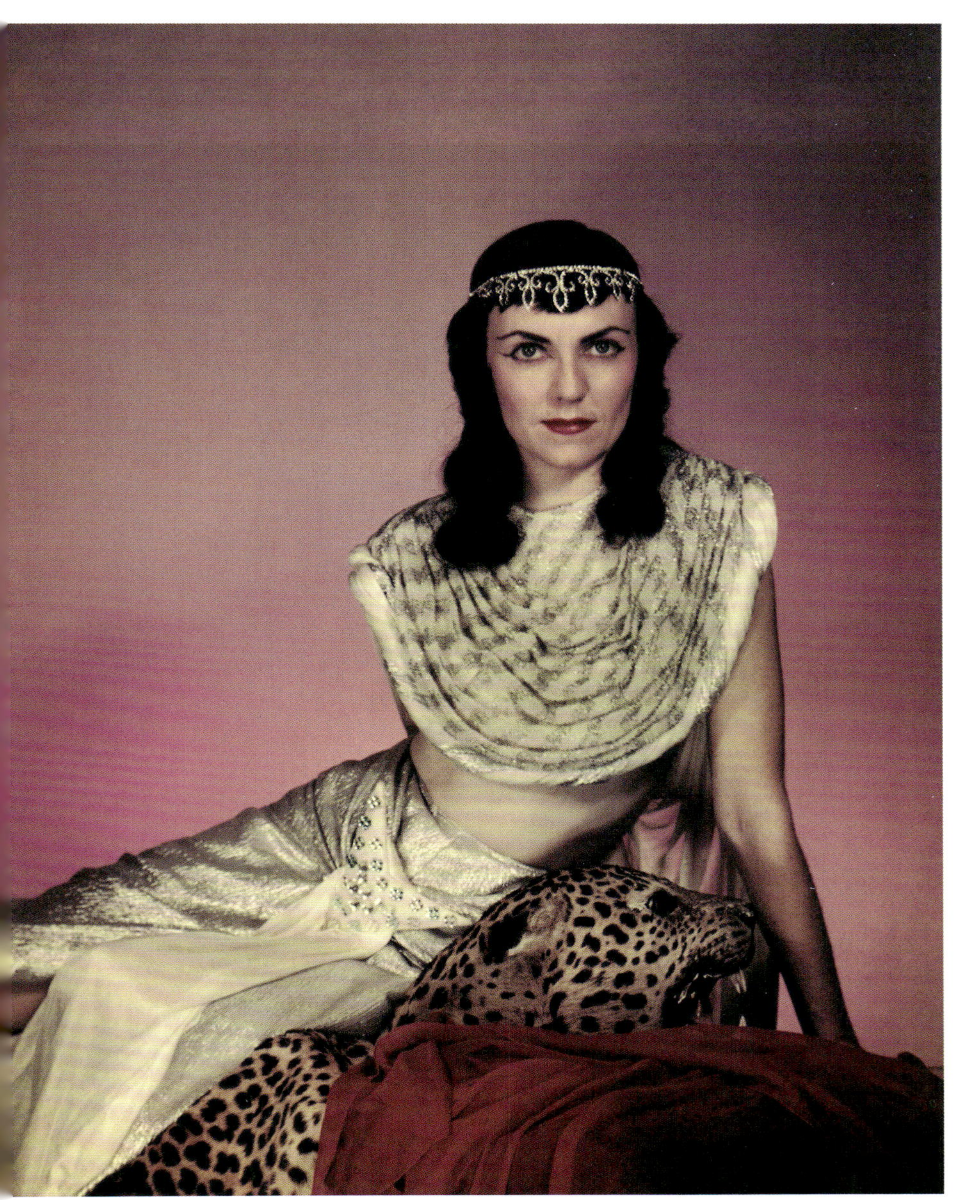

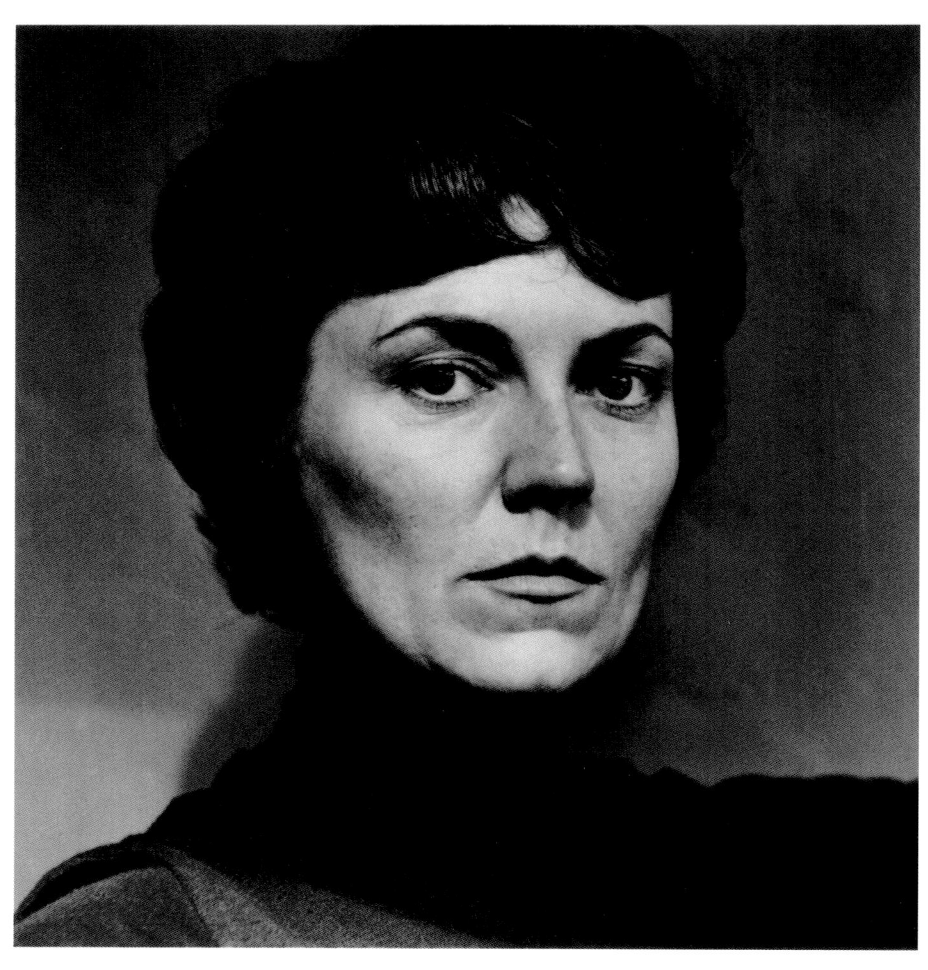

June as Hedda Gabler, Melbourne, 1960
Ramatuelle, 1962

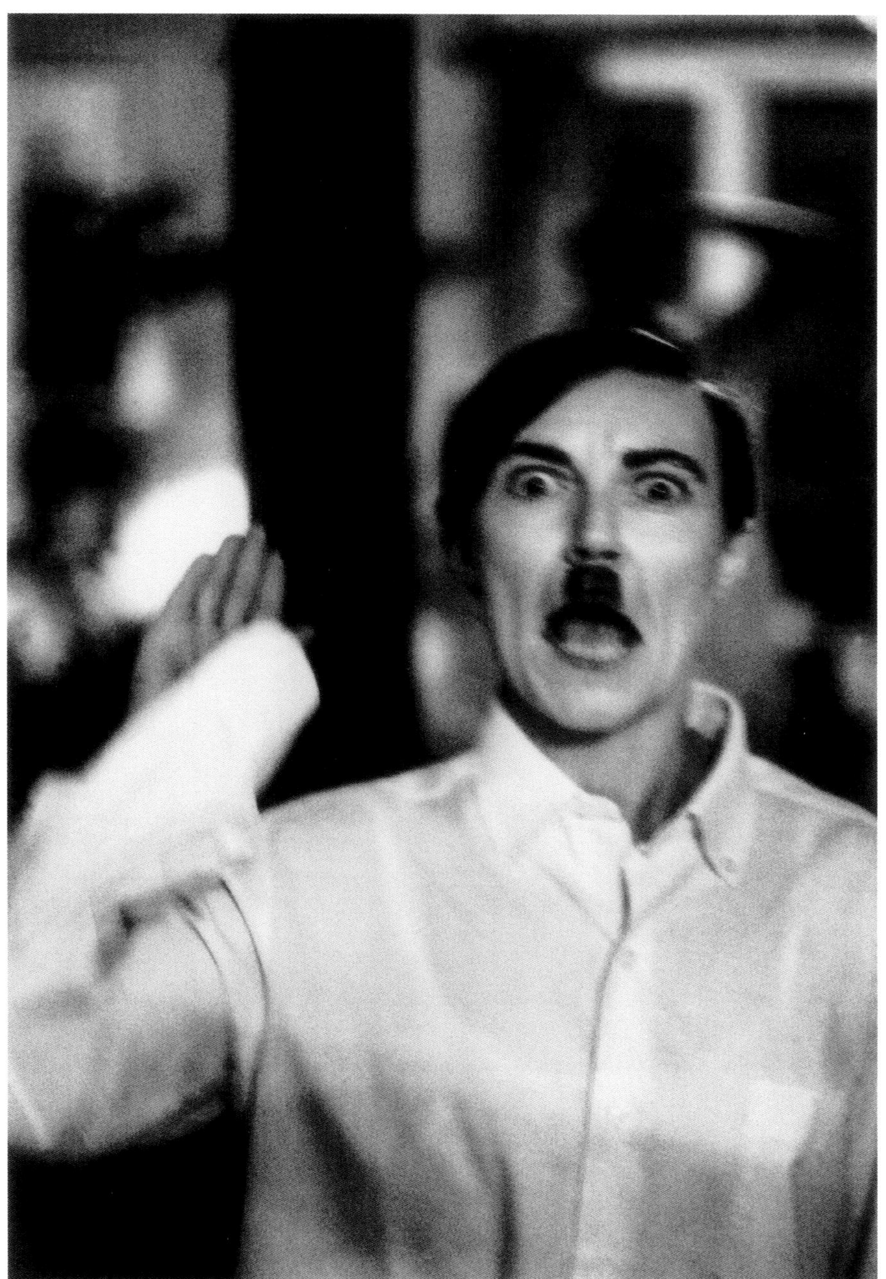

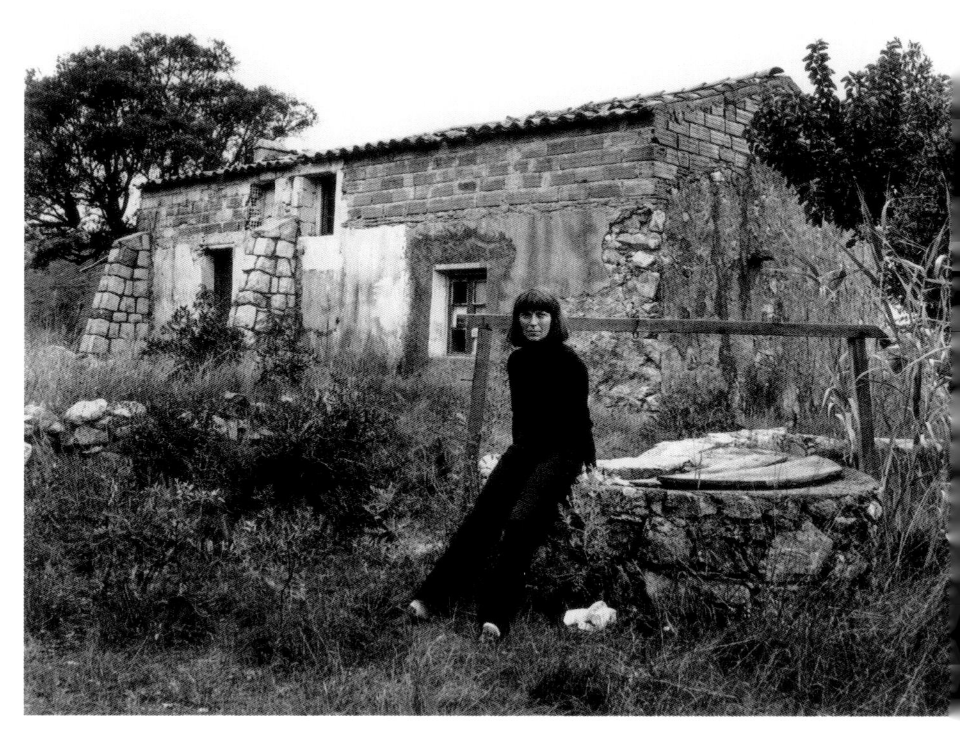

June and our house
the day we bought it, Ramatuelle, 1964

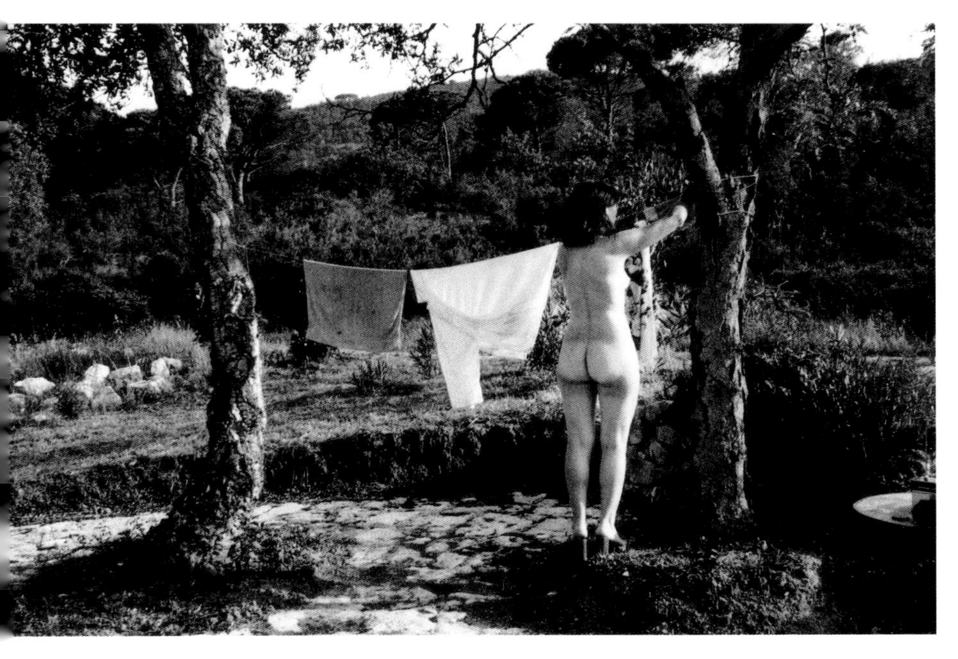

Ramatuelle, 1972

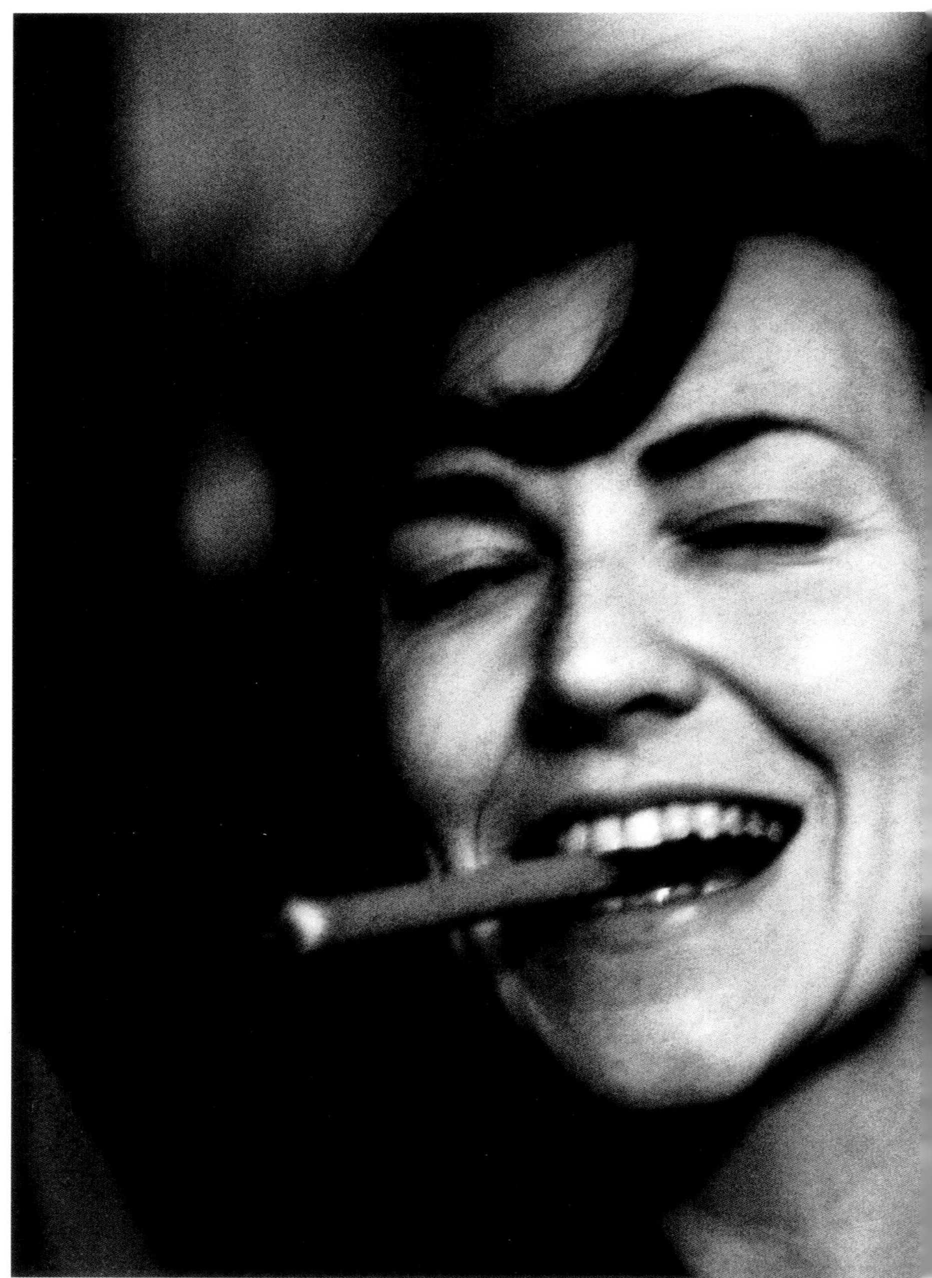

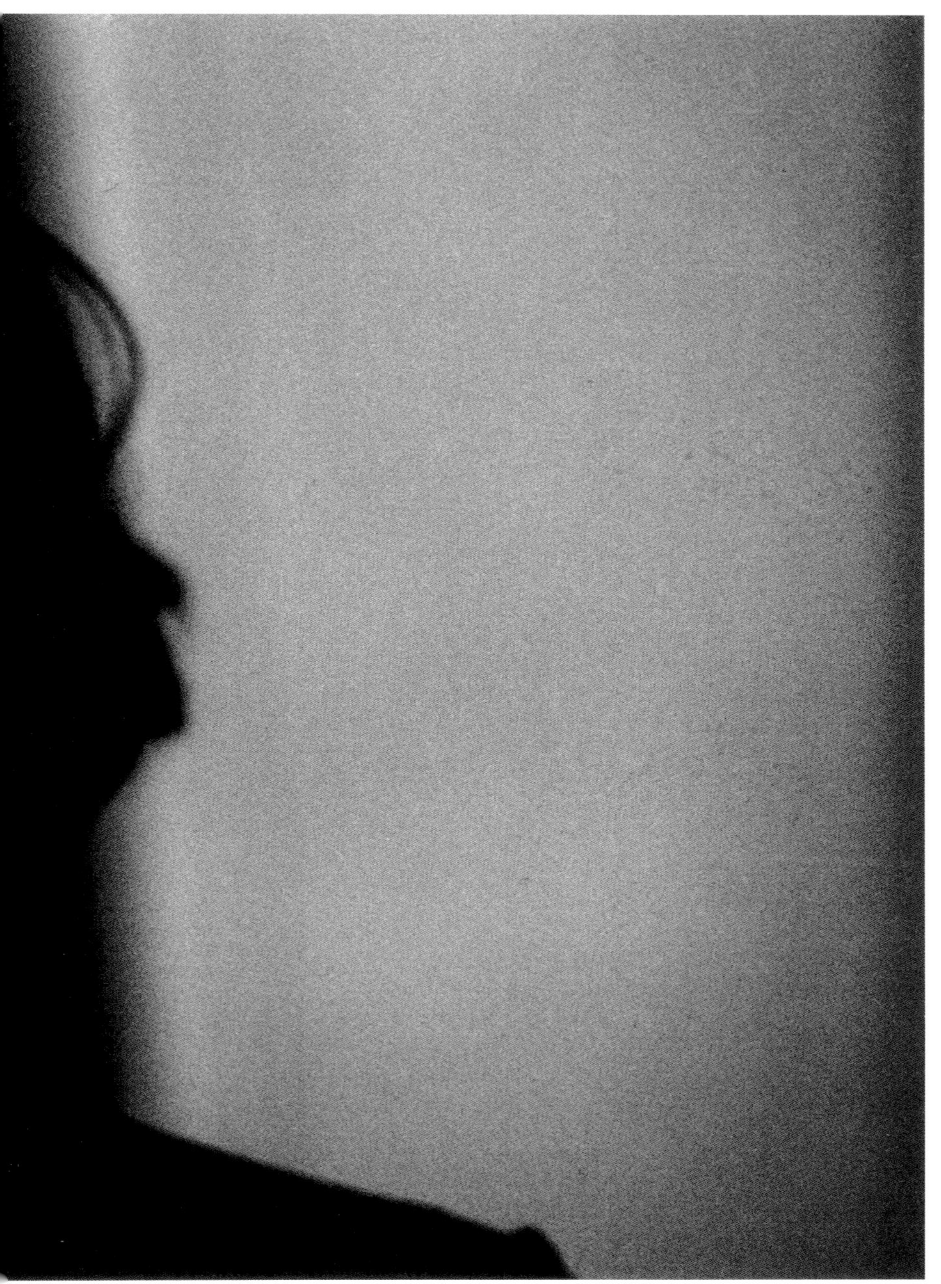

PAGES 64/65 Paris, 1962
In our kitchen, Rue Aubriot, Paris, 1972

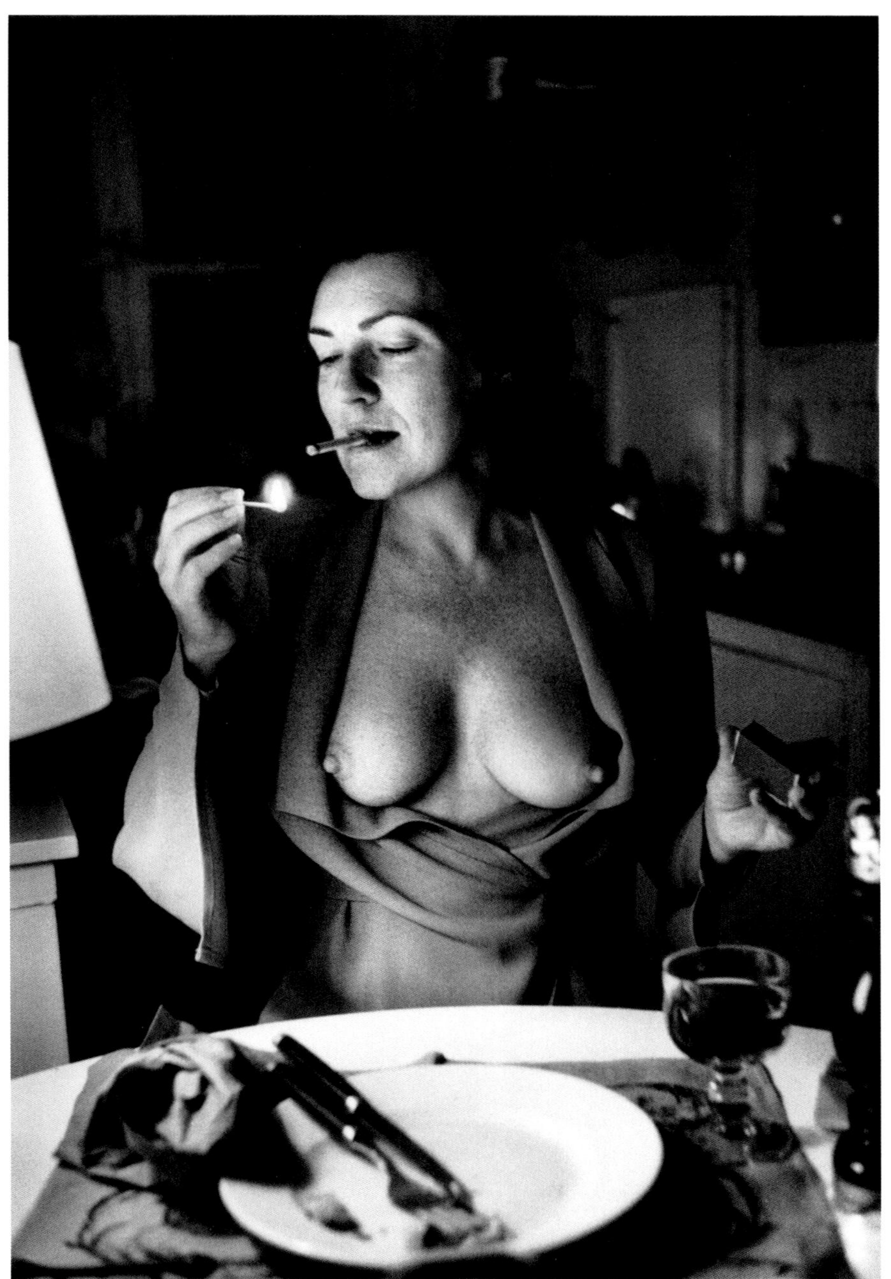

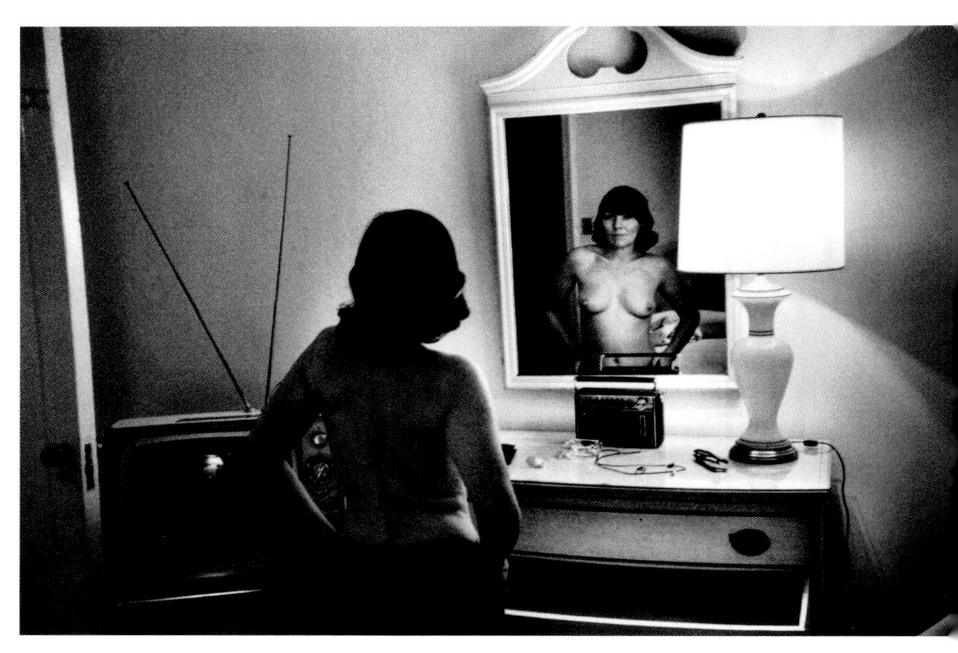

Hotel Volney, New York, 1972

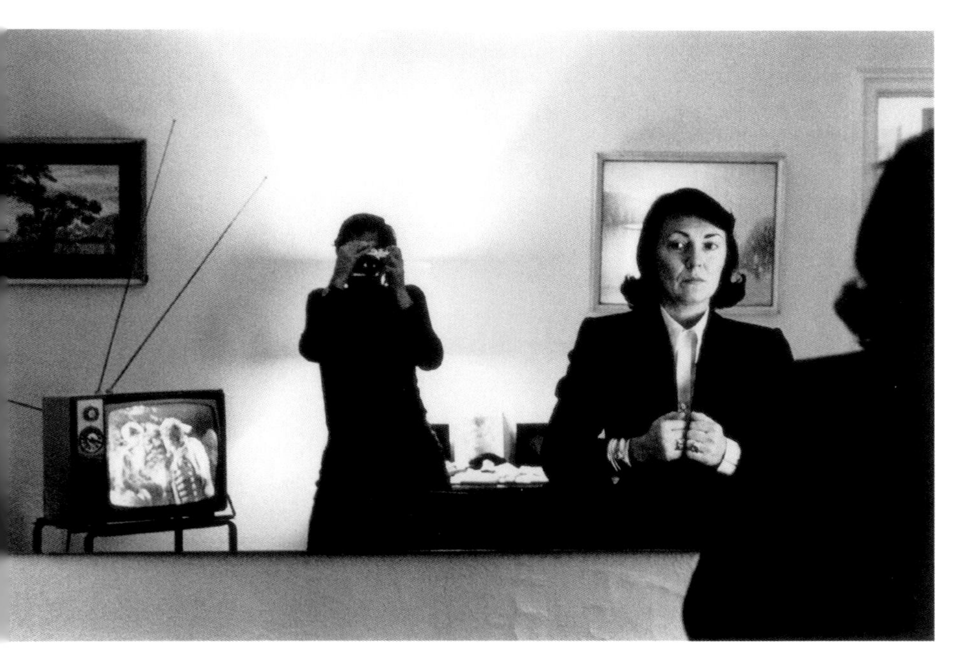

Hotel Volney, New York, 1982

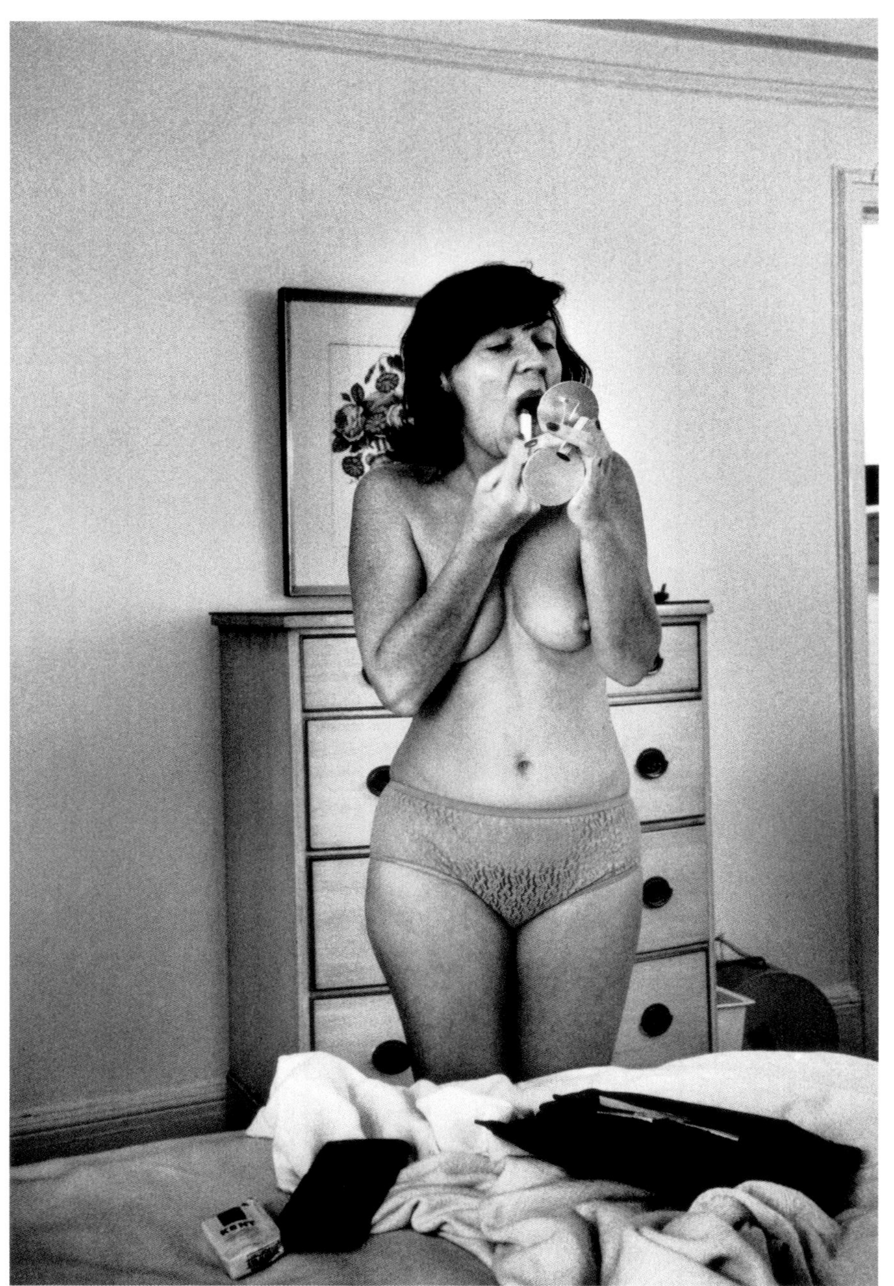

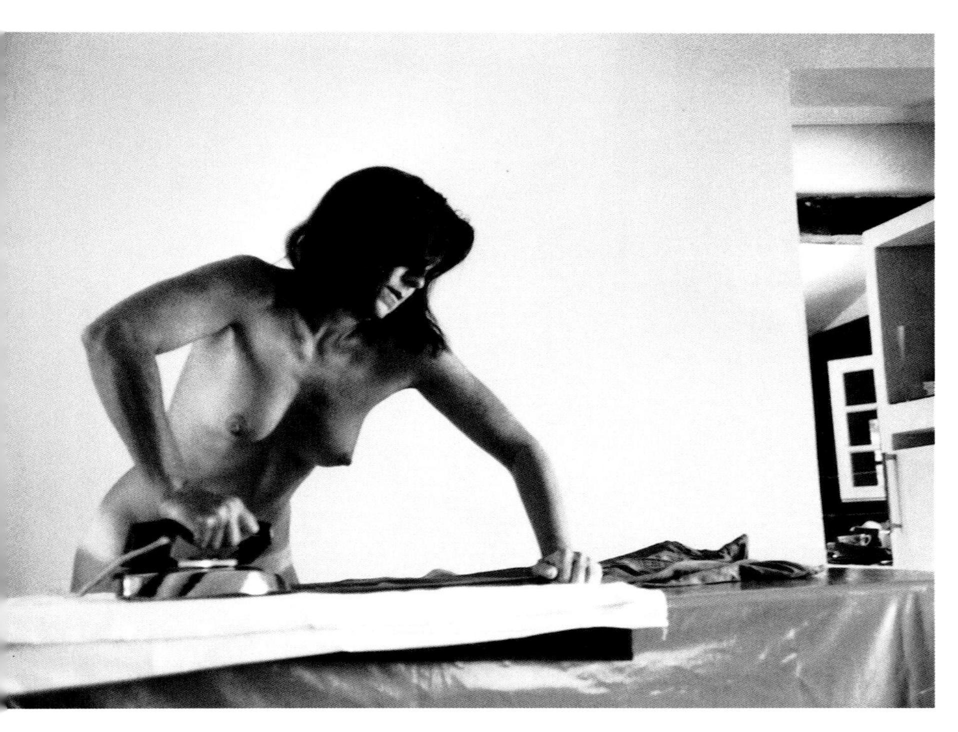

Hotel Volney, New York, 1972
Ramatuelle, 1972
PAGES 72/73 Ramatuelle, 1973

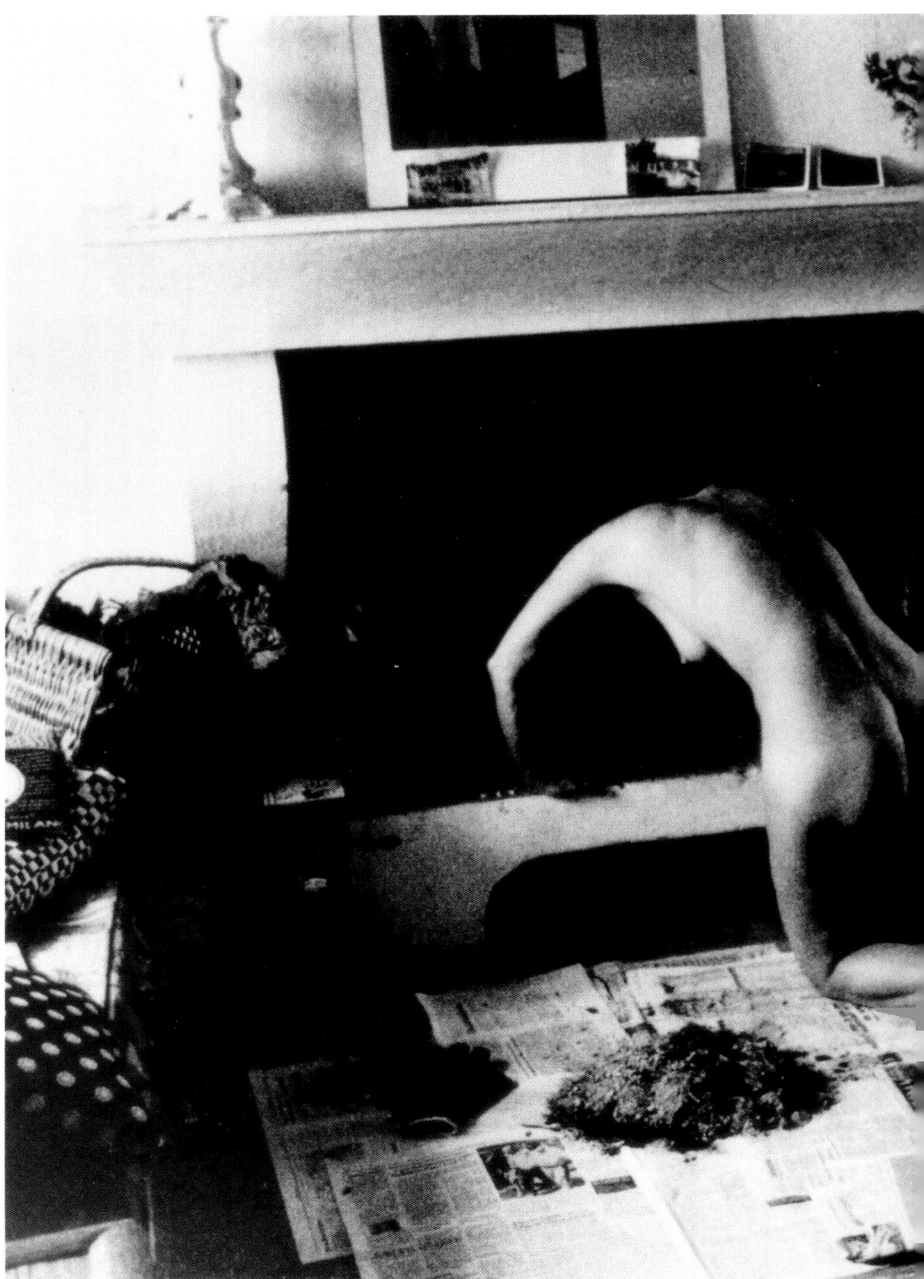

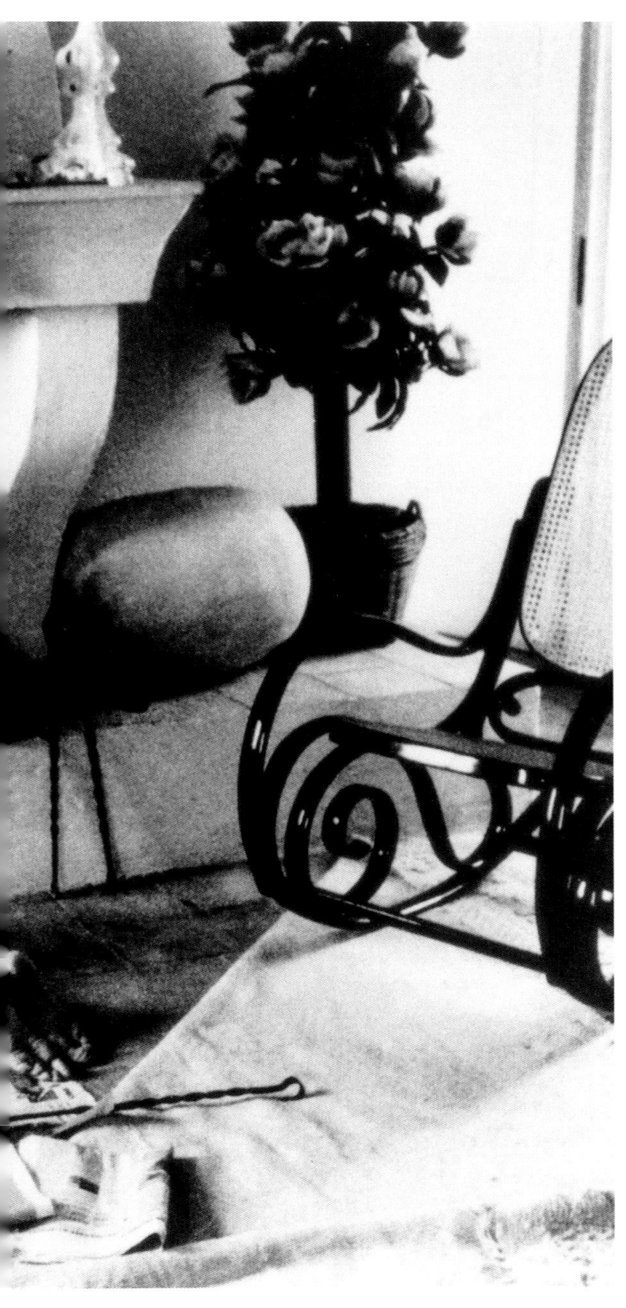

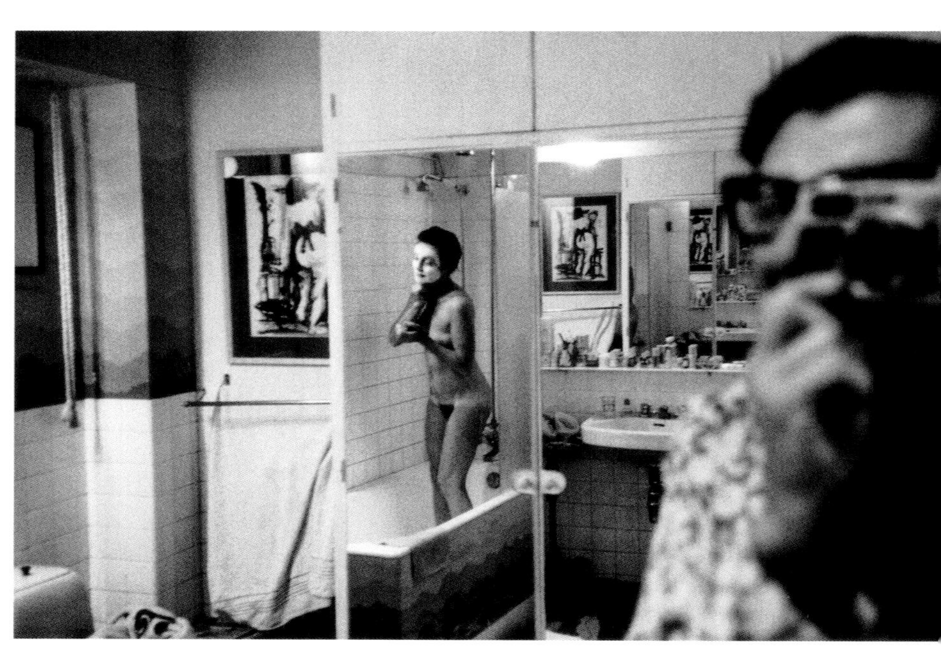

Rue Aubriot, Paris, 1974

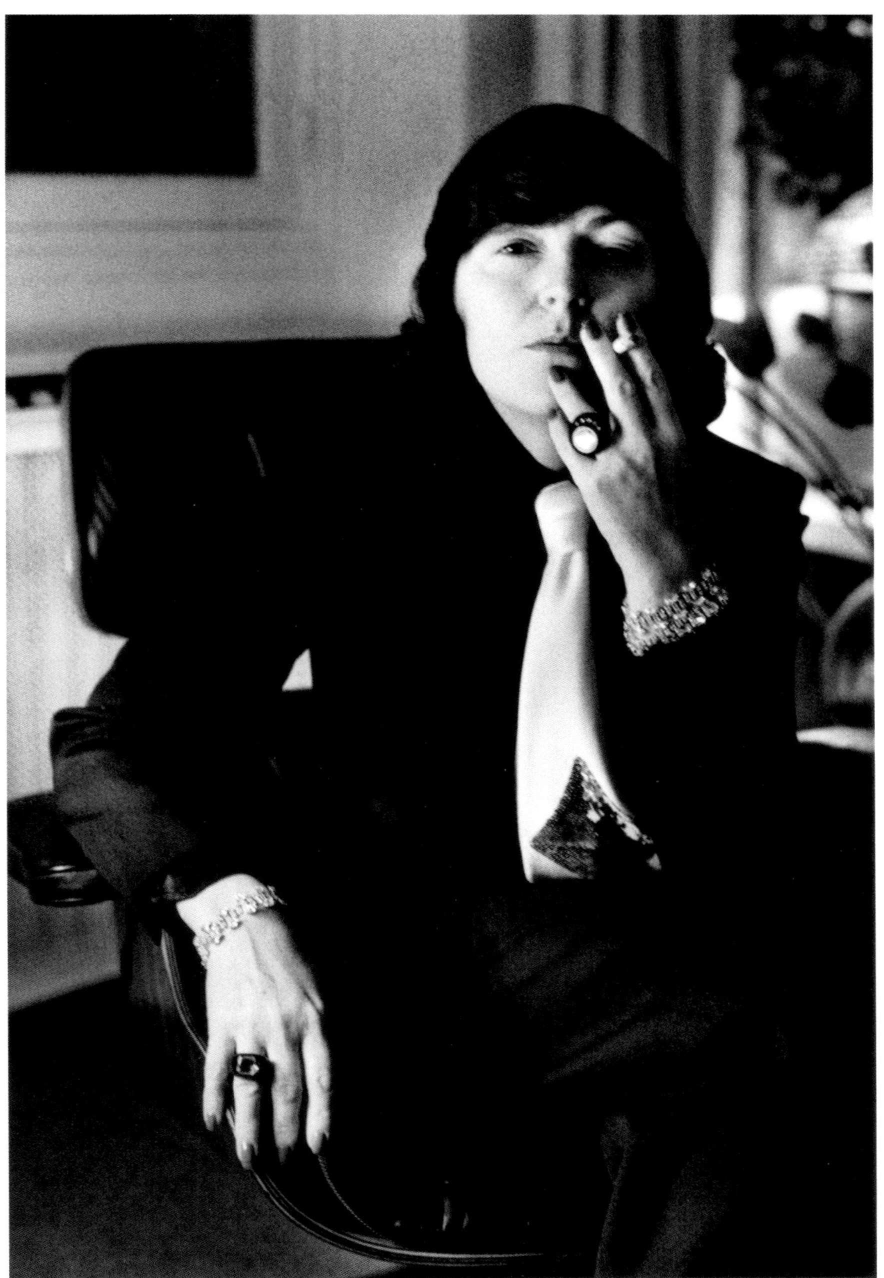

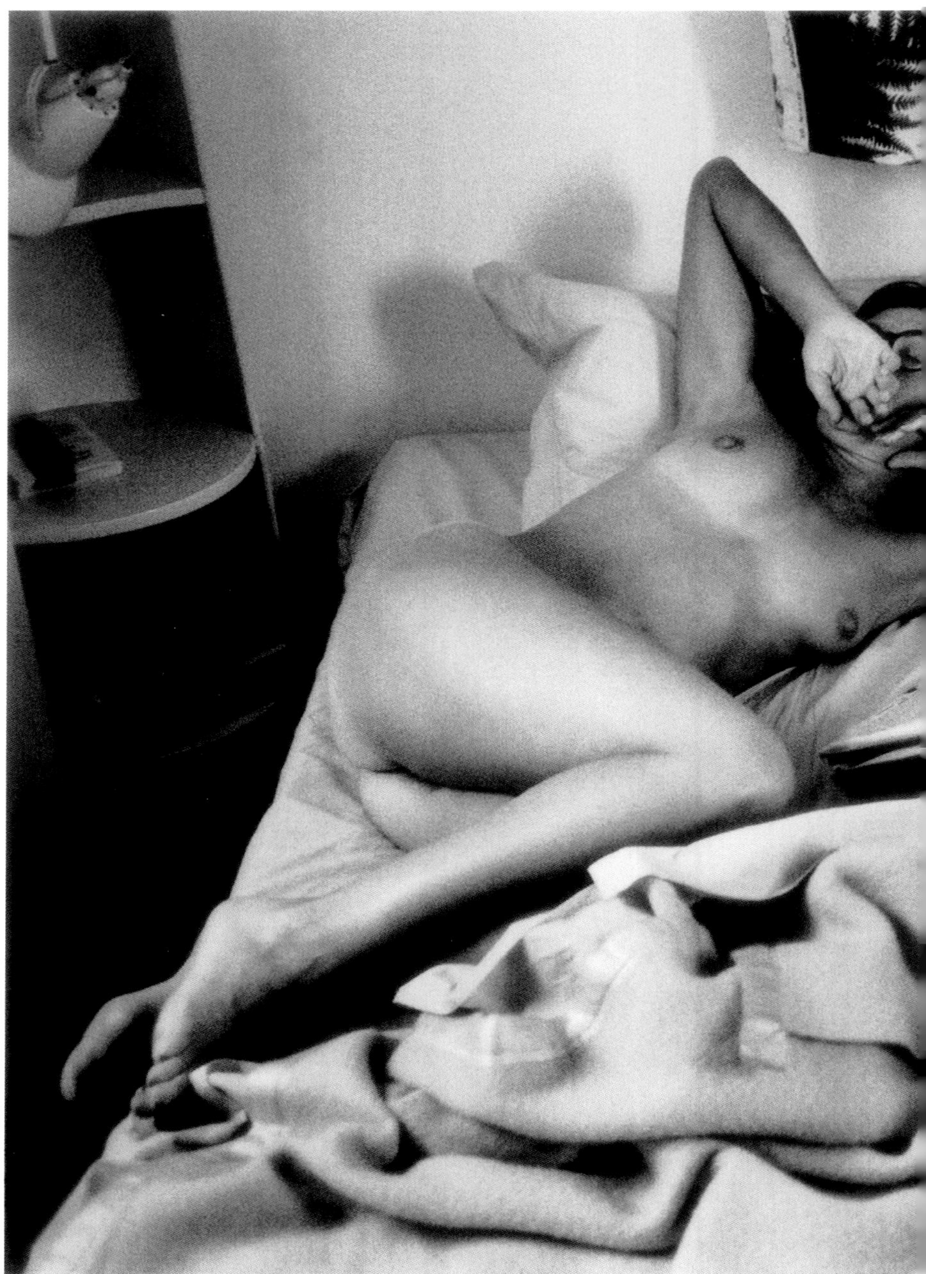

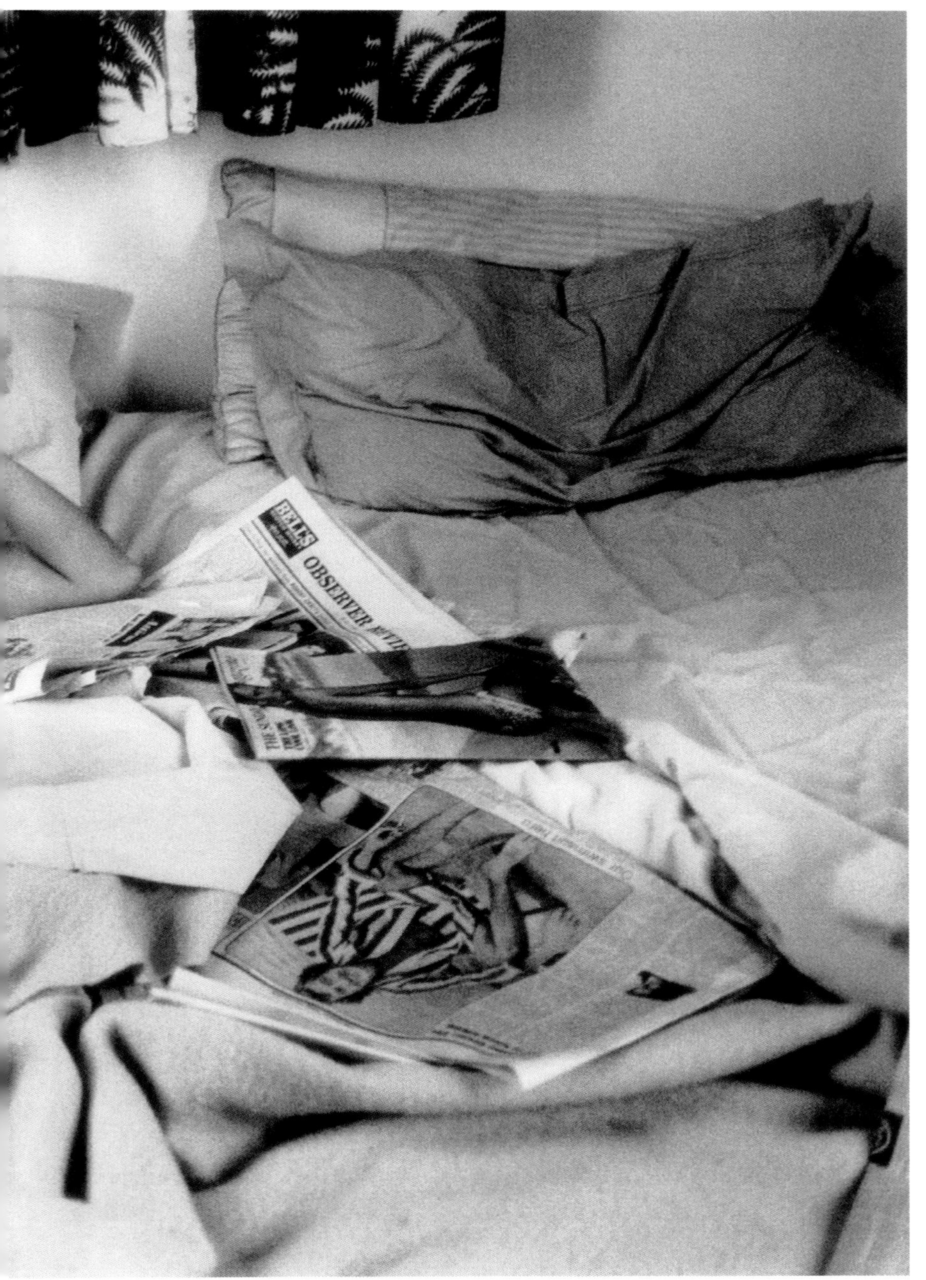

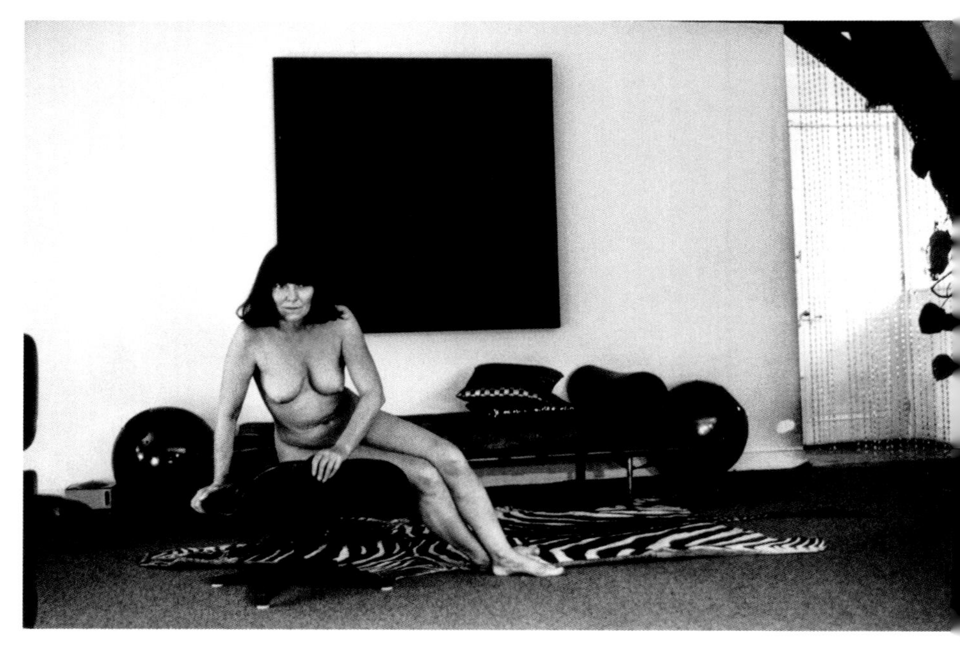

PAGES 76/77 Rue Aubriot, Paris, 1974
In our apartment, Rue Aubriot, Paris, 1975
Hotel Due Torri, Verona, 1978

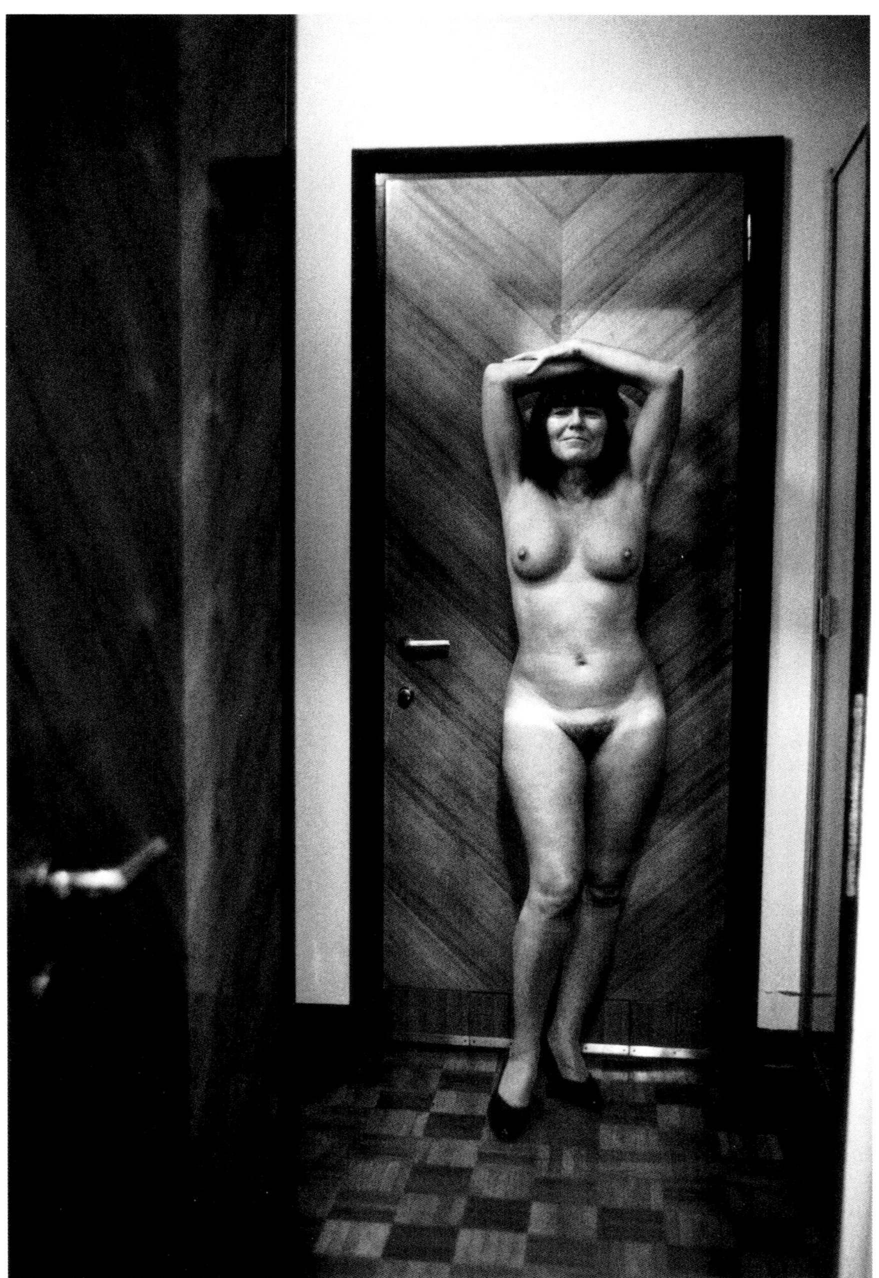

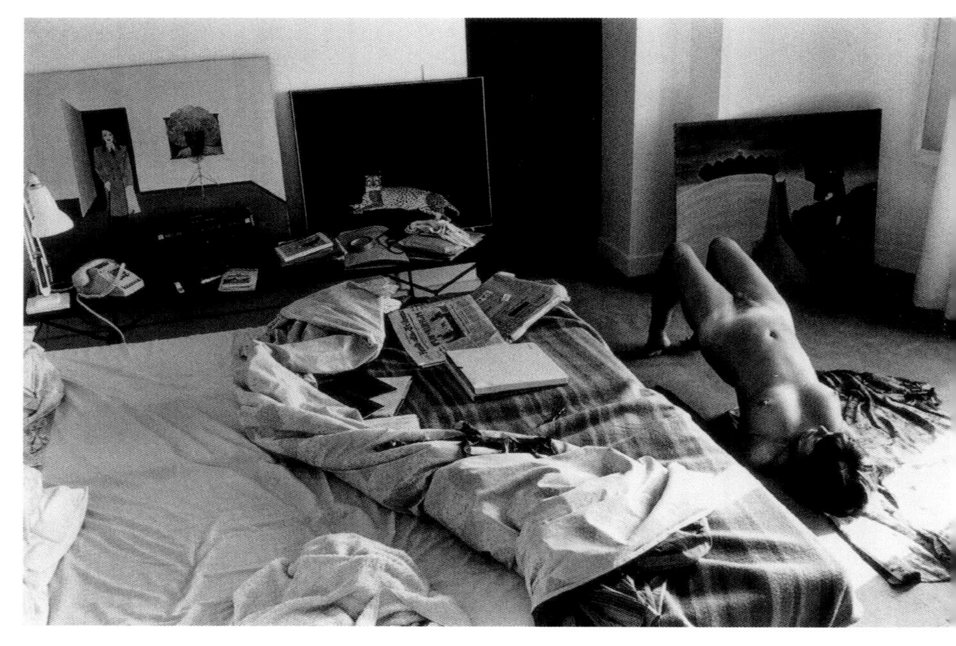

Our apartment, Rue de l'Abbé de l'Épée, Paris, 1978
Ramatuelle, 1980
PAGES 82/83 Ramatuelle, 1976

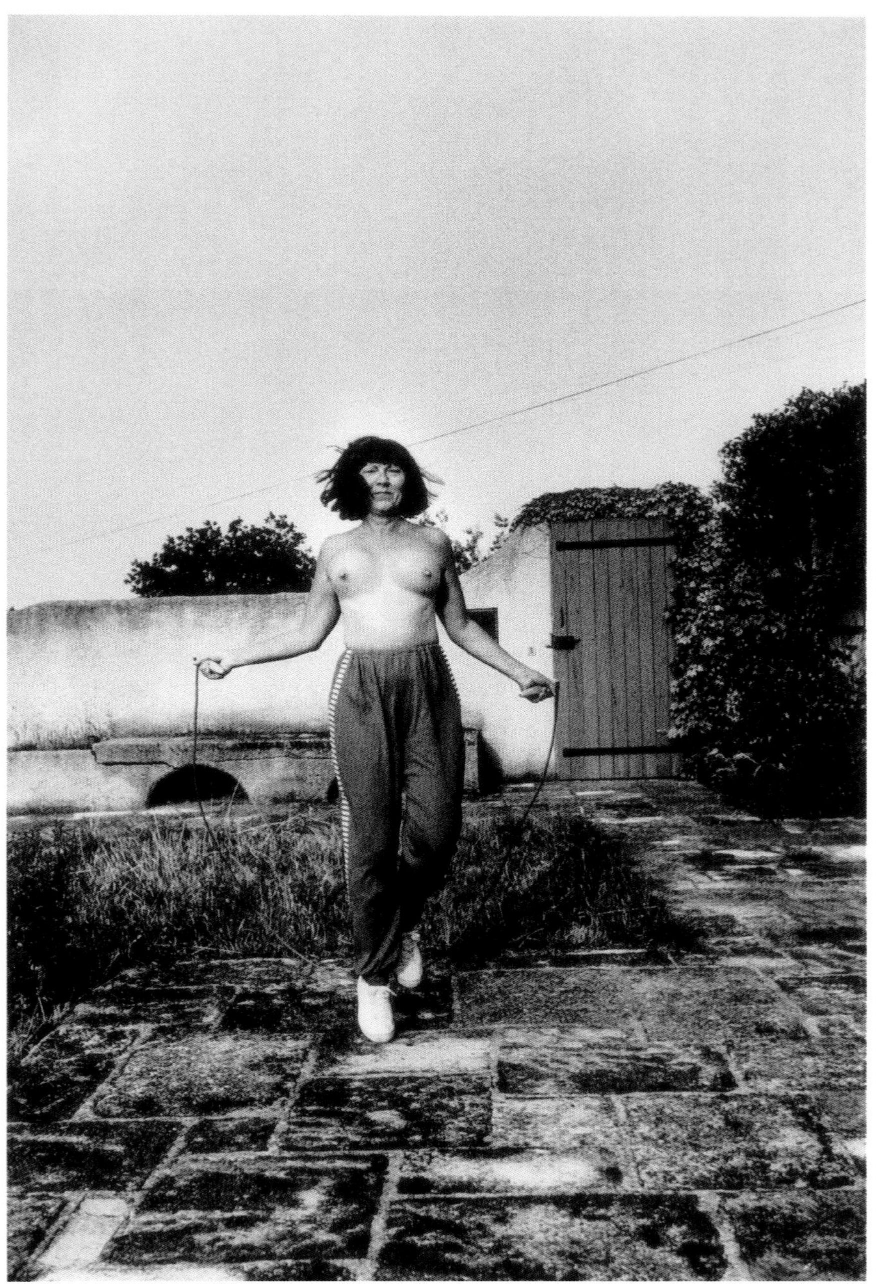

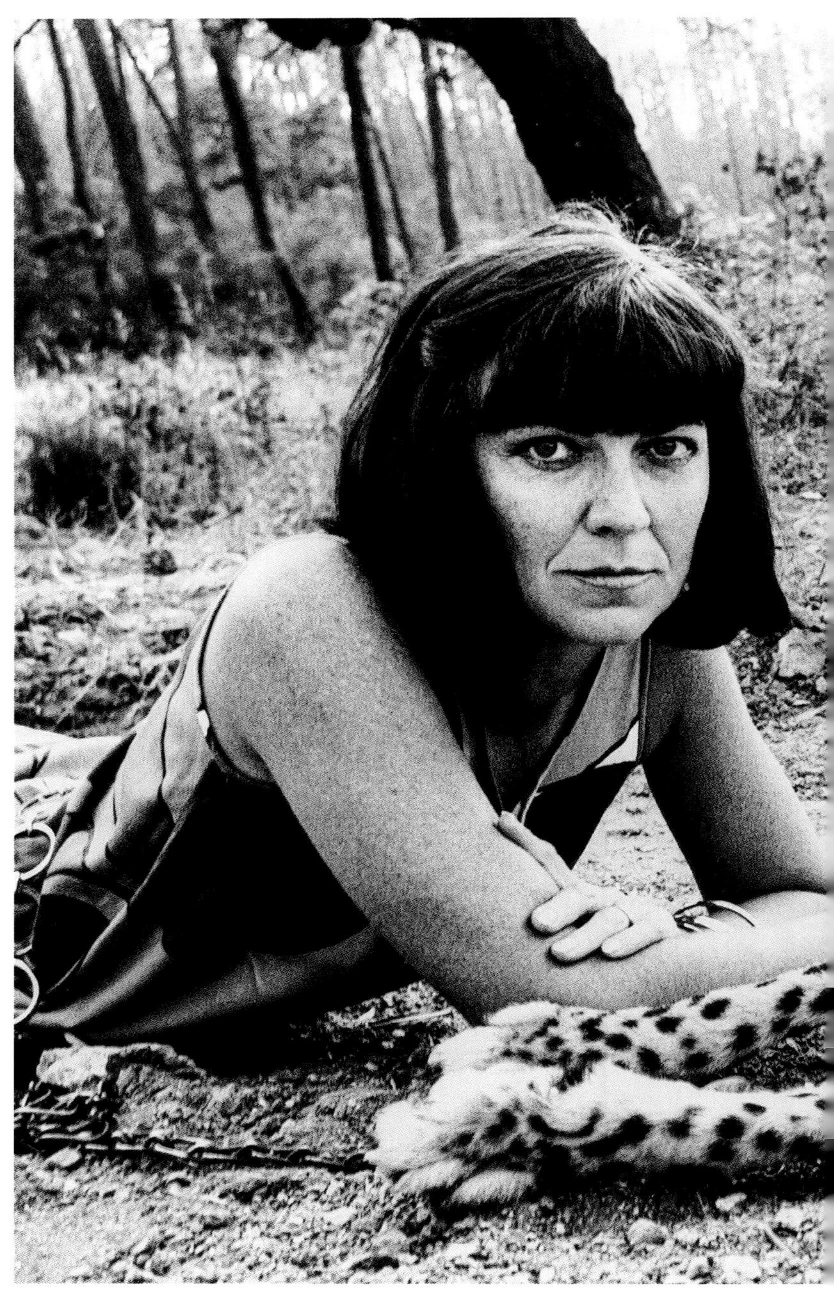

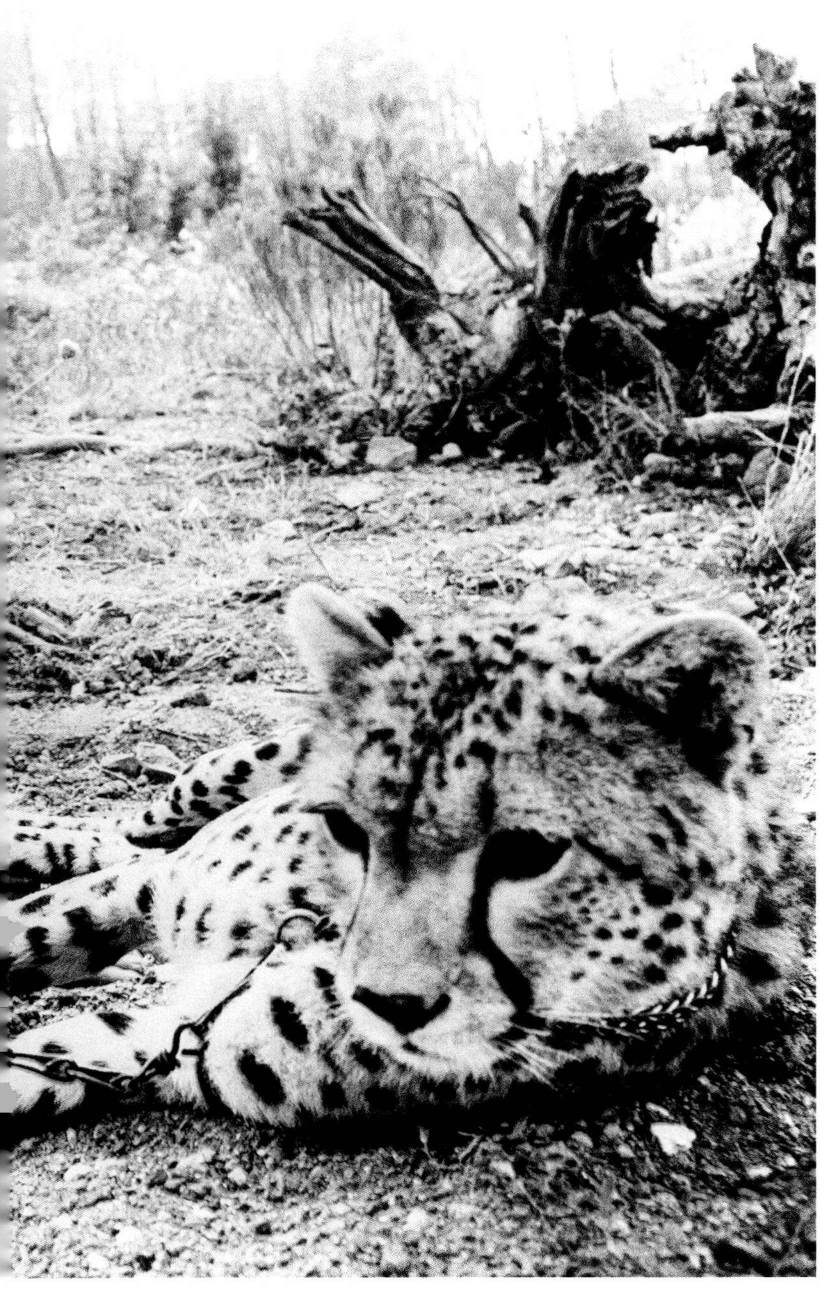

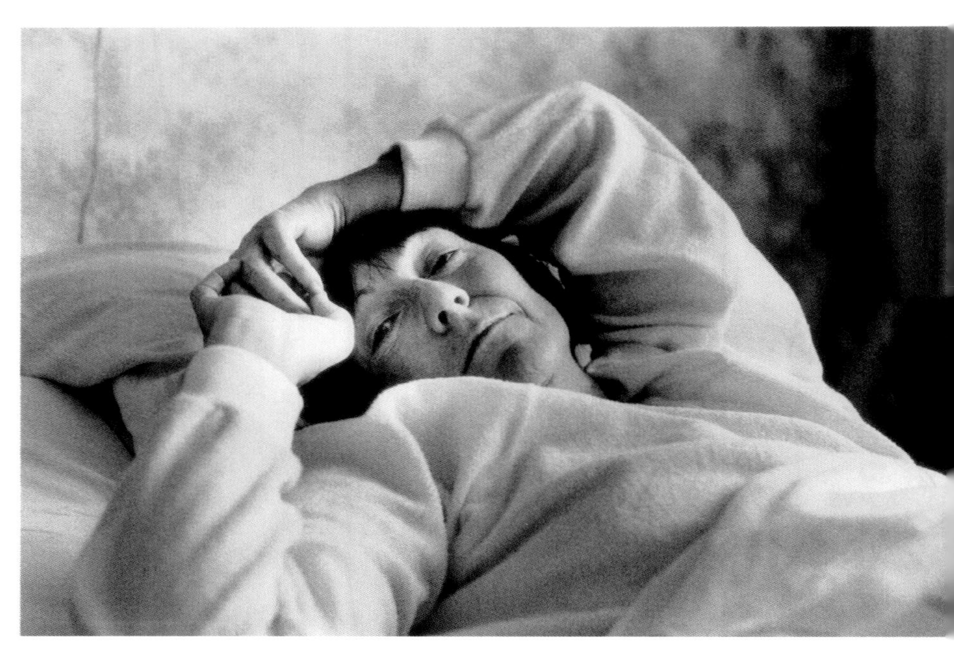

Hospital, Paris, 1982

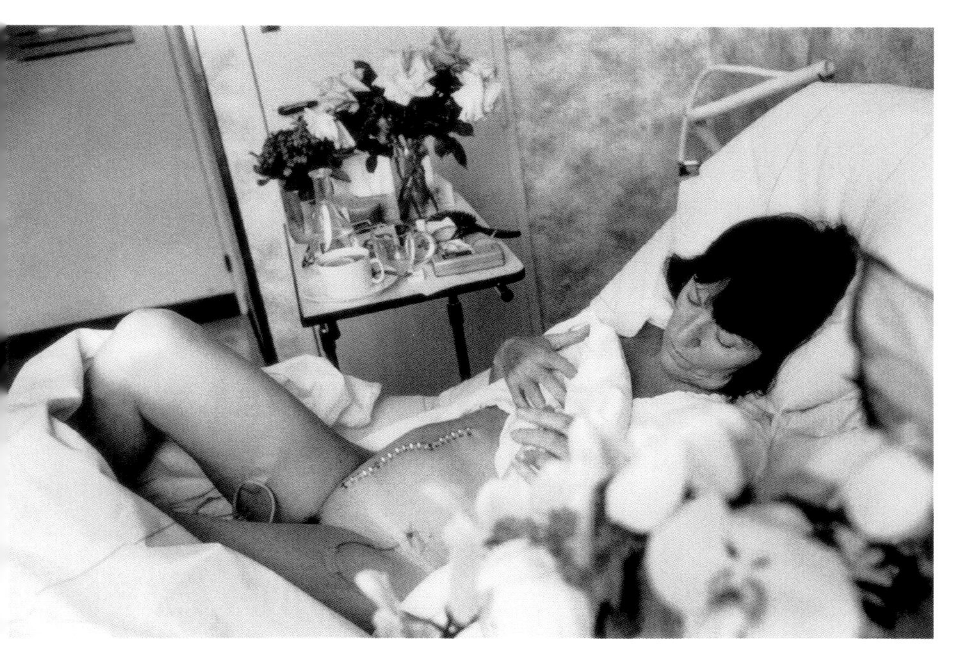

PAGES 86/87 Monte Carlo, 1982

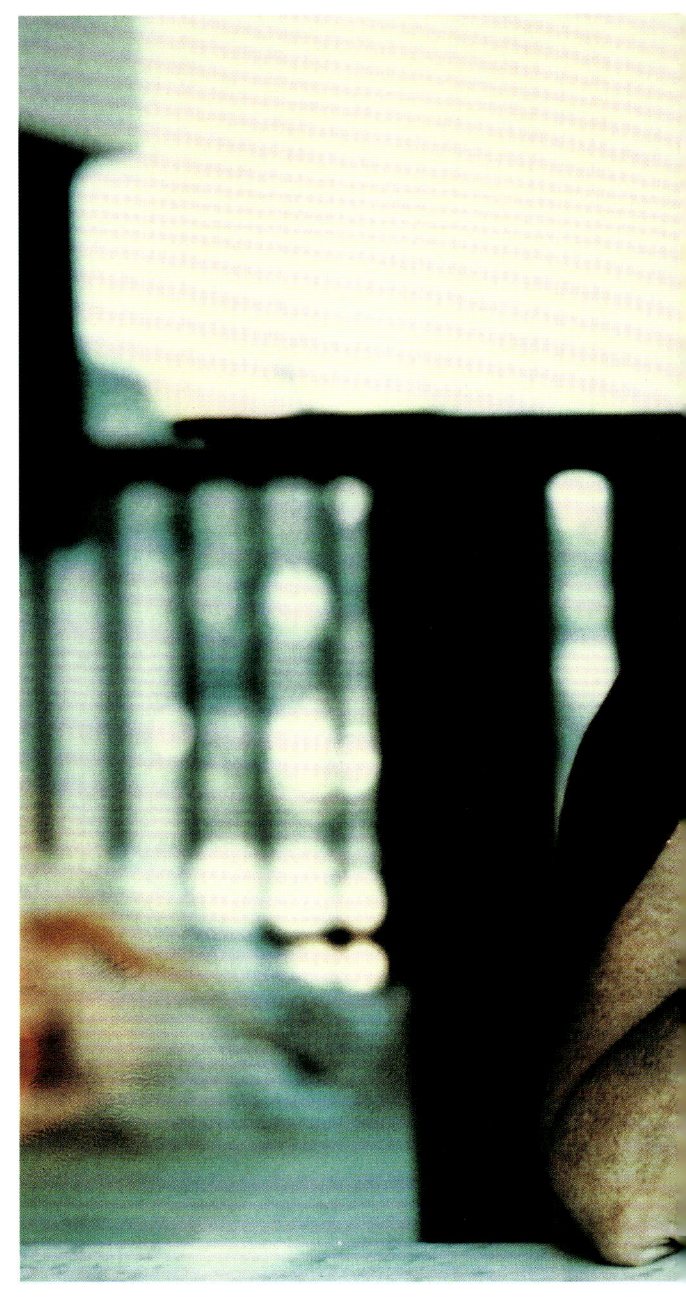

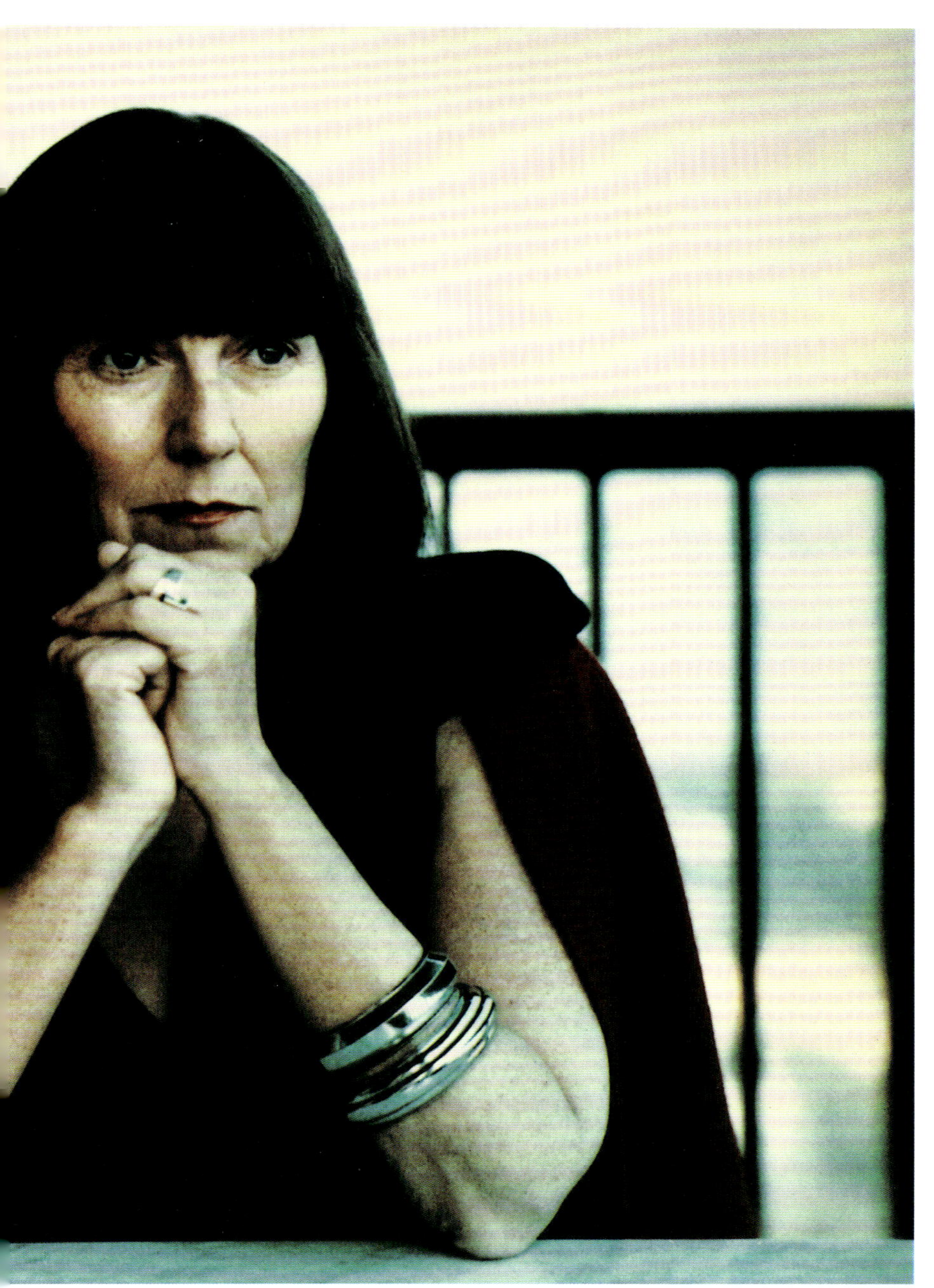

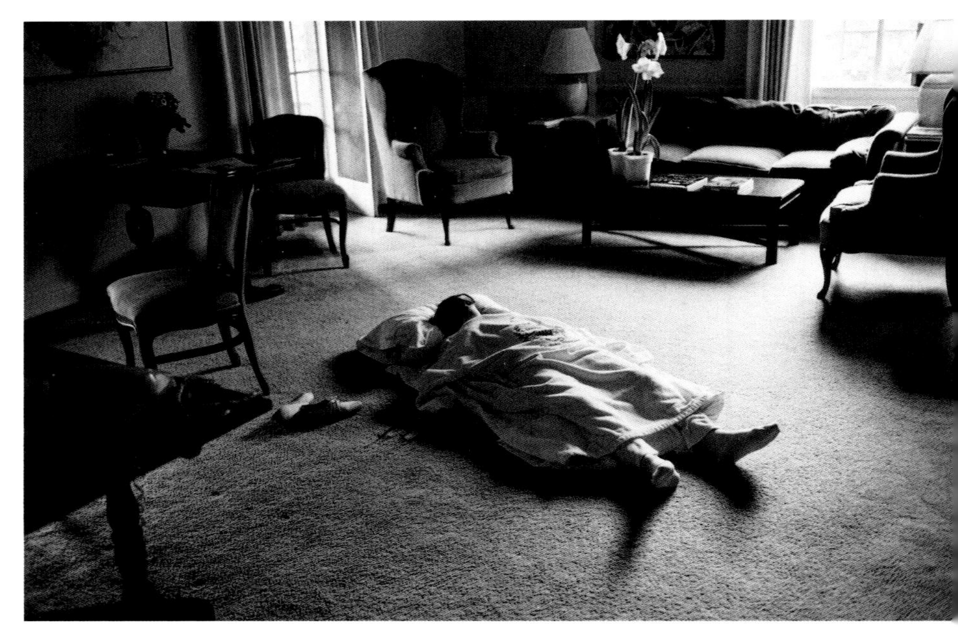

Chateau Marmont, Hollywood, 1991
Monte Carlo, 1997

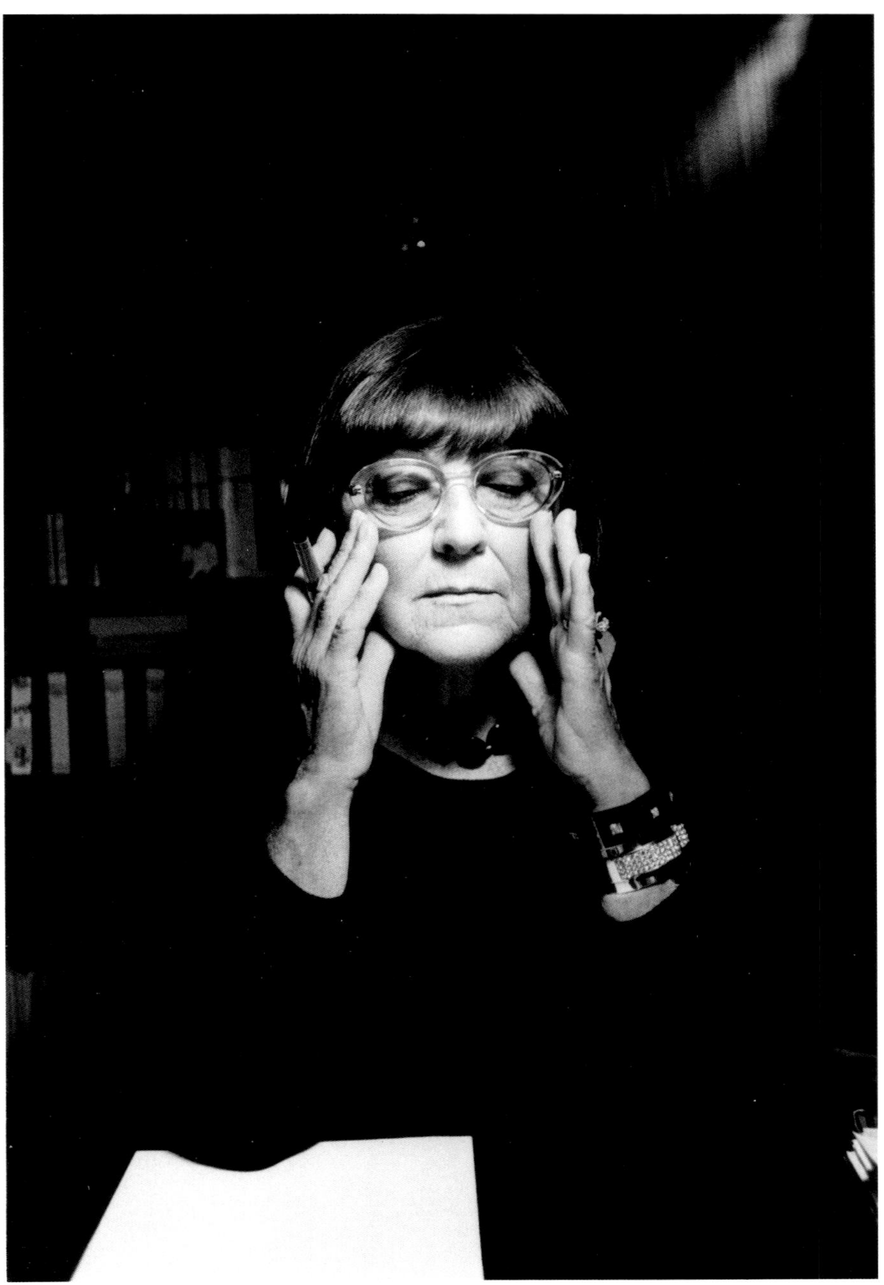

HELMUT NEWTON

SELF-PORTRAITS

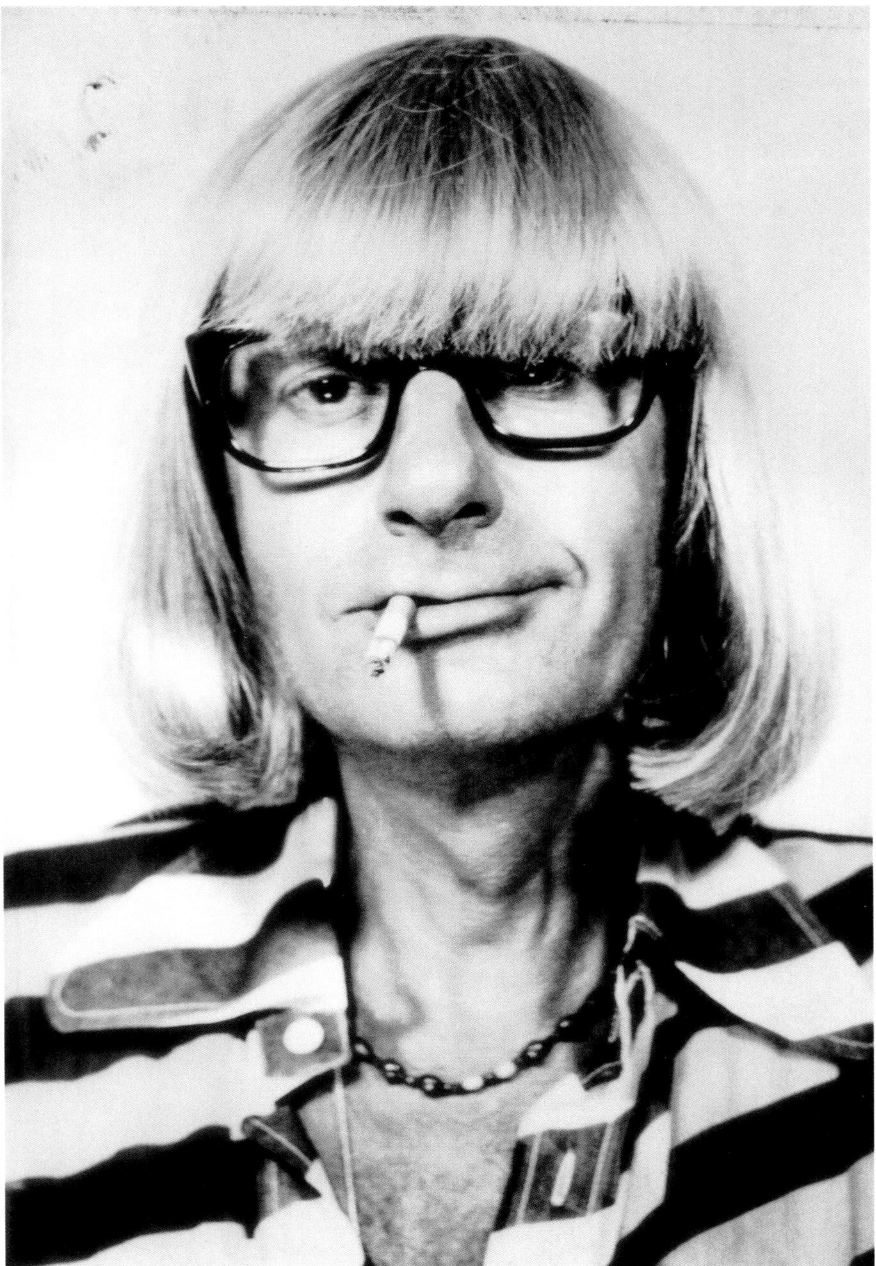

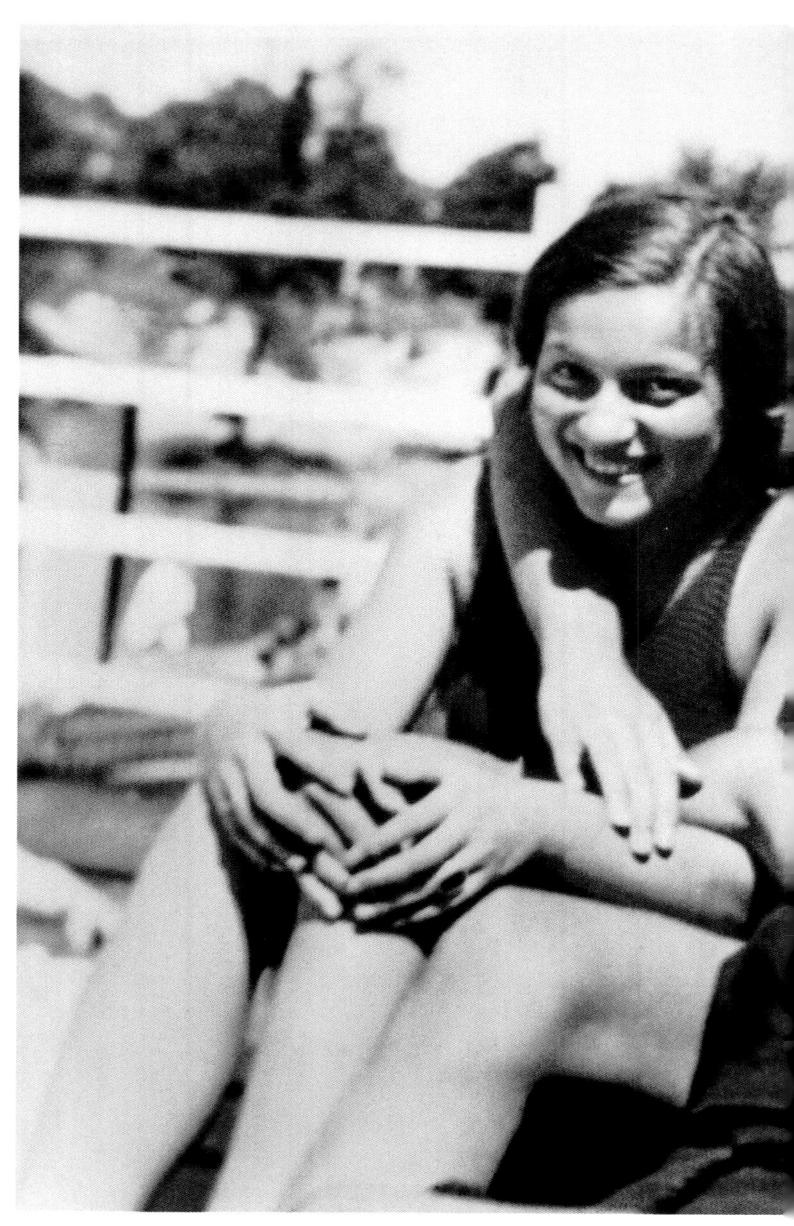

PAGE 91 Photomaton, Paris, 1973

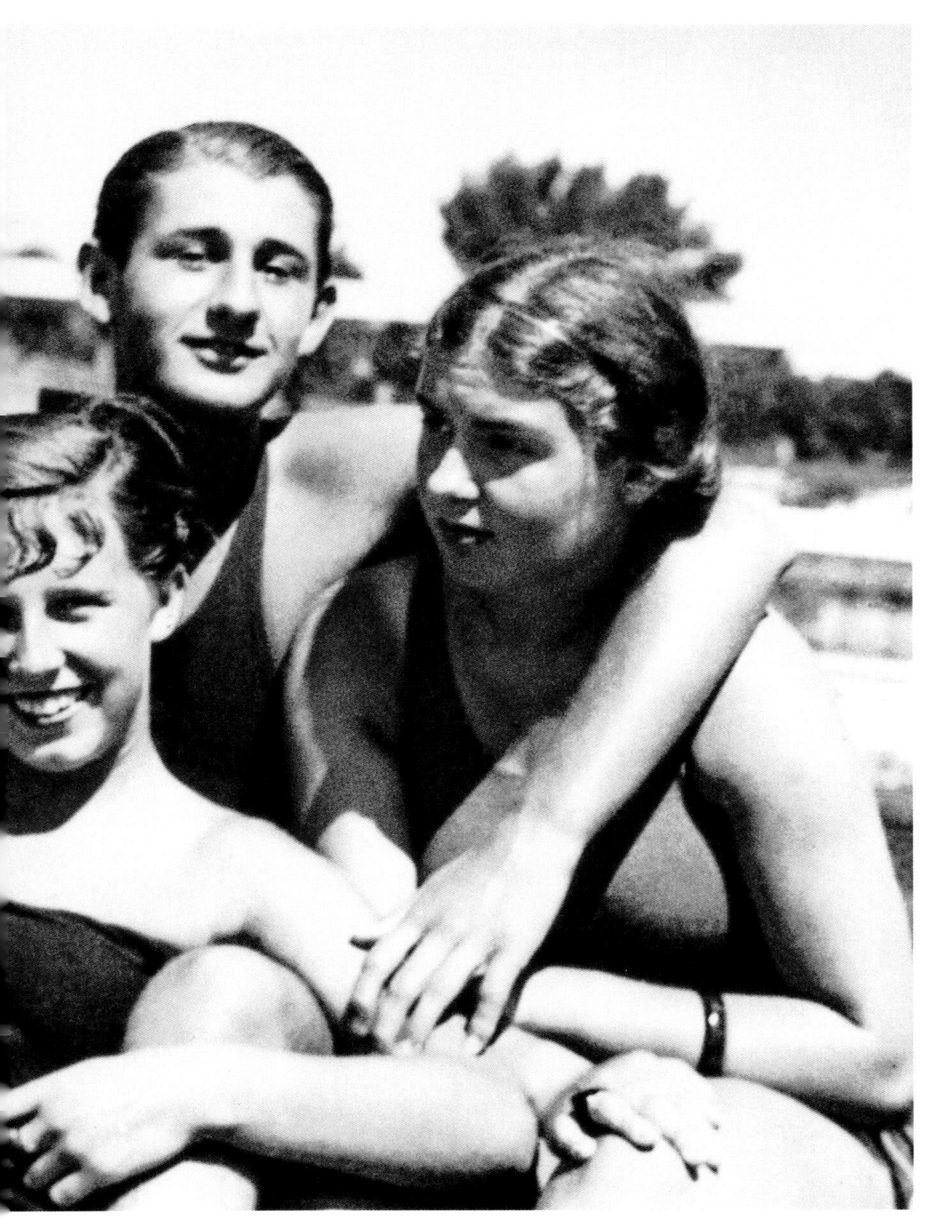

Halensee public bath, Berlin, 1936

In Yva's studio, Berlin, 1936

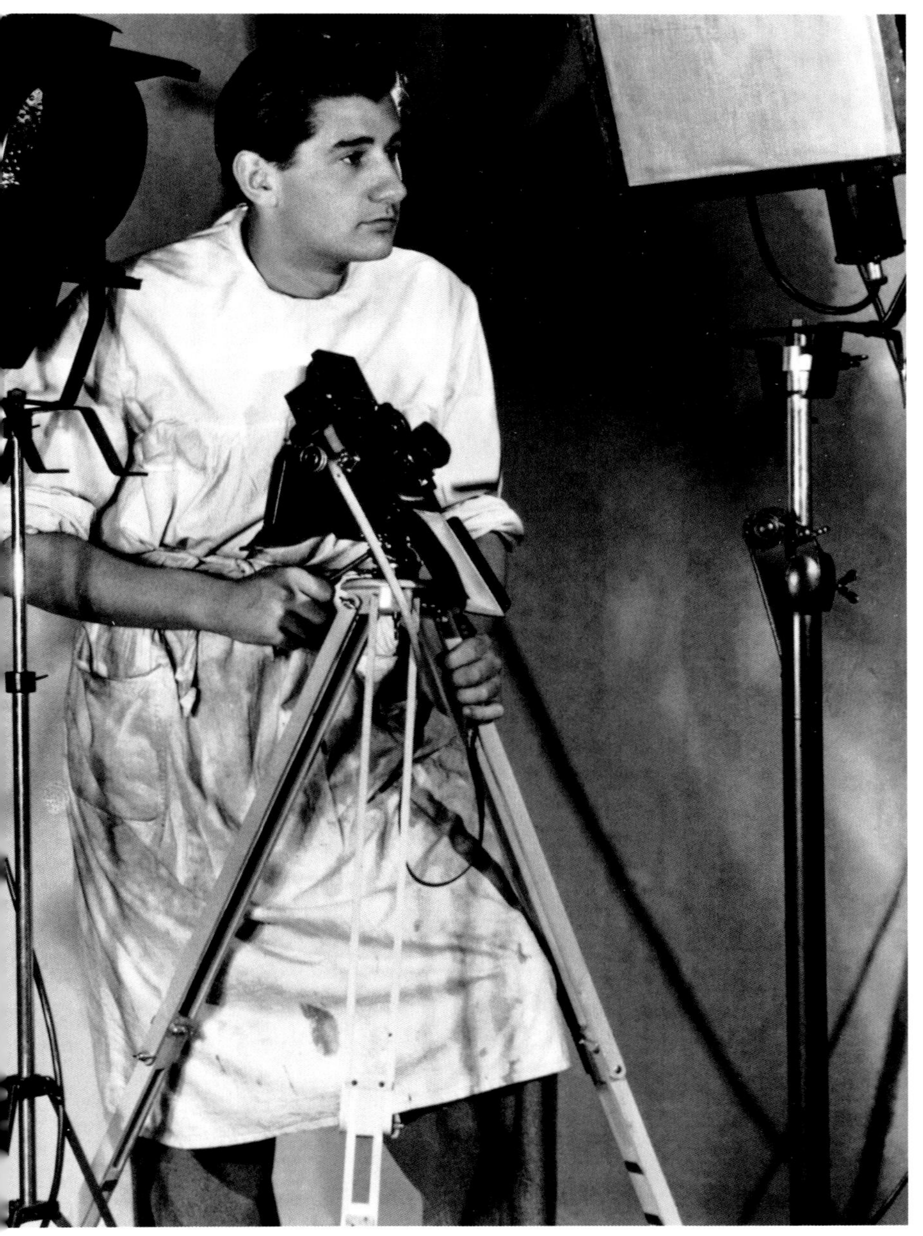

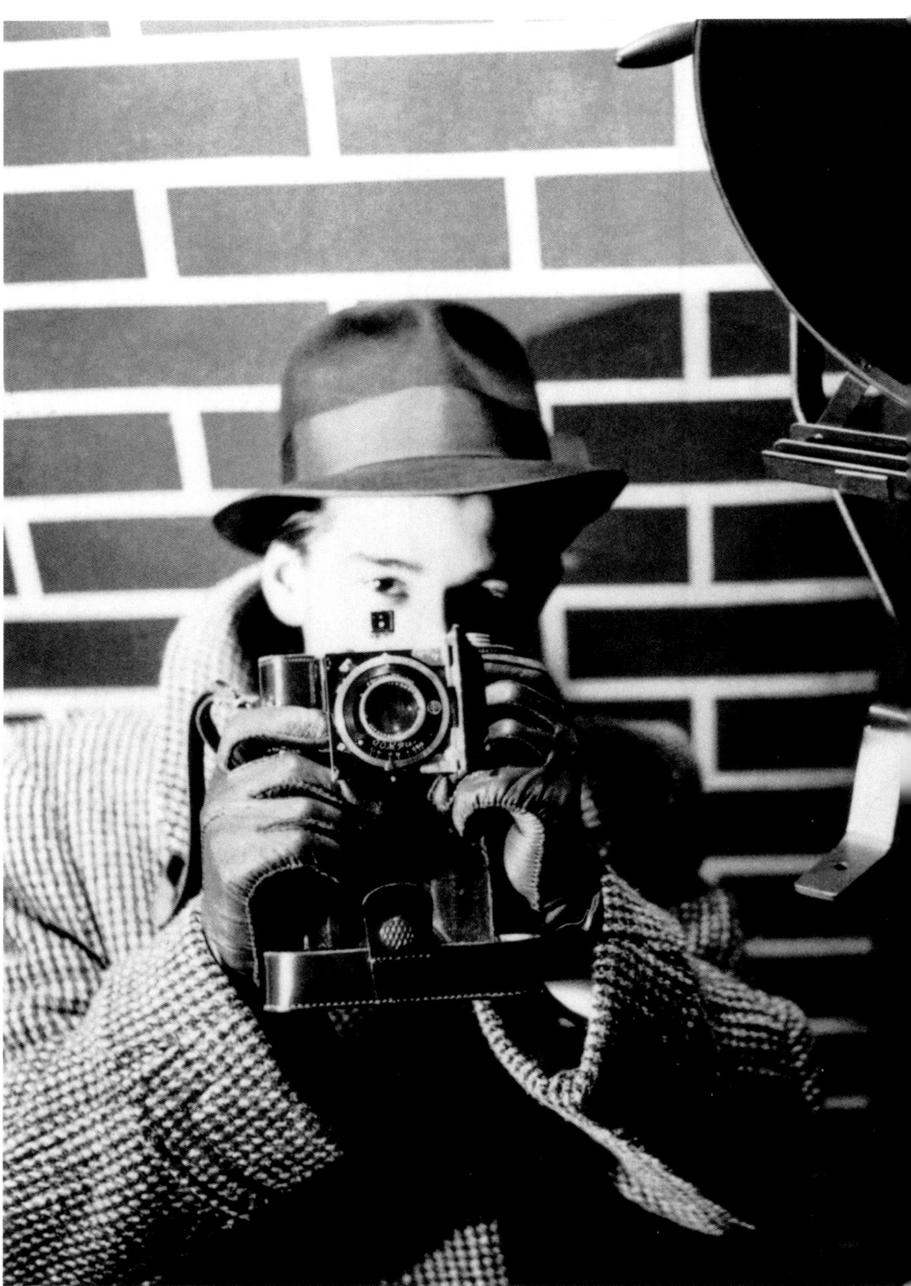

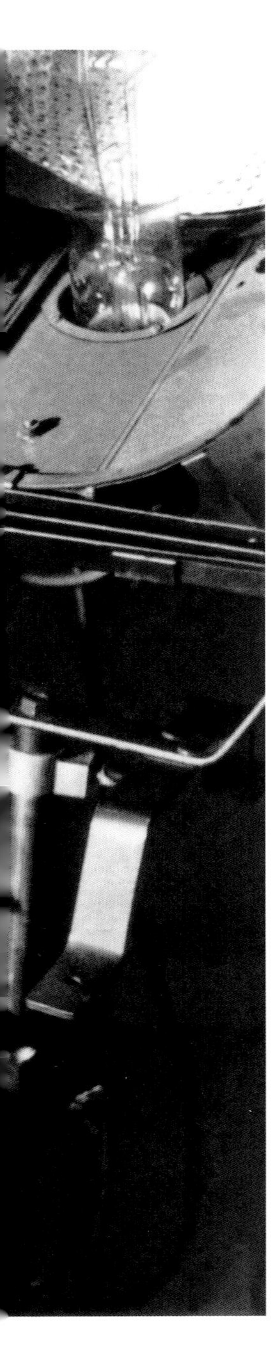

In Yva's studio, Berlin, 1936

Self-portrait with model, Paris, 1973

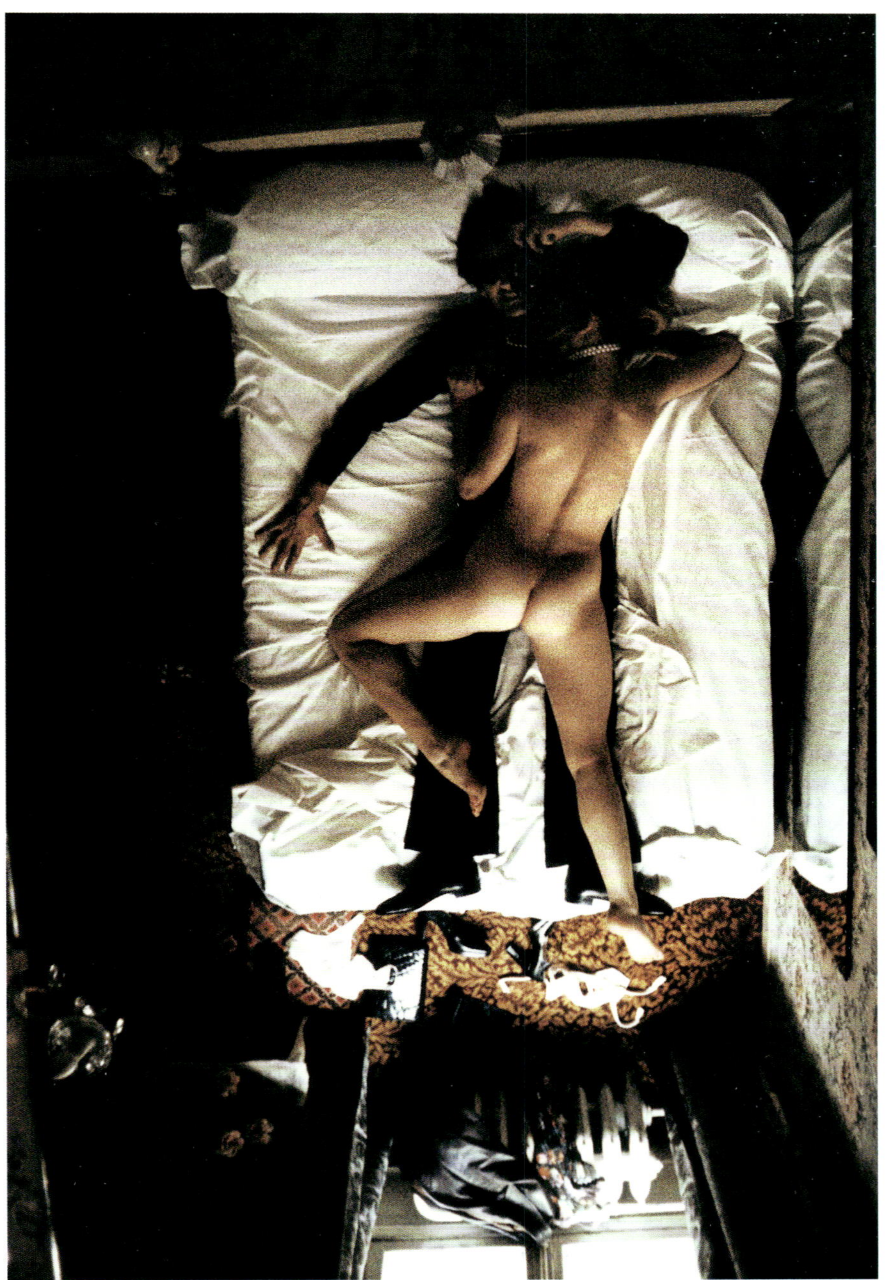

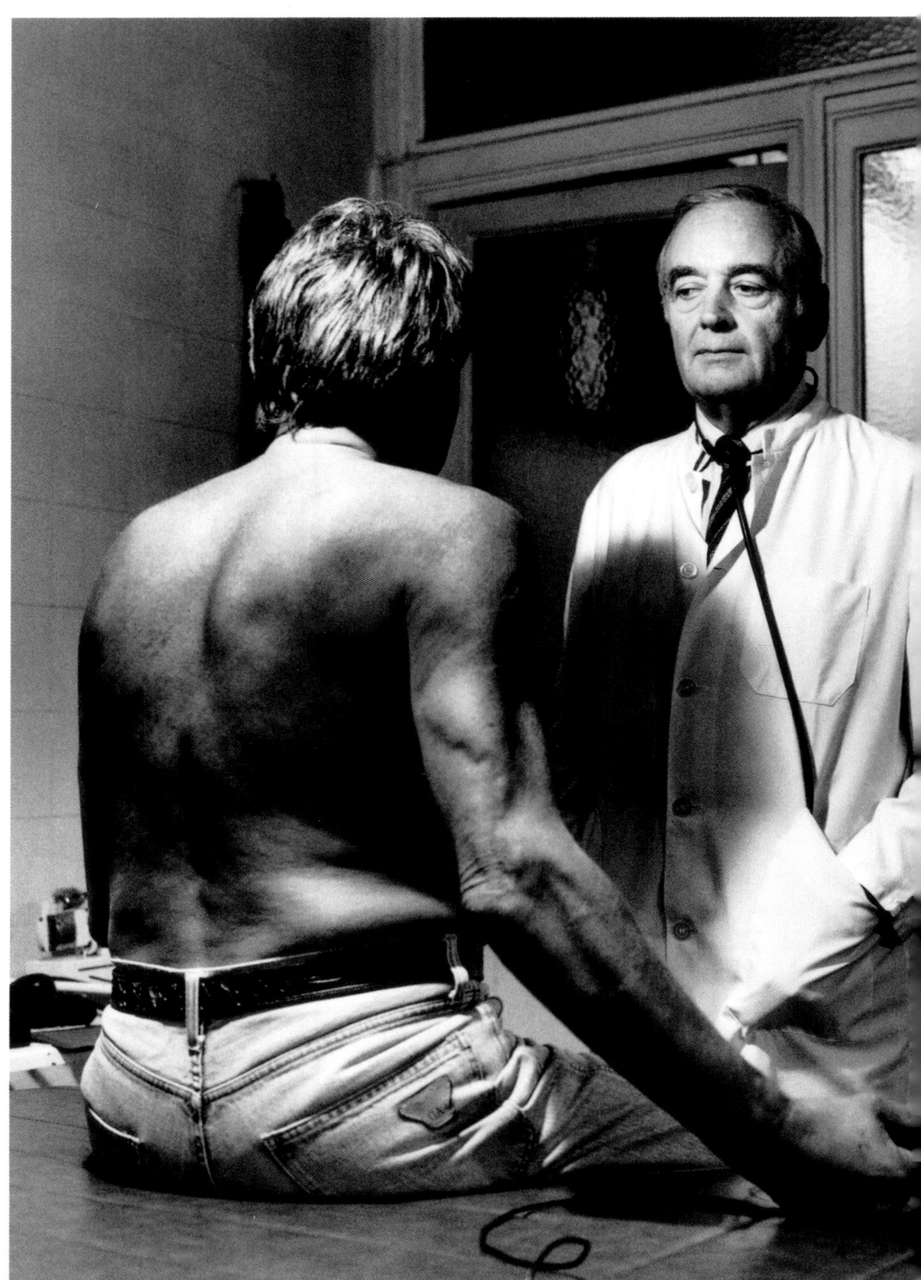

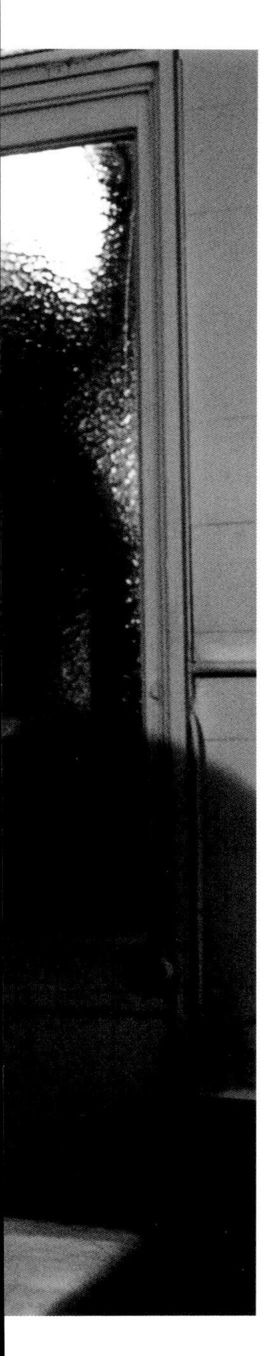

Self-portrait with
Dr. Jean Dax, Paris, 1985

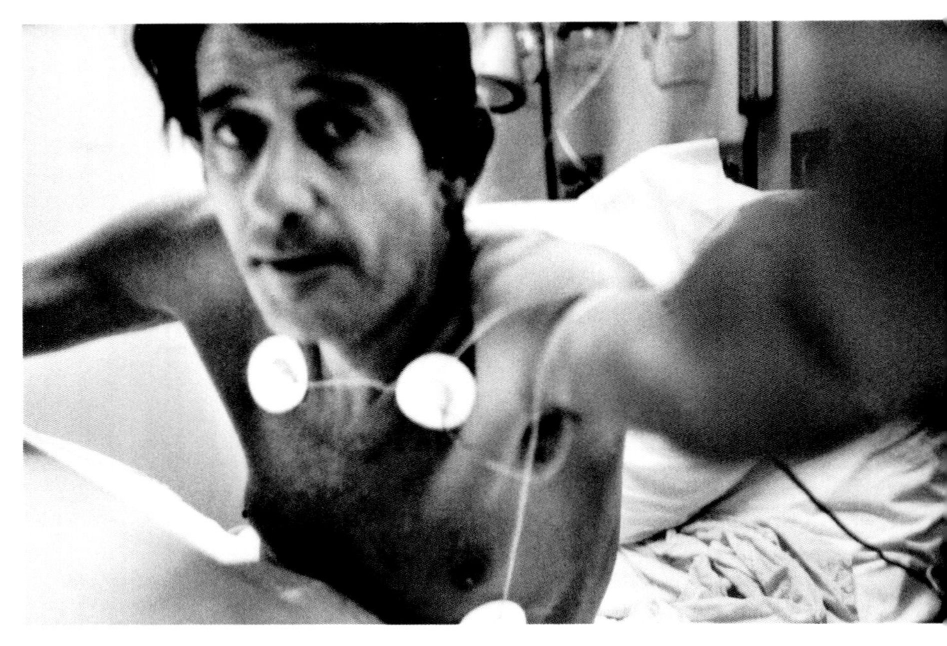

Lenox Hill Hospital, New York, 1973
PAGES 104/105 Hotel Due Torri, Verona, 1976

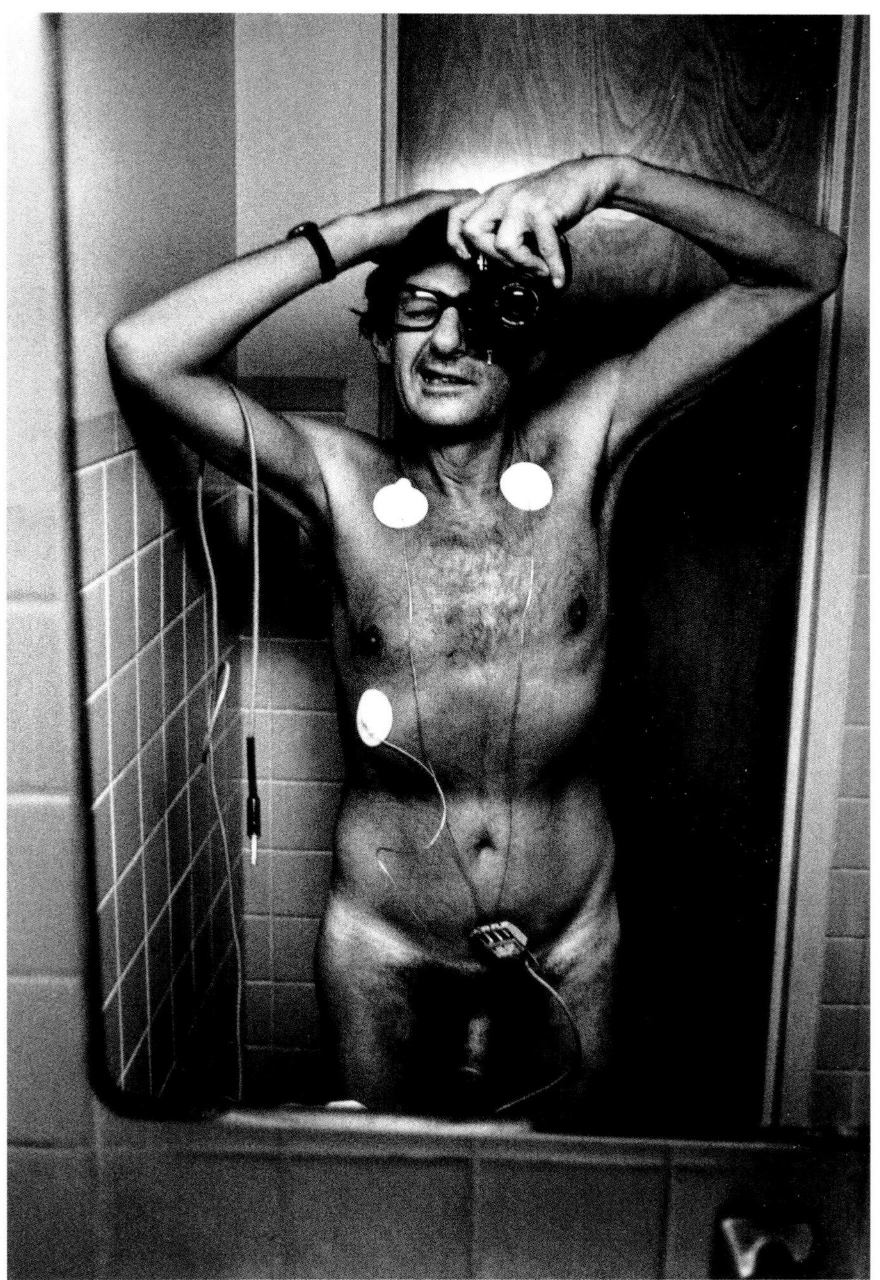

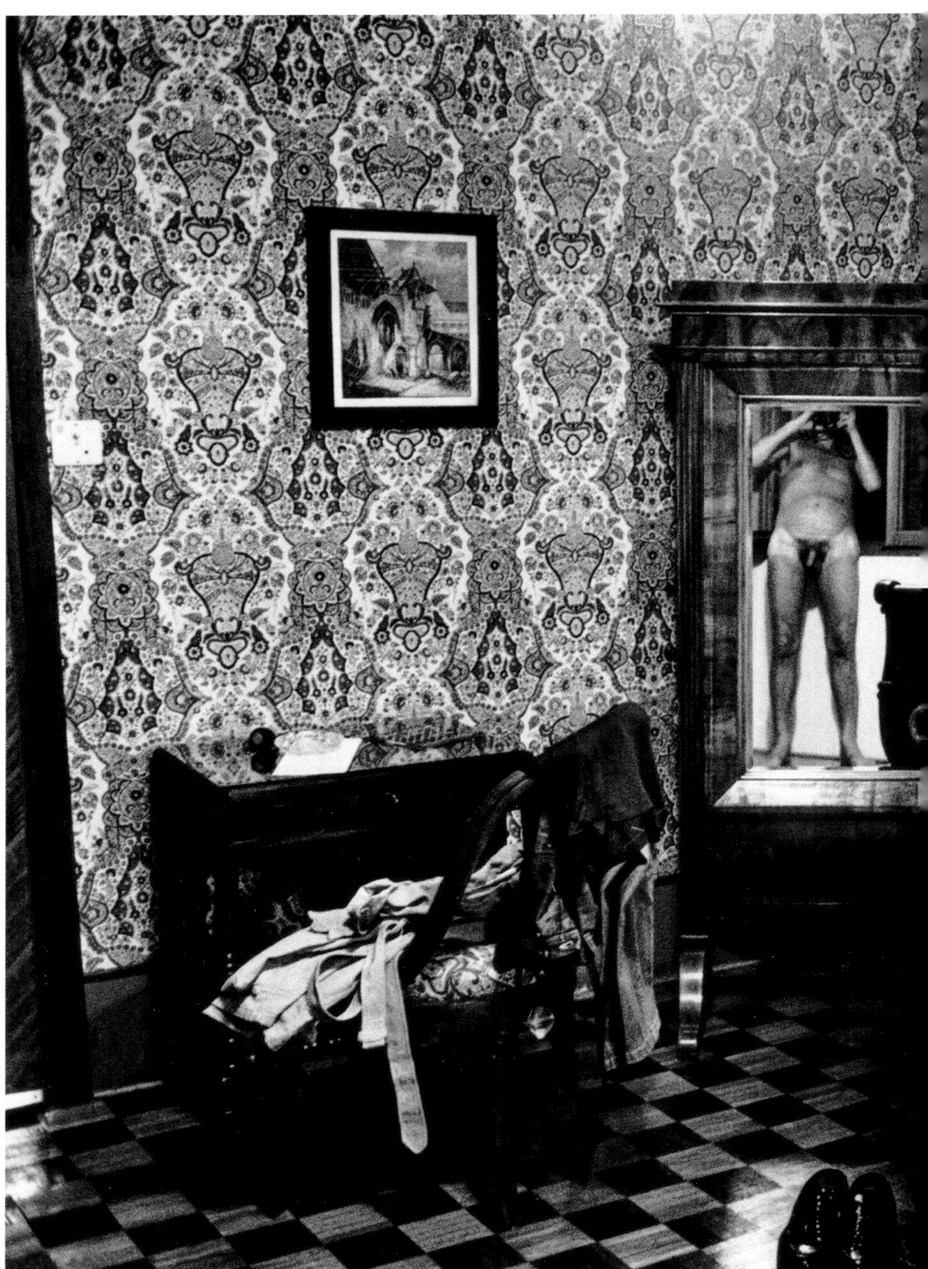

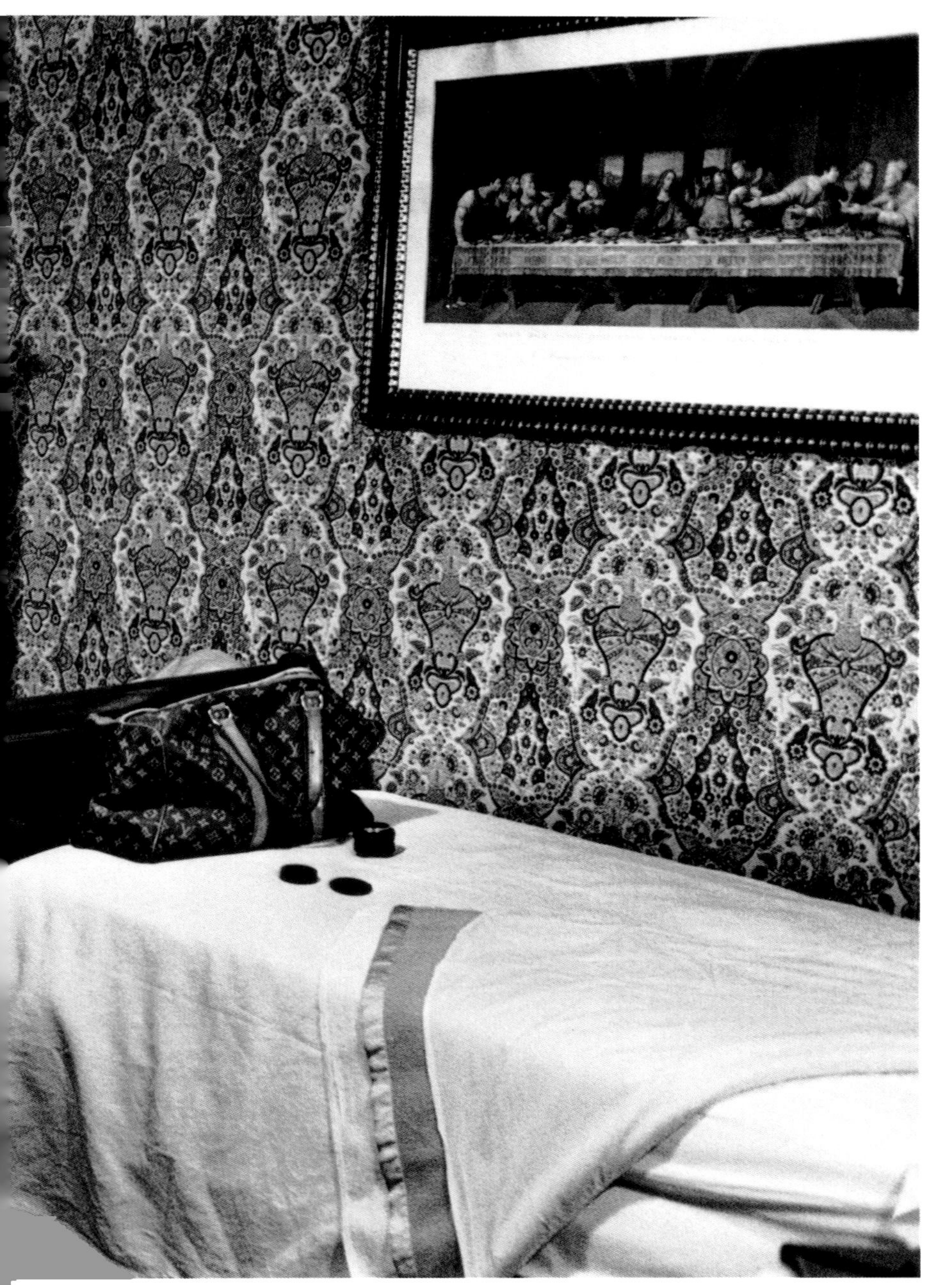

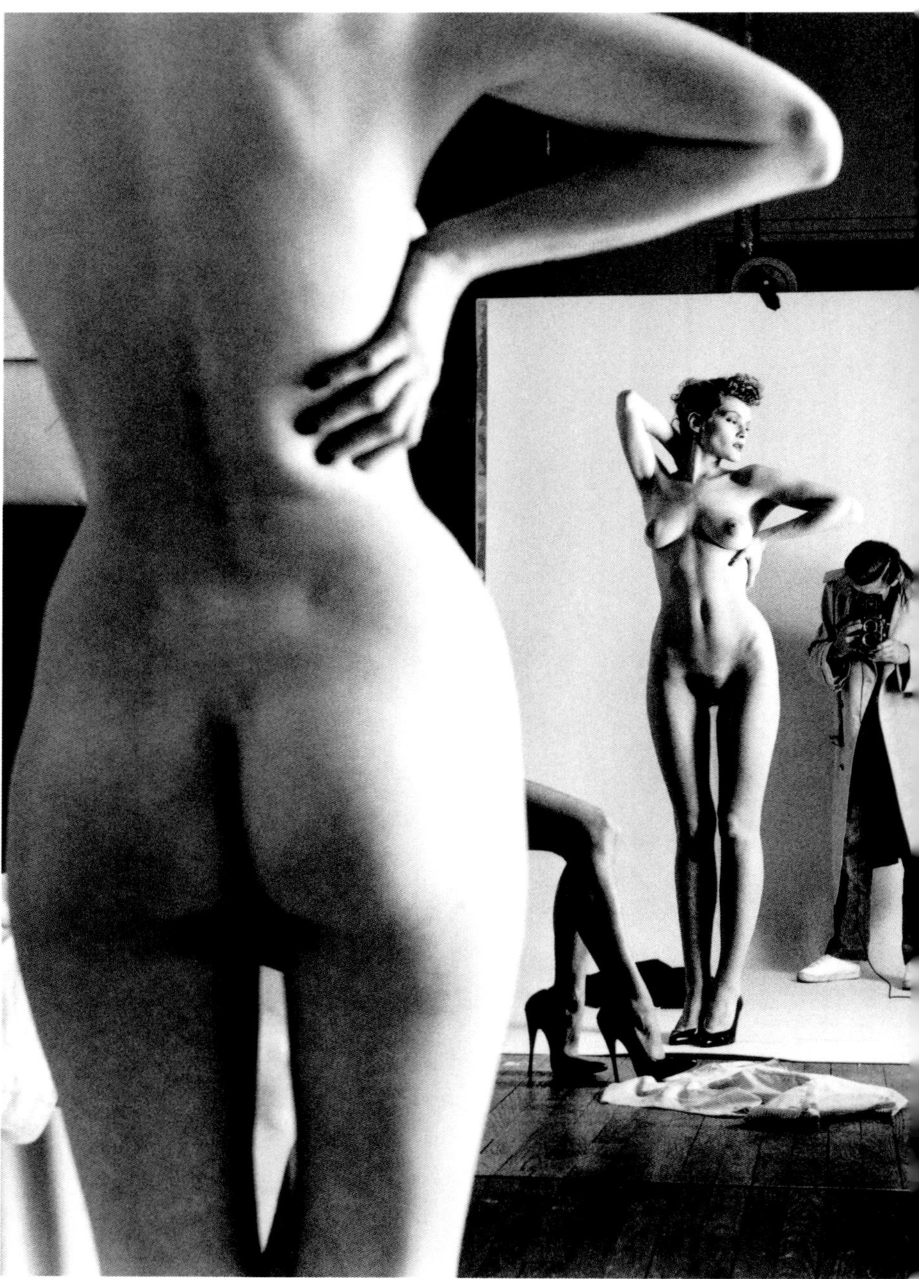

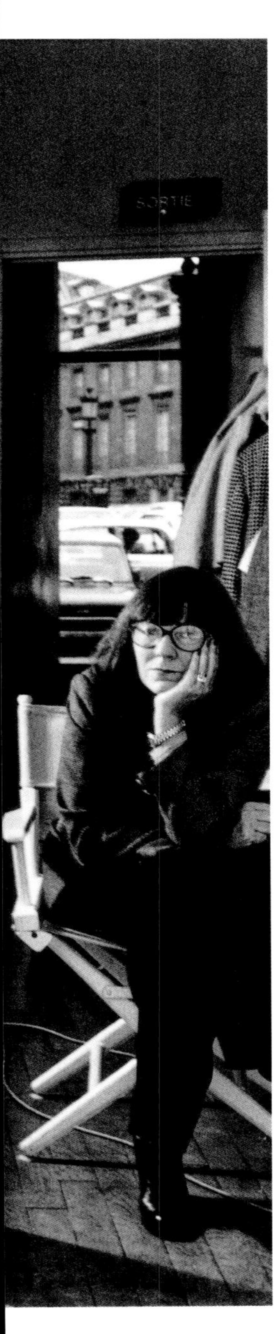

Self-portrait with wife and models, 1981

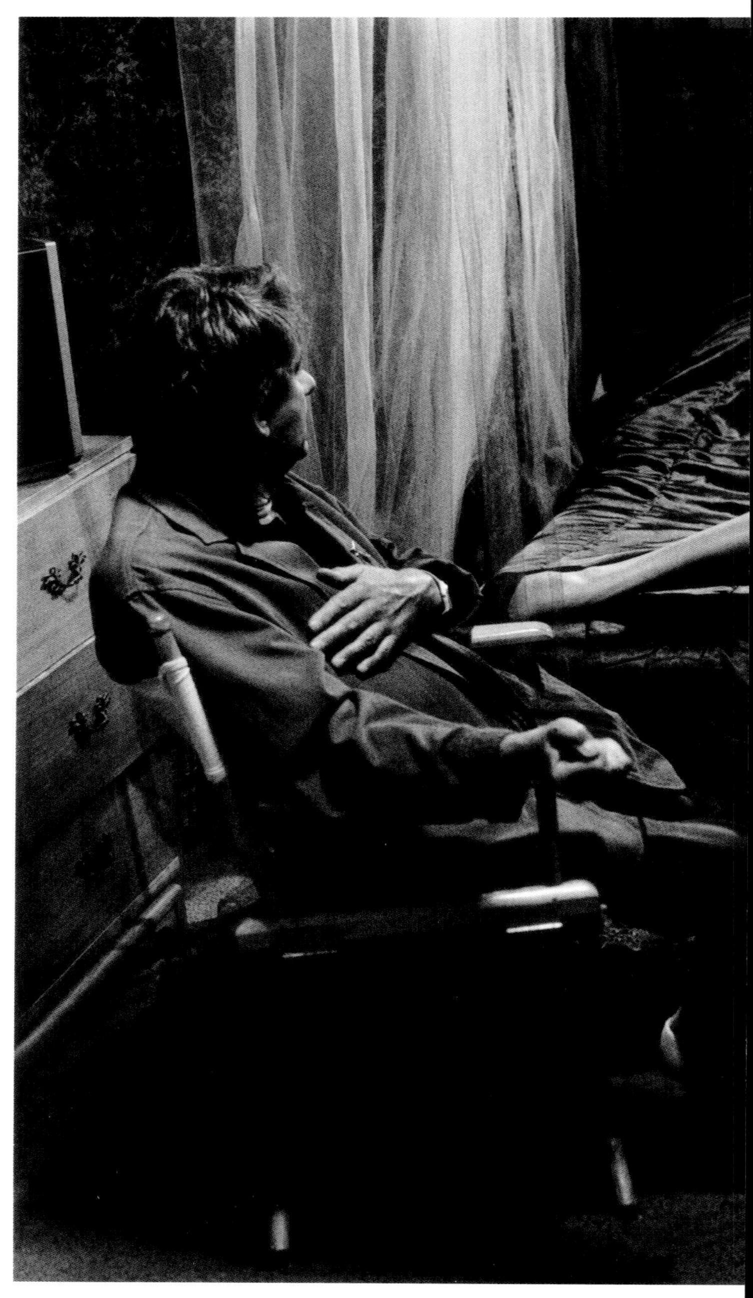

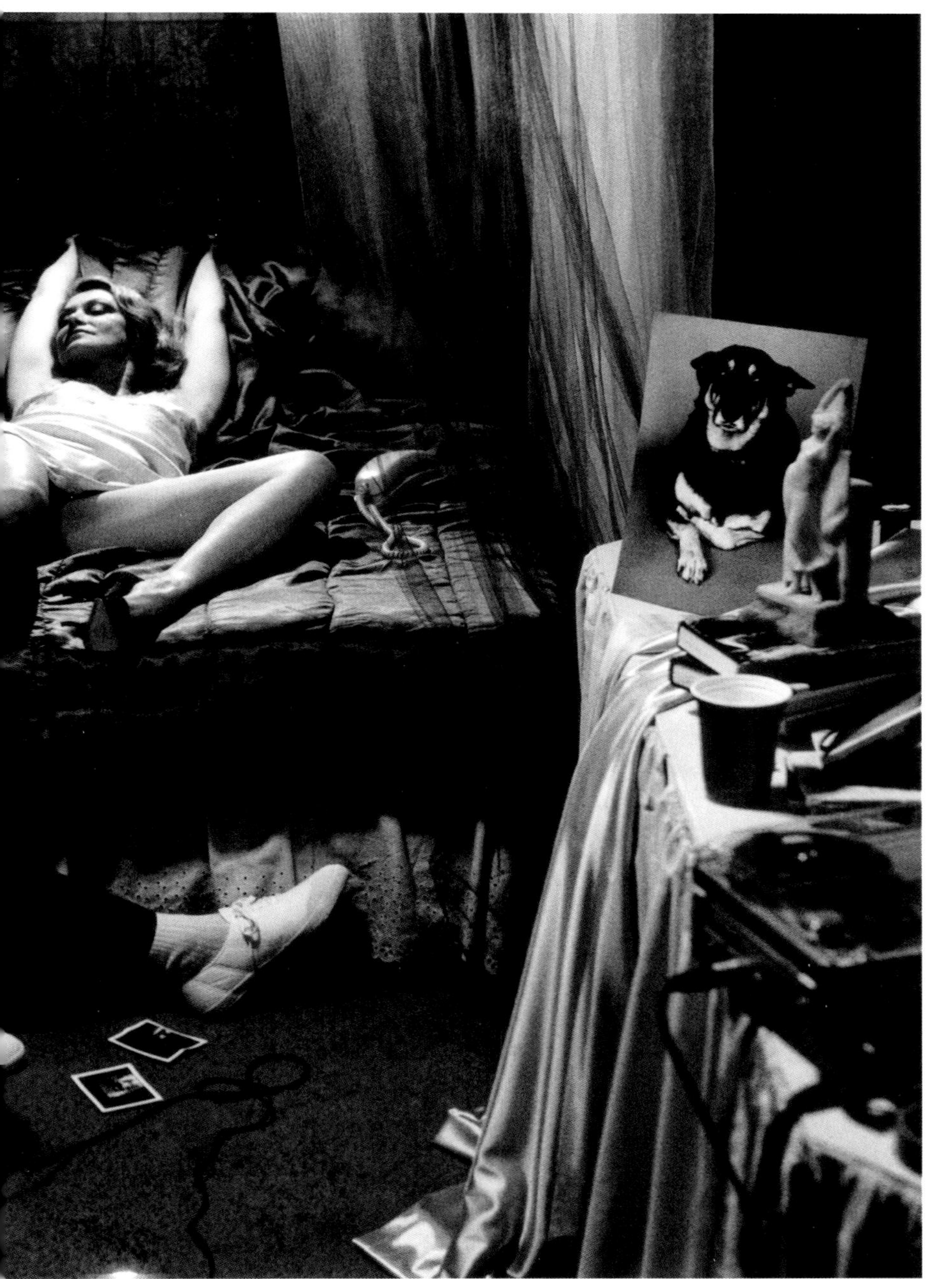

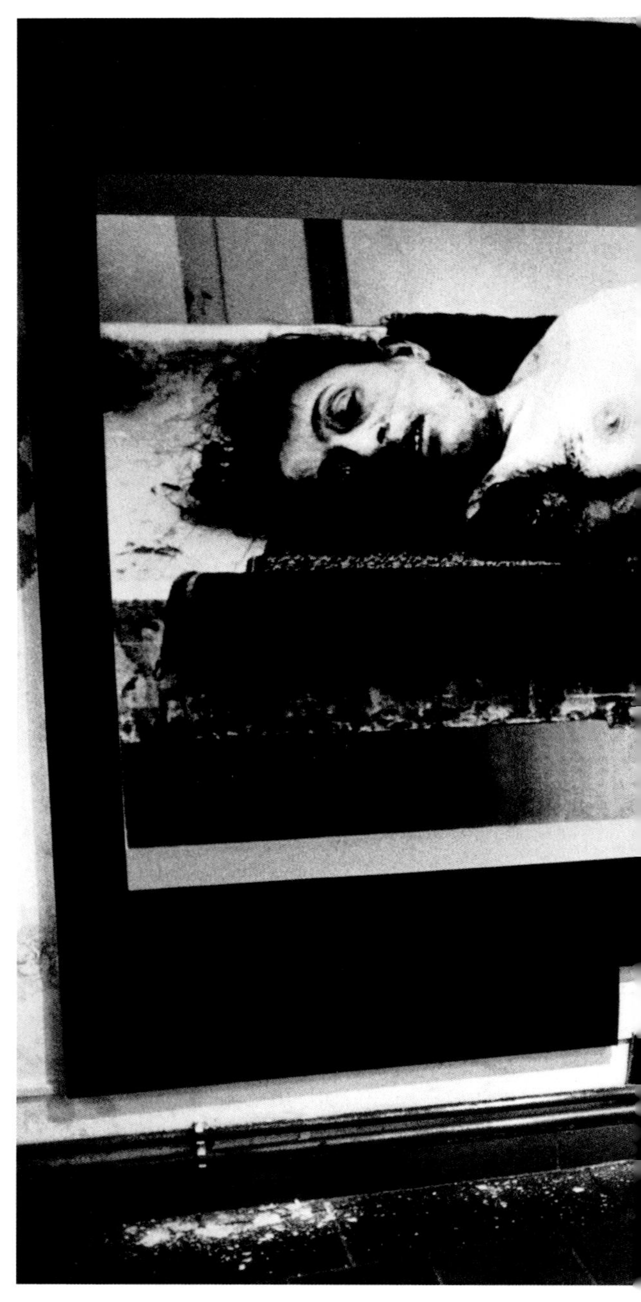

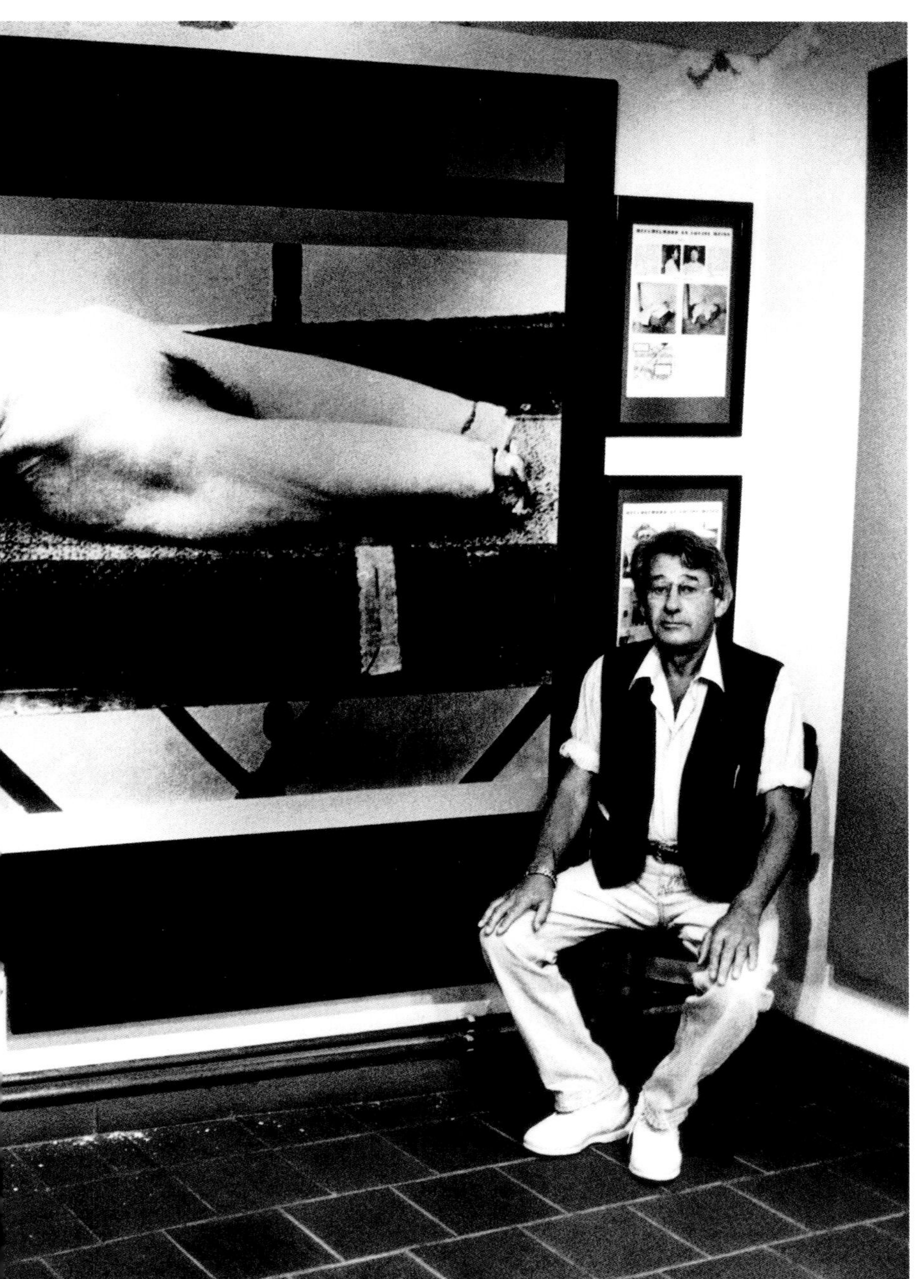

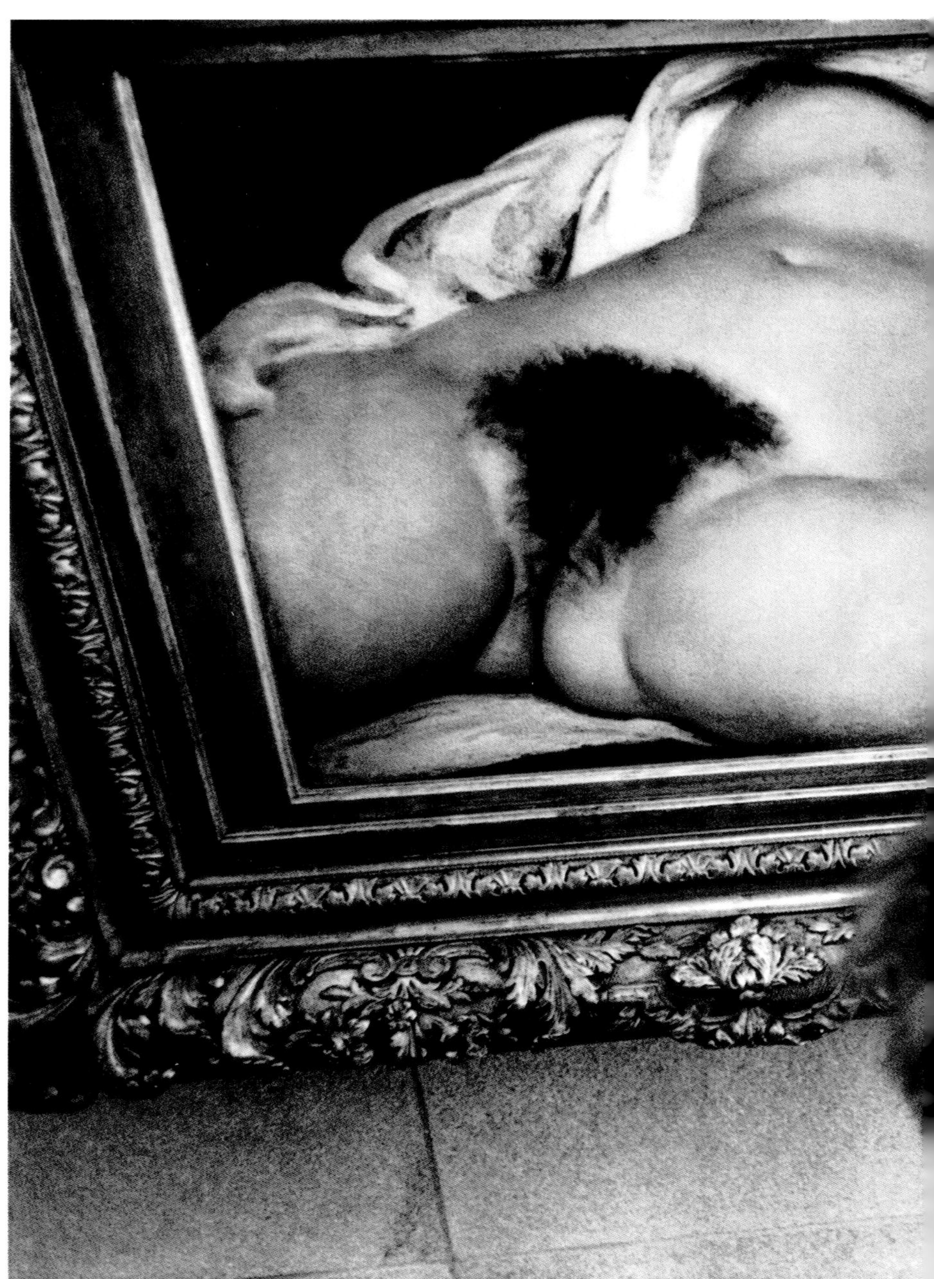

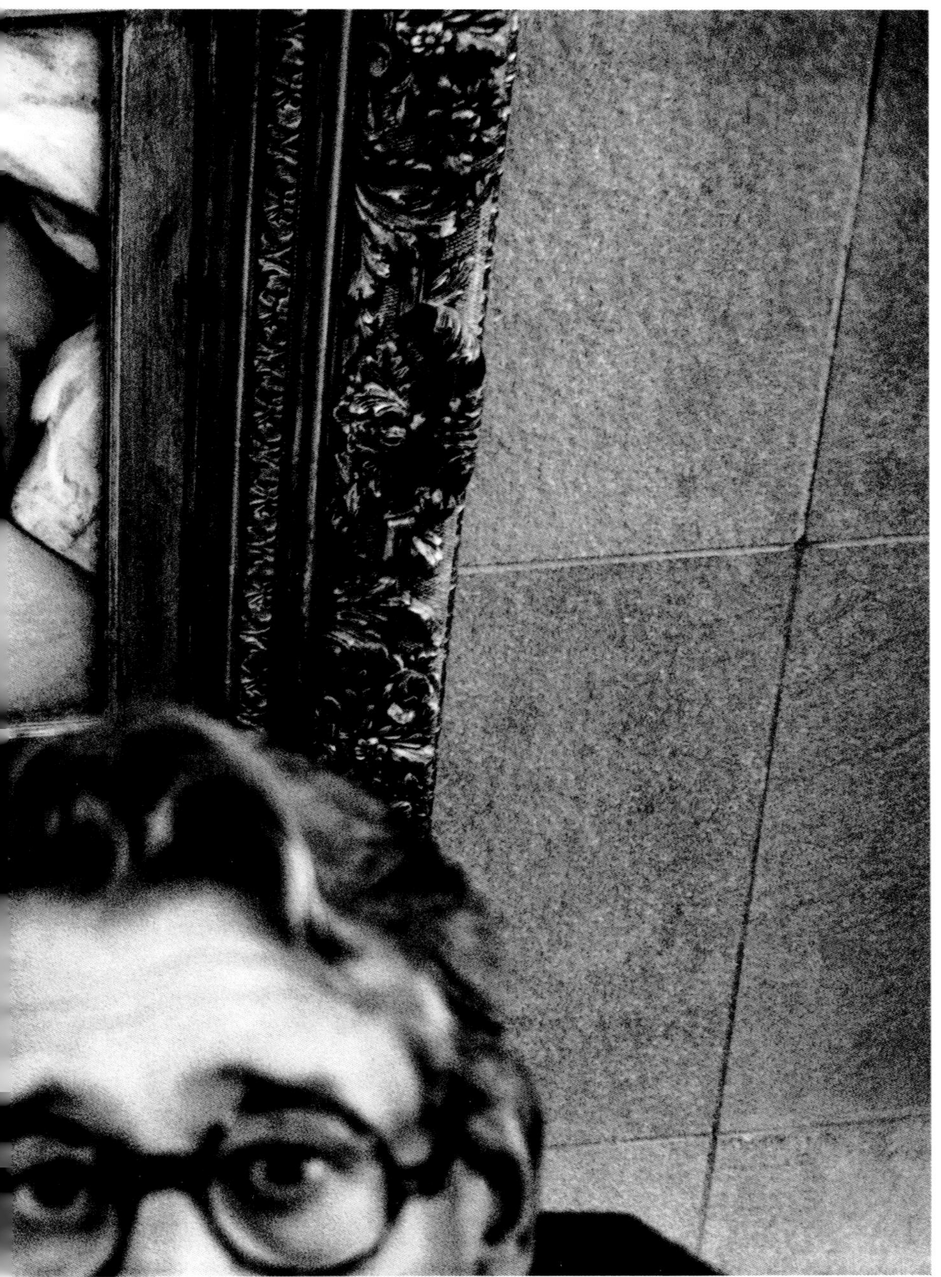

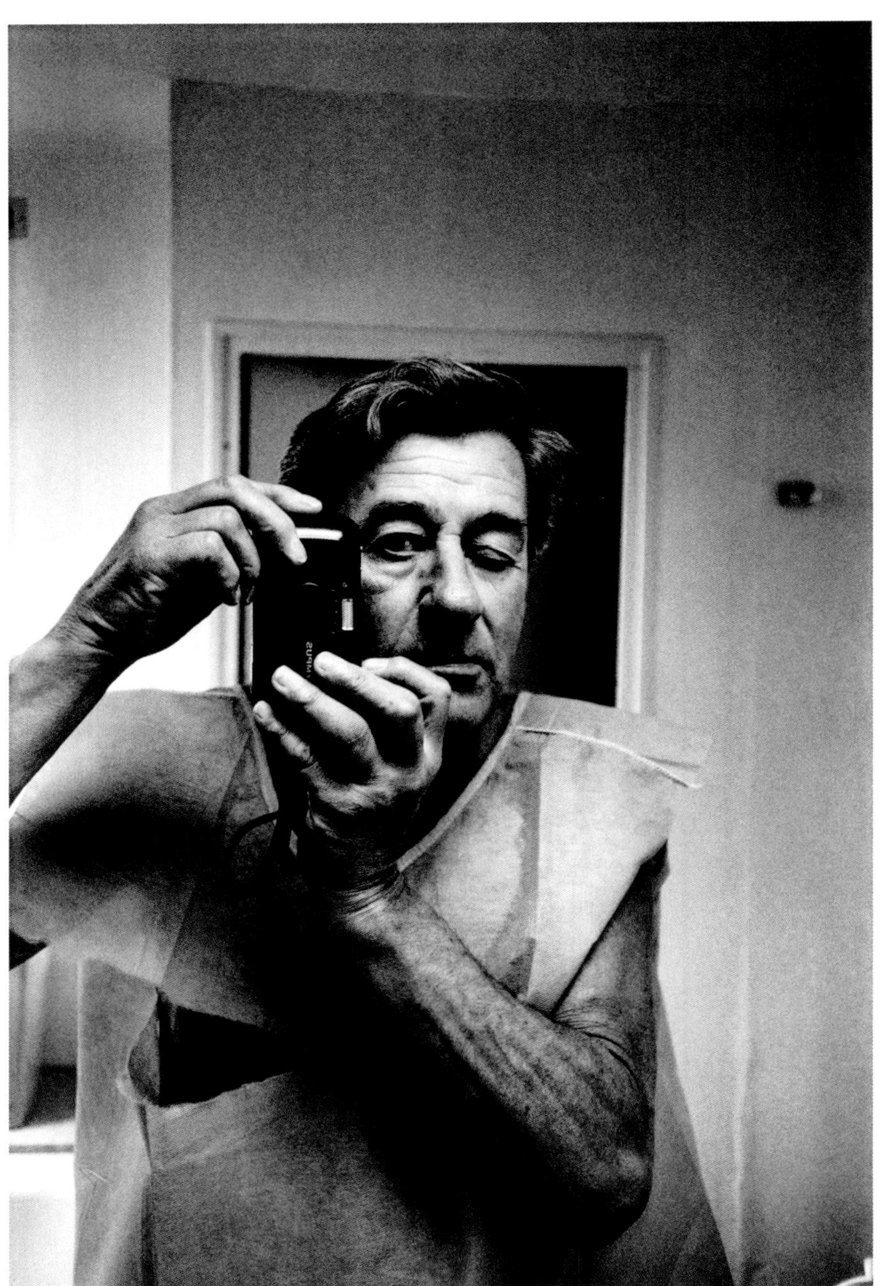

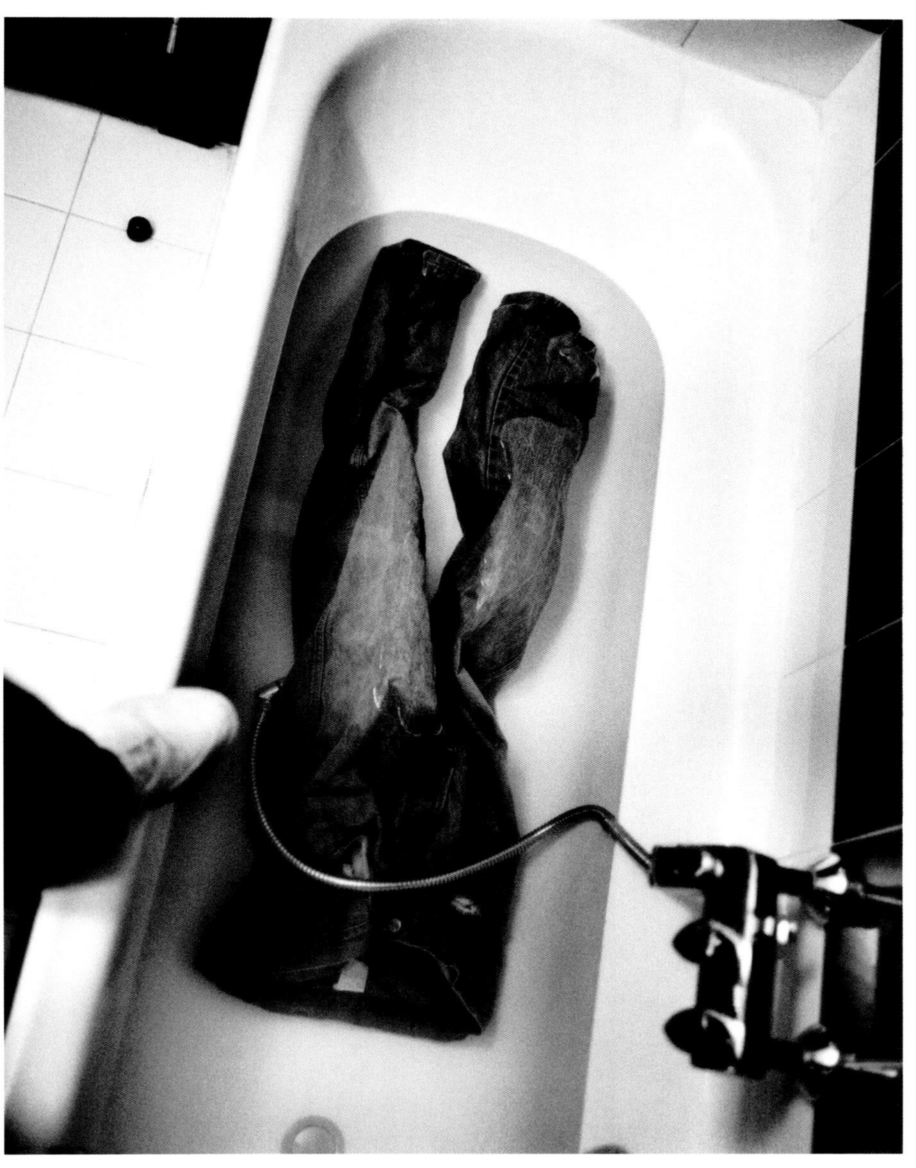

Hotel Royal Monceau, Paris, 1994
My jeans in the bath, Monte Carlo, 1985
PAGES 118 & 119 Clinique St. Jean, Cagnes-sur-Mer, September 1997

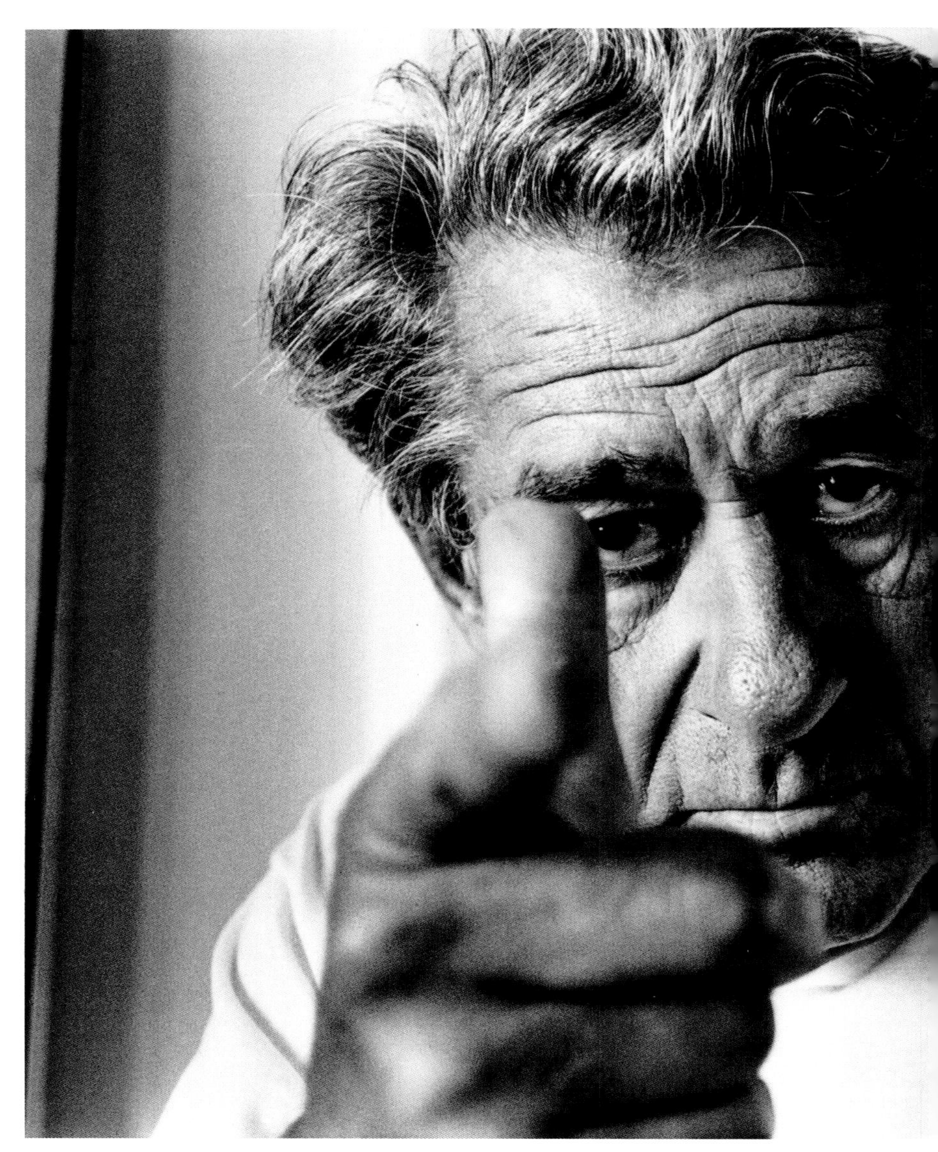

Monte Carlo, October 1993

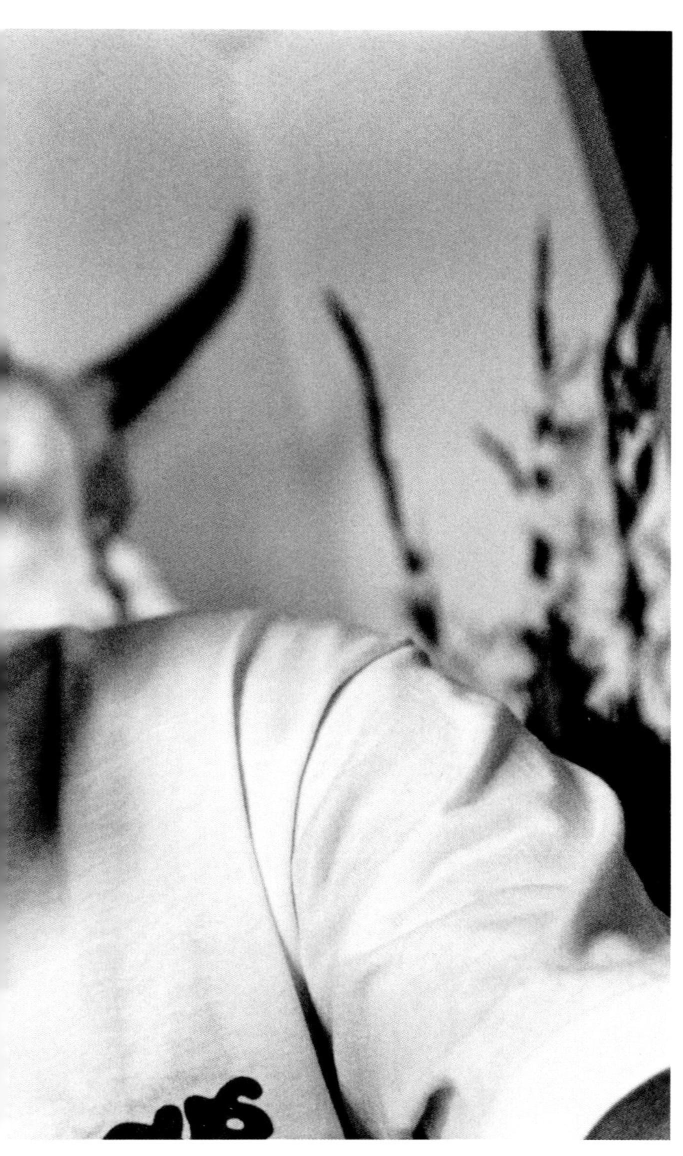

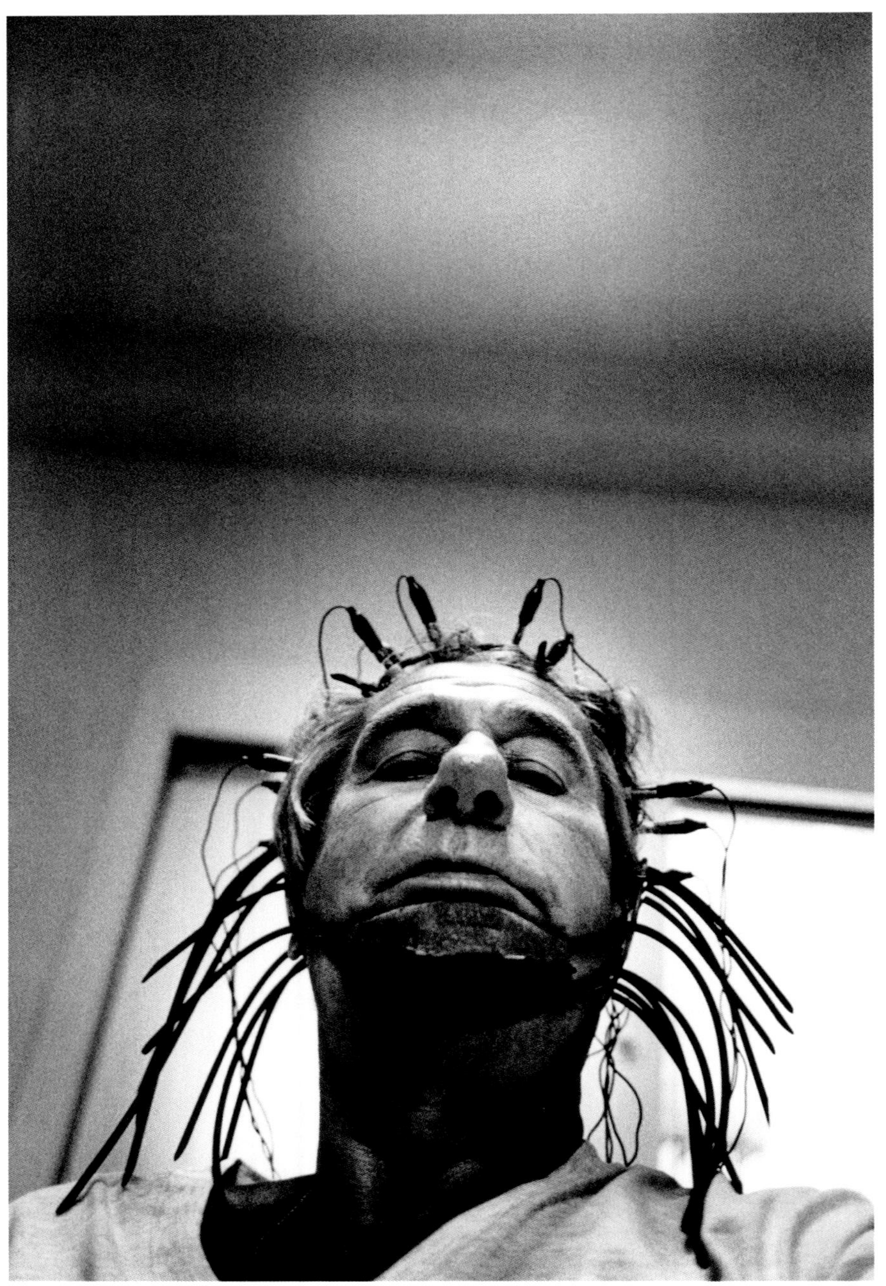

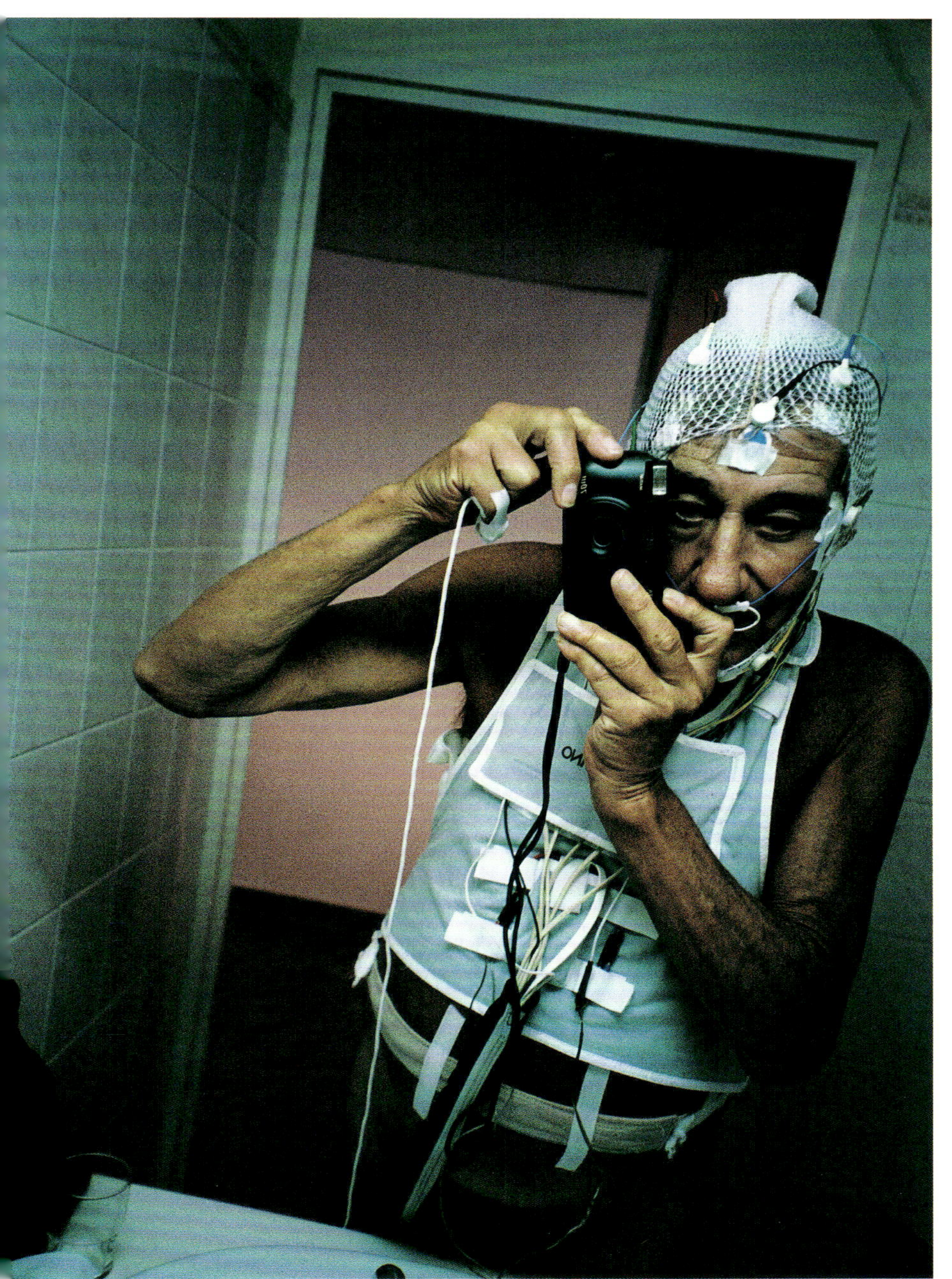

HELMUT NEWTON
ALICE SPRINGS
THEM

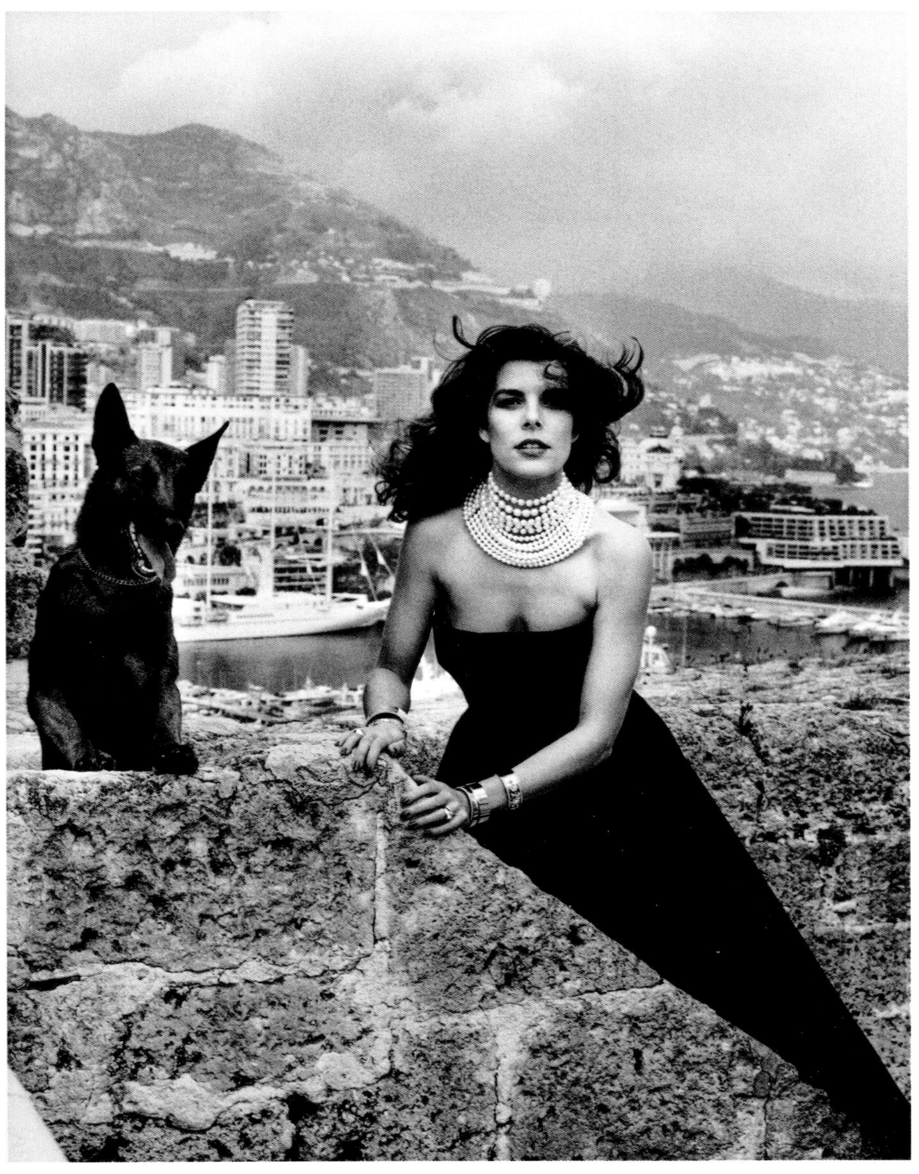

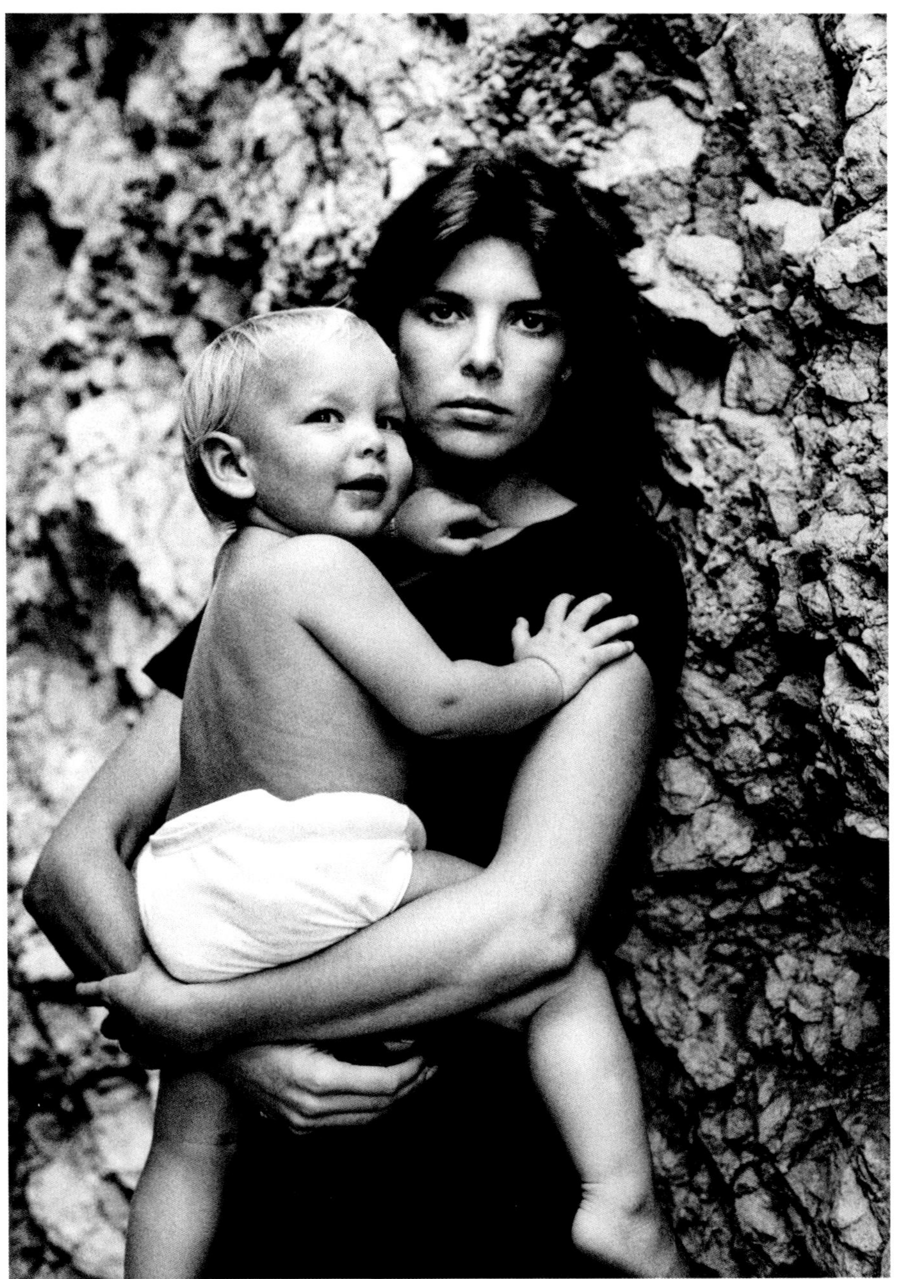

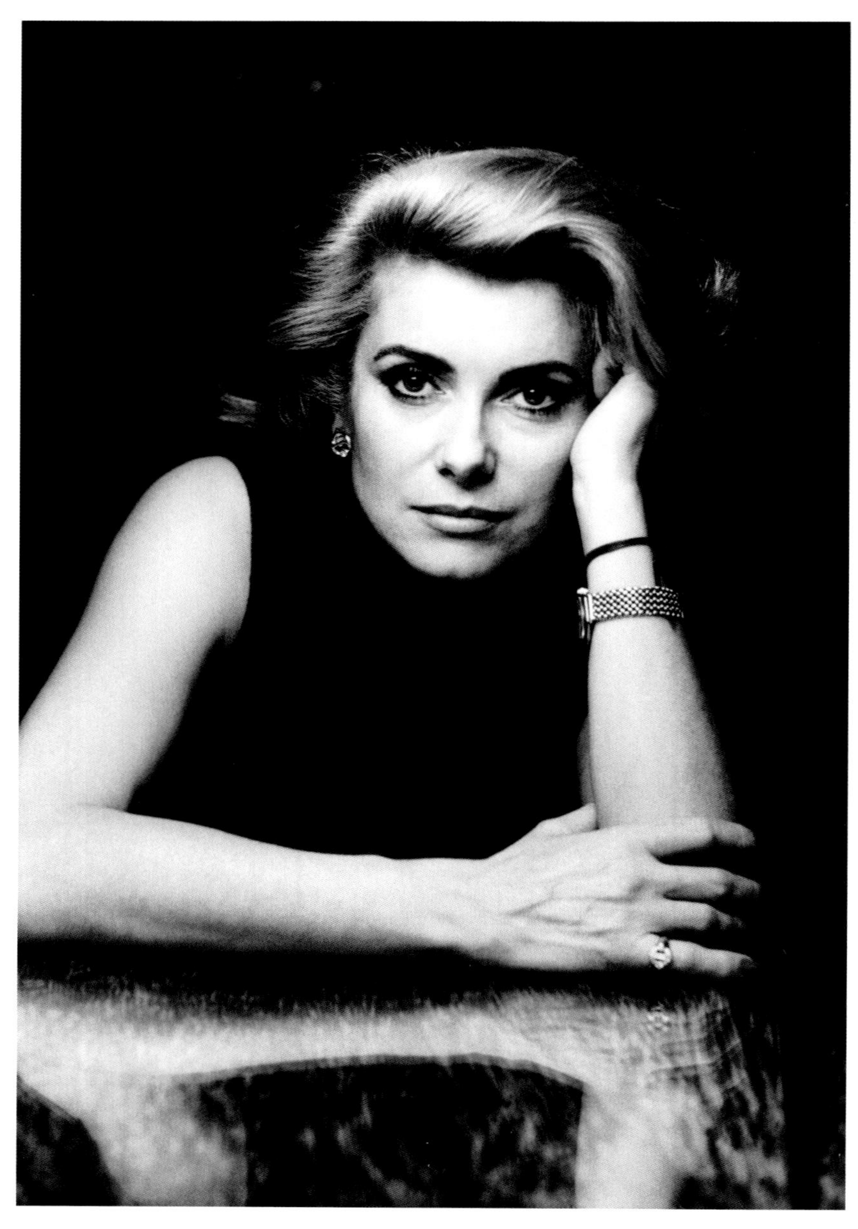

AS: Catherine Deneuve, Paris, 1984

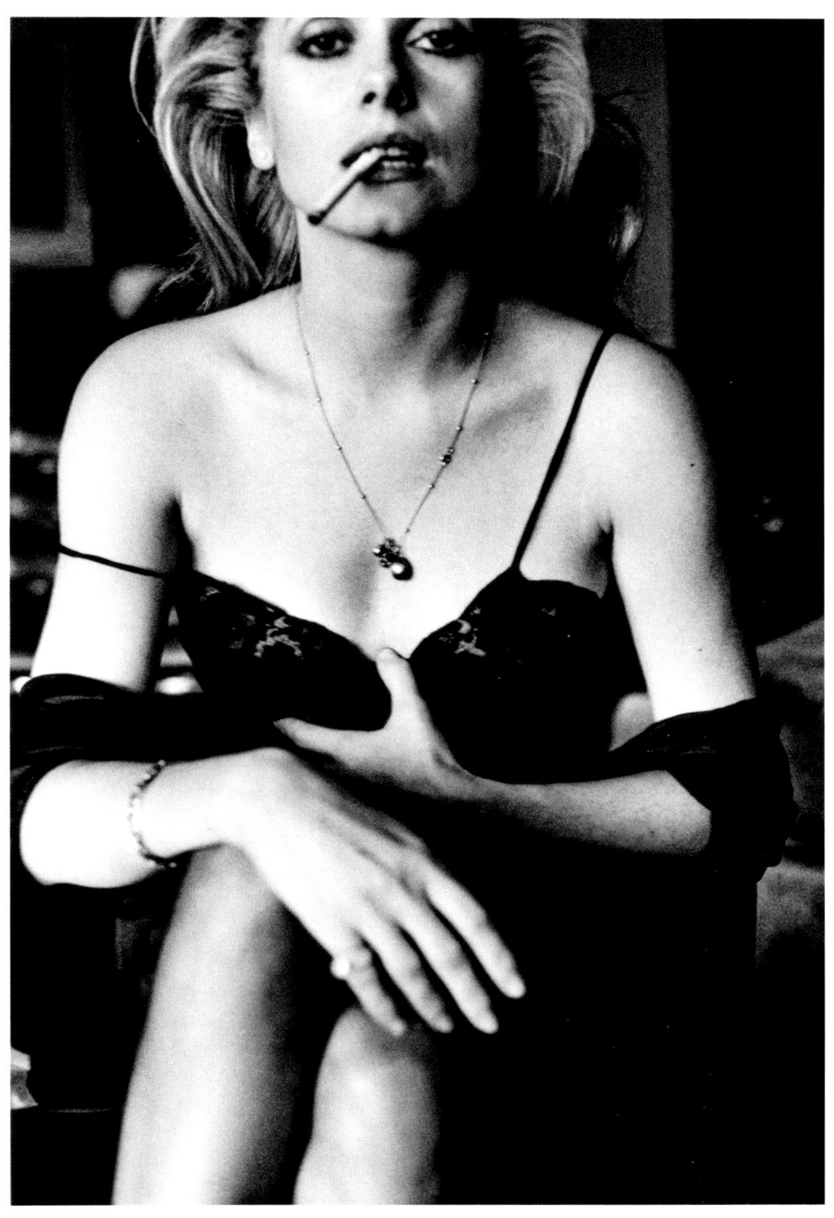

HN: Catherine Deneuve, Paris, 1976

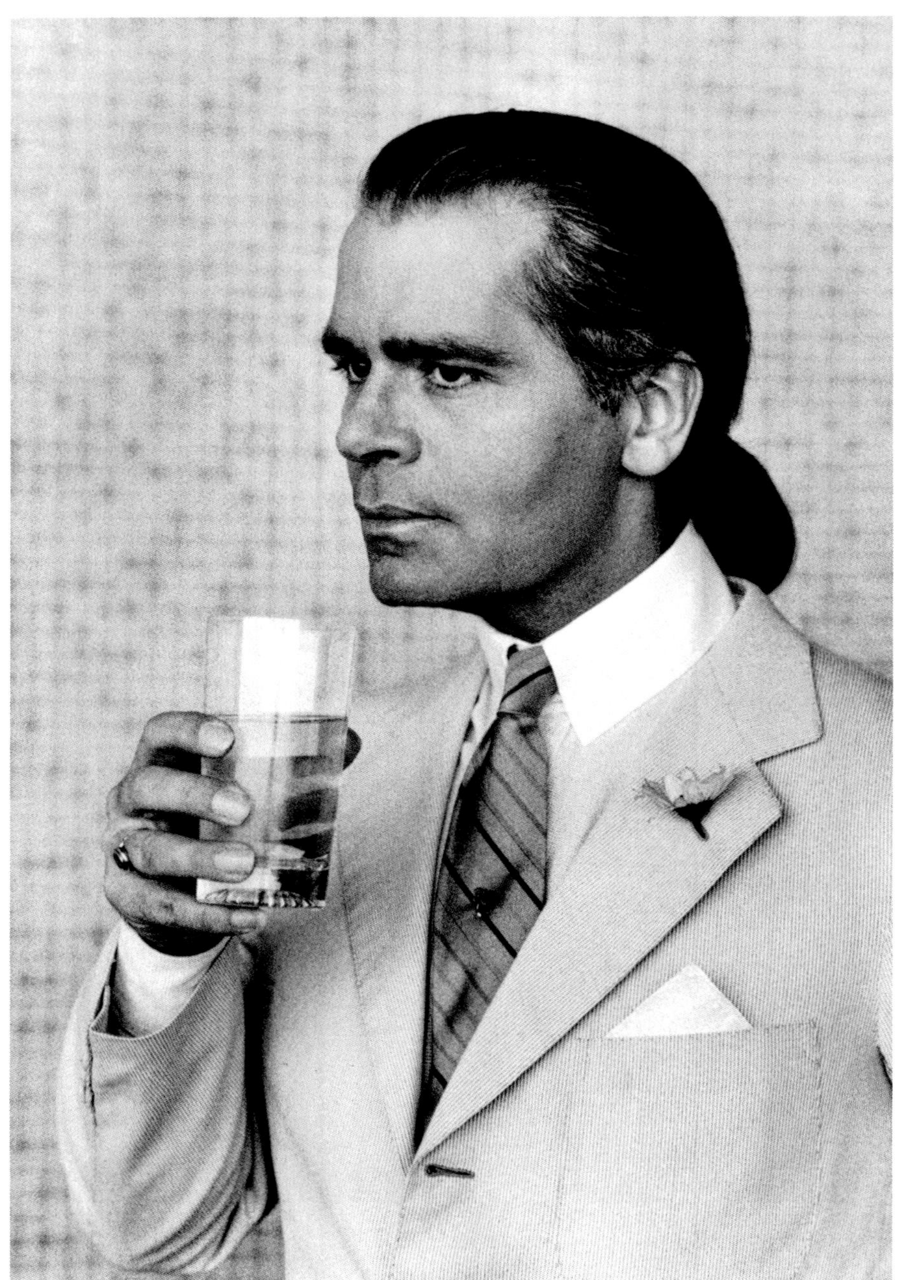

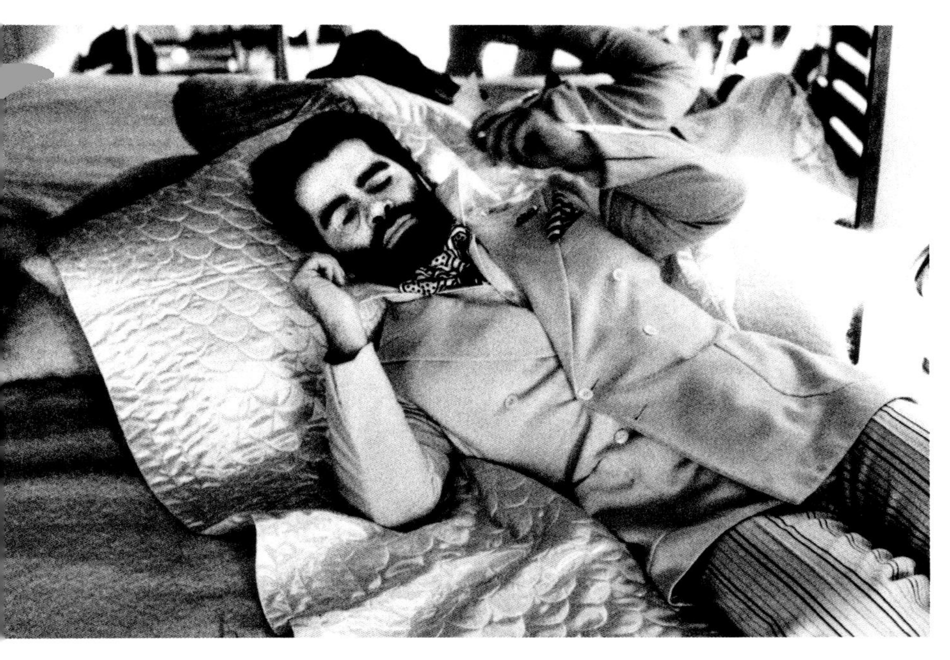

AS: Karl Lagerfeld, Monte Carlo, 1983
HN: Karl Lagerfeld, Paris, 1974

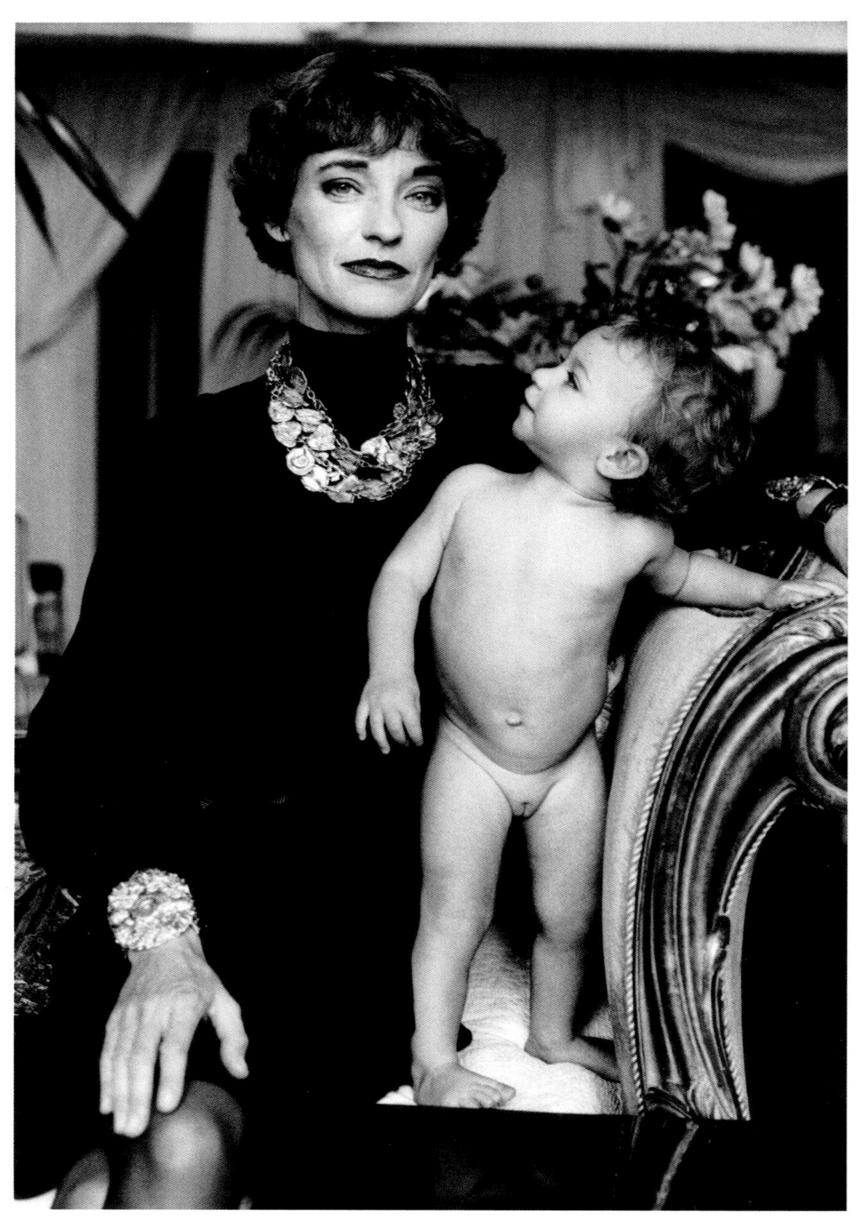

AS: Loulou de la Falaise and Anna, Paris, 1986
HN: Loulou de la Falaise, Hotel Pont Royal, Paris, 1975

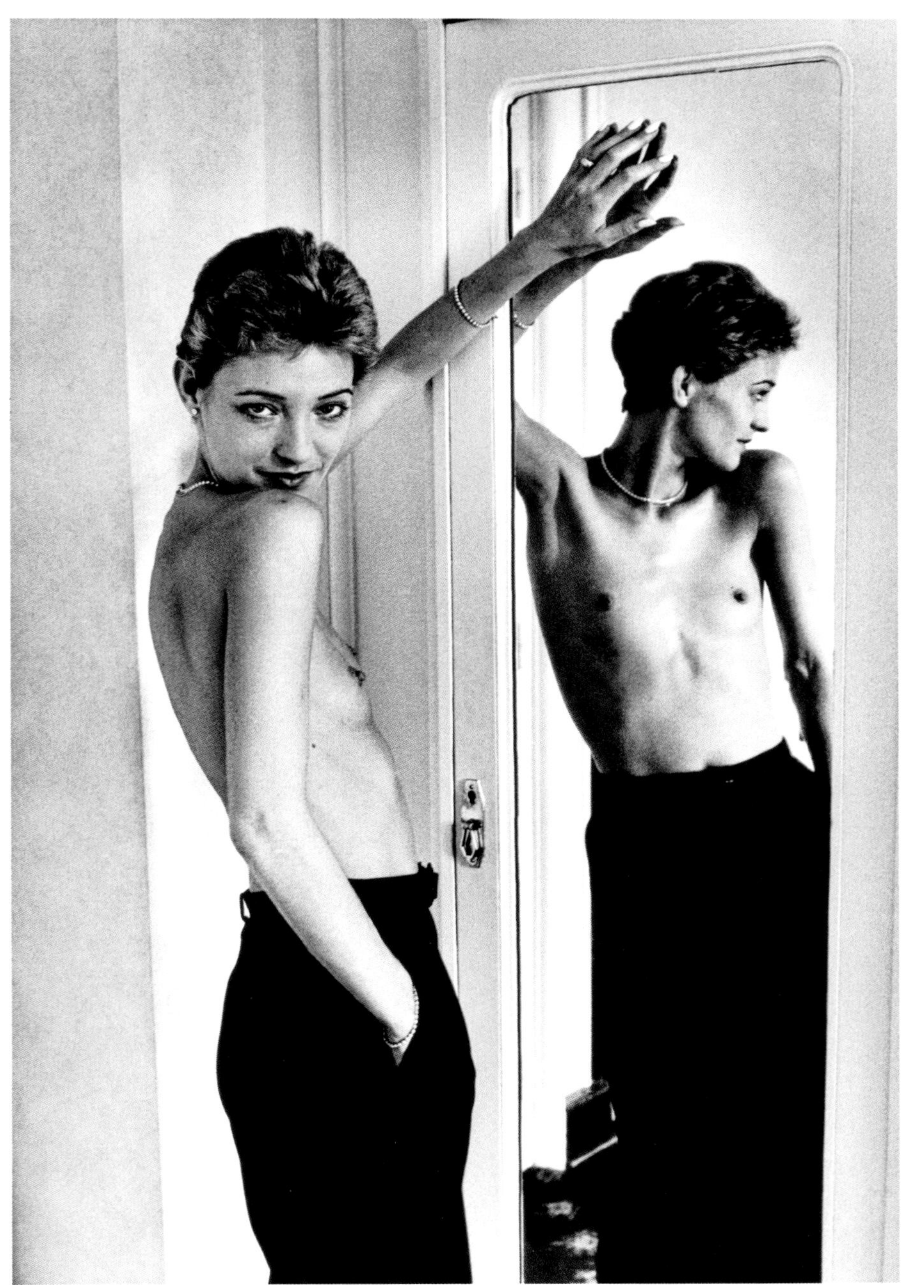

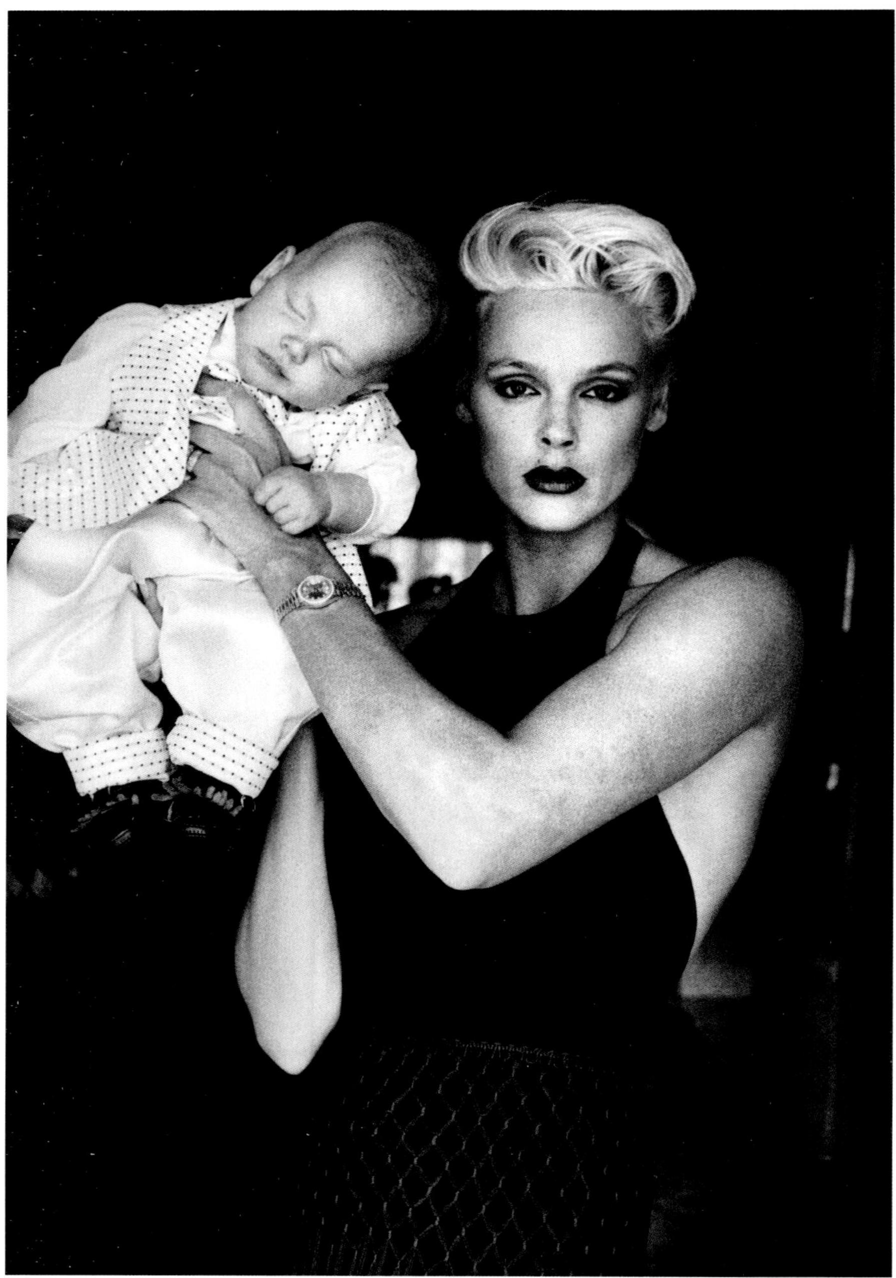

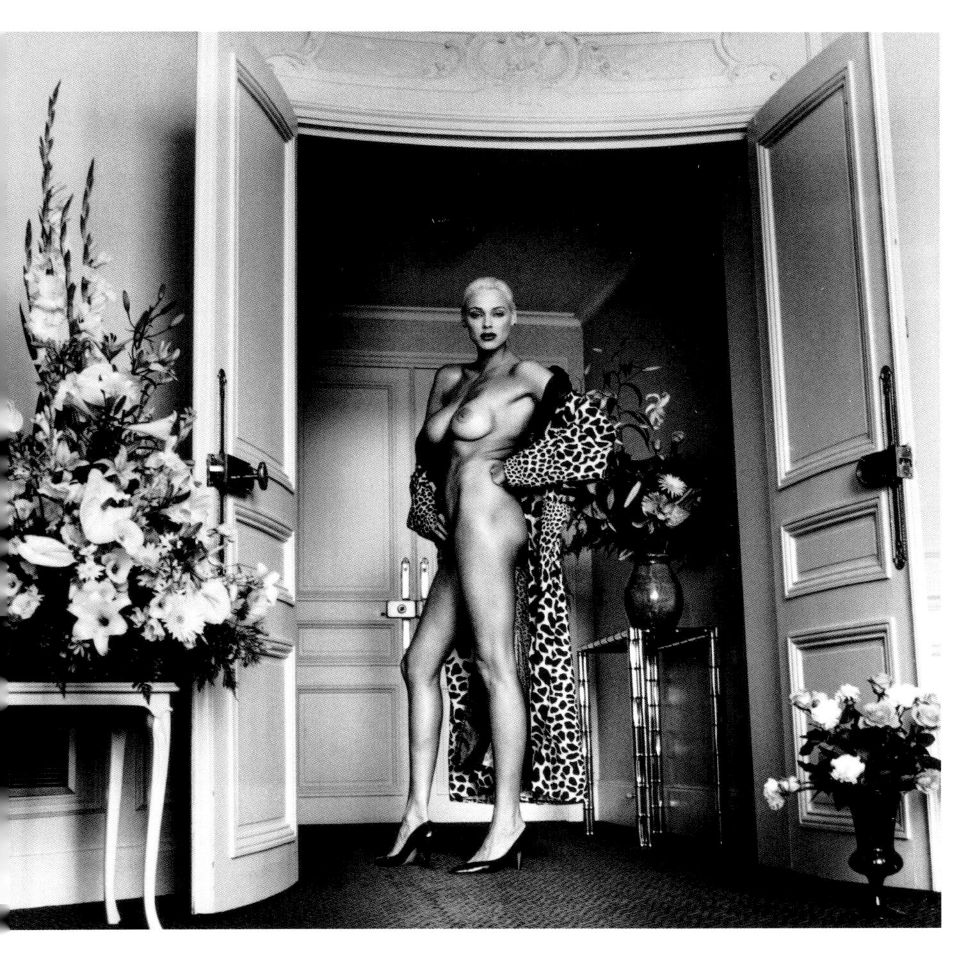

AS: Brigitte Nielsen and son, Beverly Hills, 1990
HN: Brigitte Nielsen, Hotel Hermitage, Monte Carlo, 1987

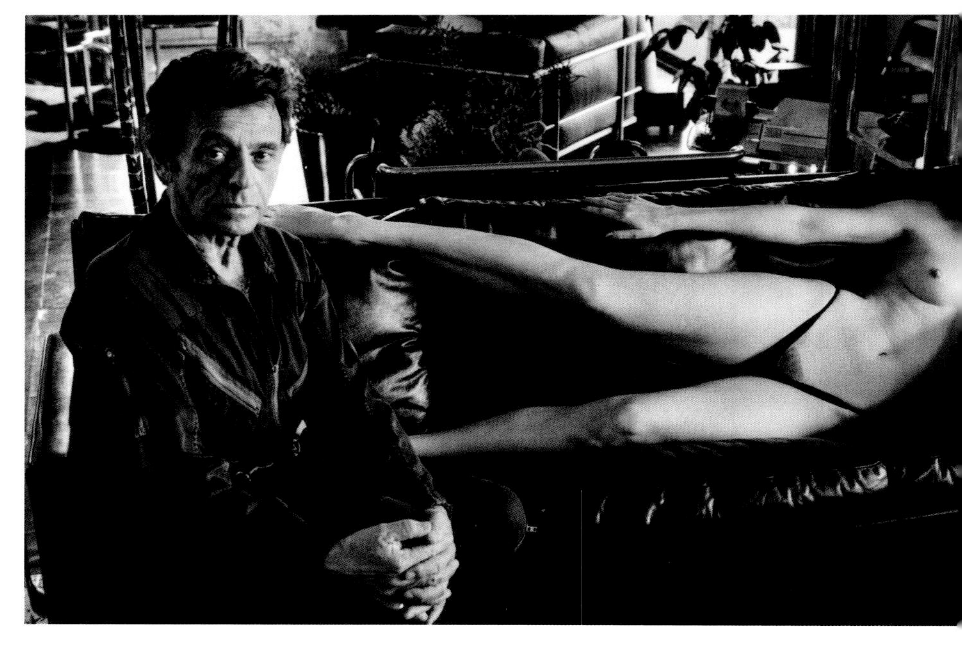

HN: Rudi Gernreich, Los Angeles, 1985
AS: Rudi Gernreich, Los Angeles, 1985

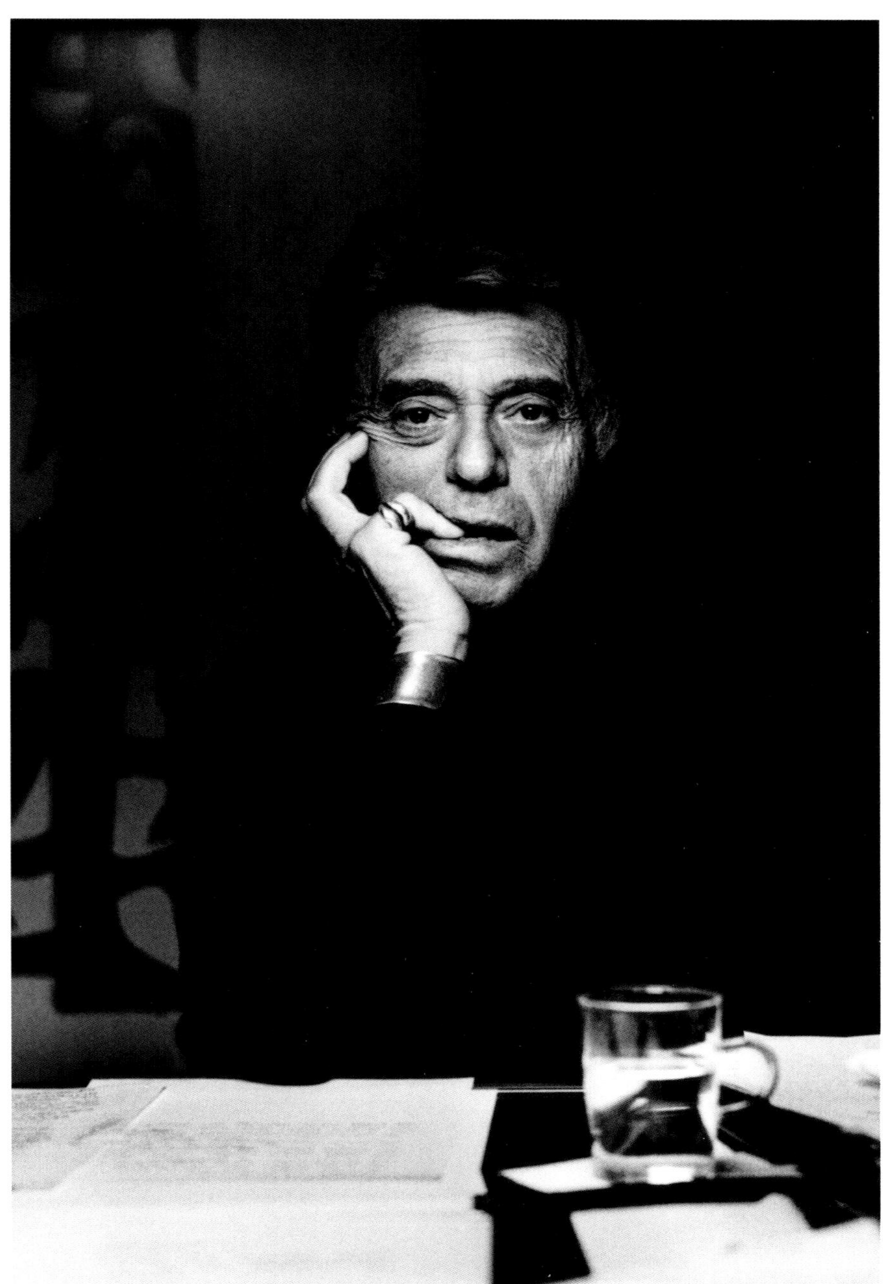

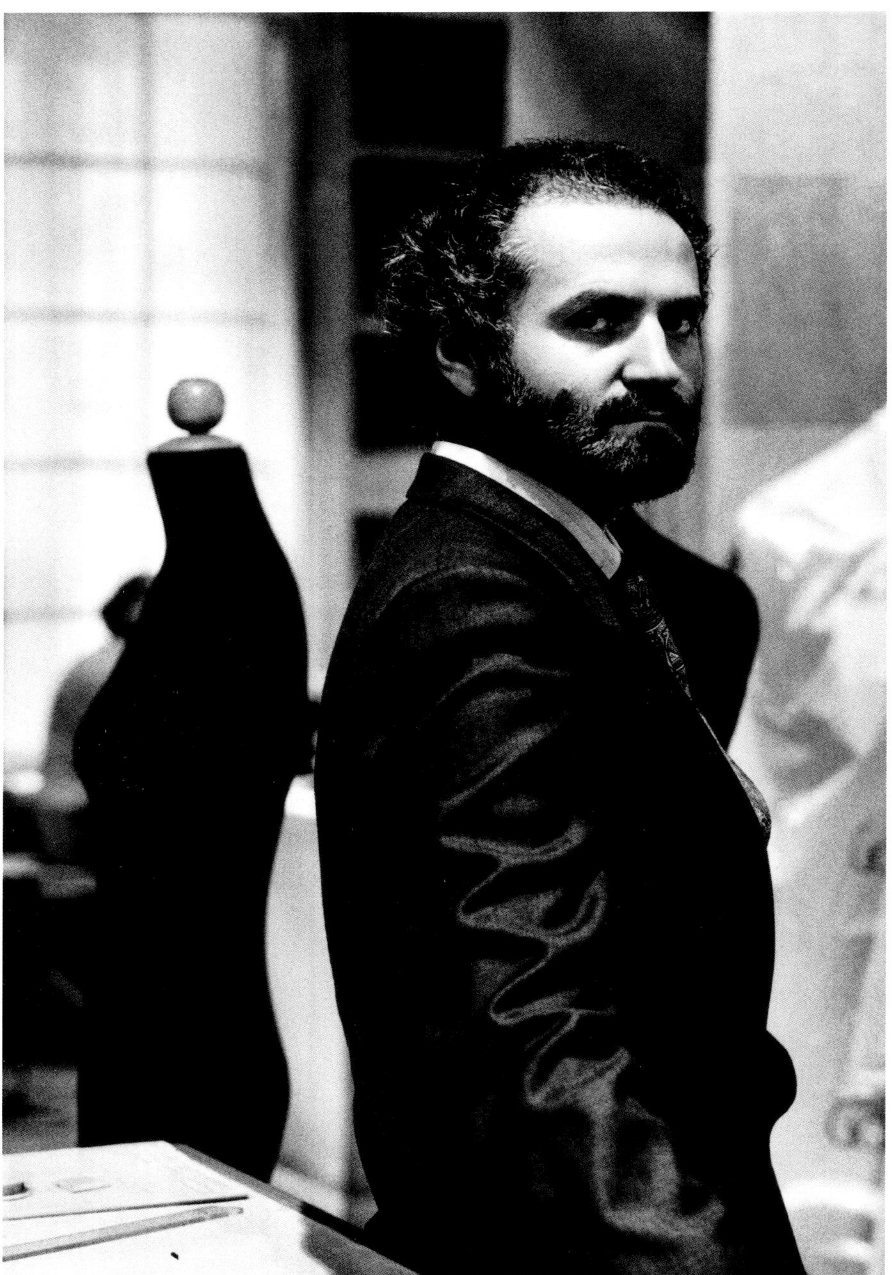

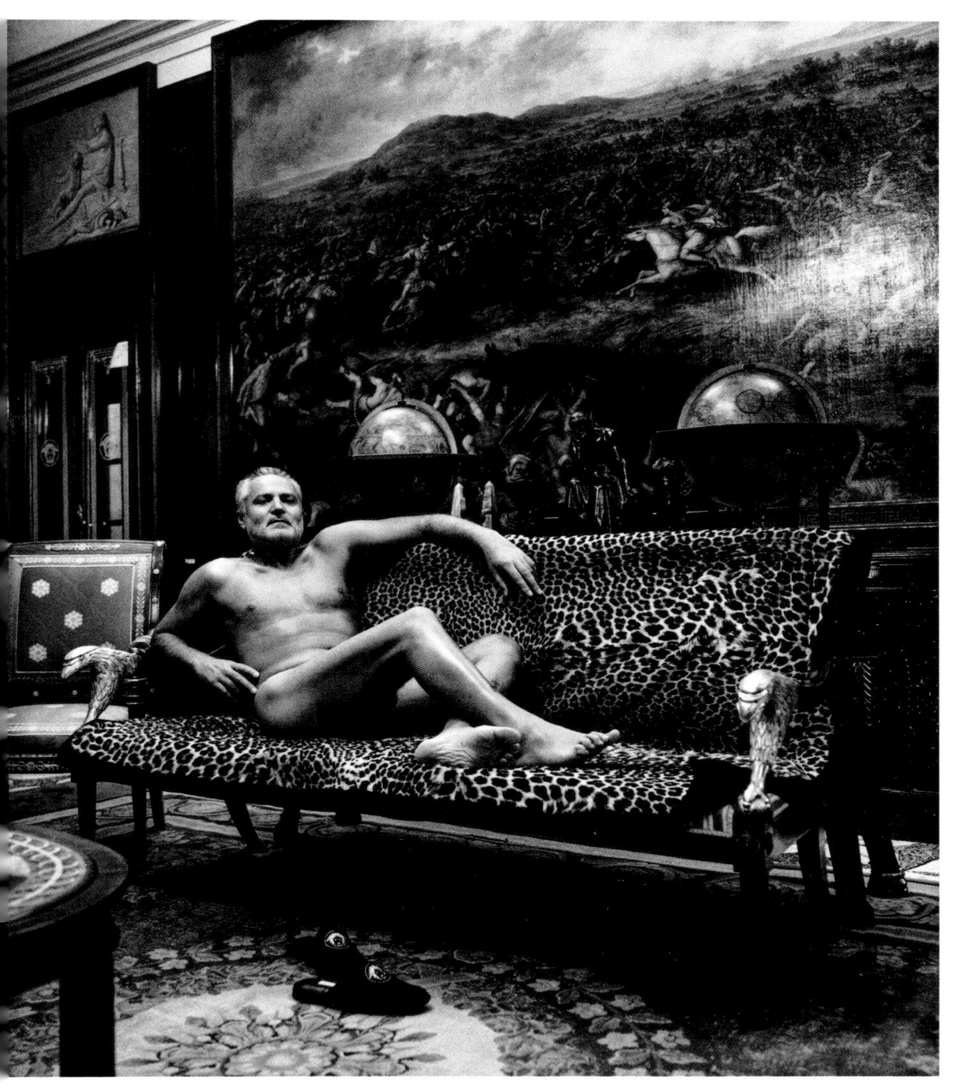

AS: Gianni Versace, Milan, 1985
HN: Gianni Versace, Lake Como, 1994

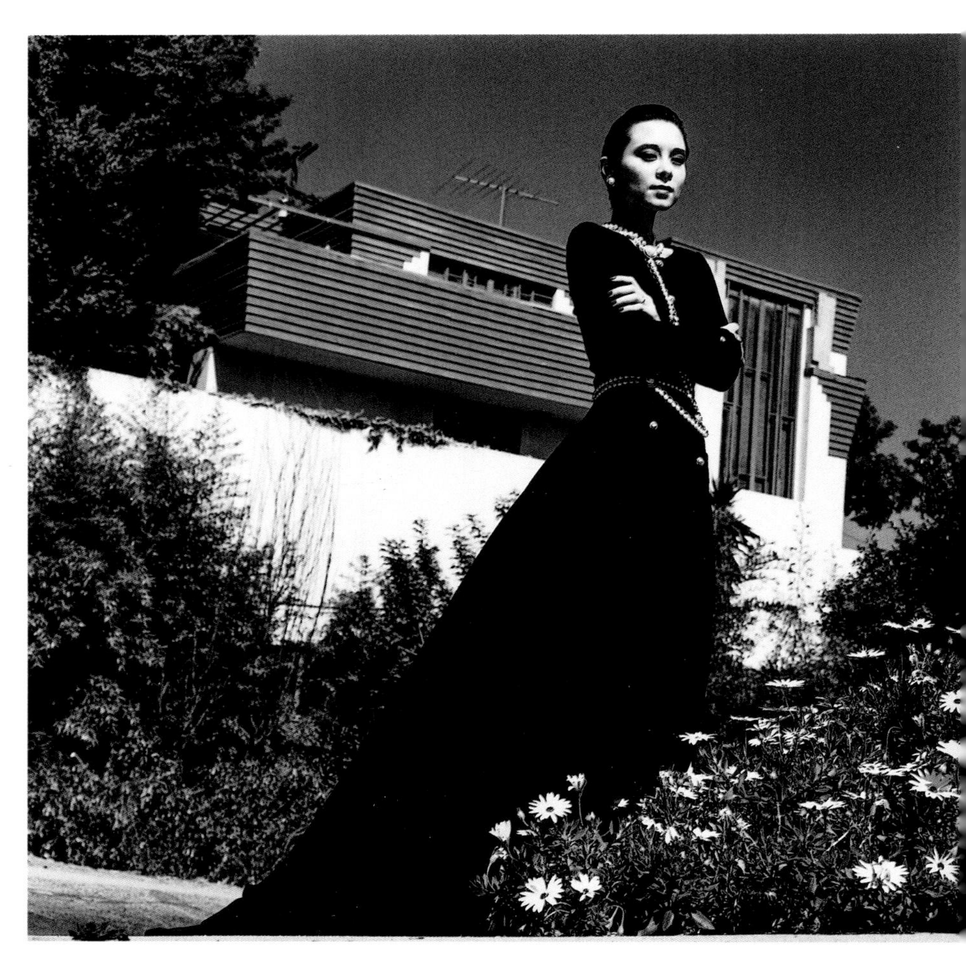

HN: Tina Chow, Beverly Hills, 1984
AS: Tina Chow, Beverly Hills, 1986

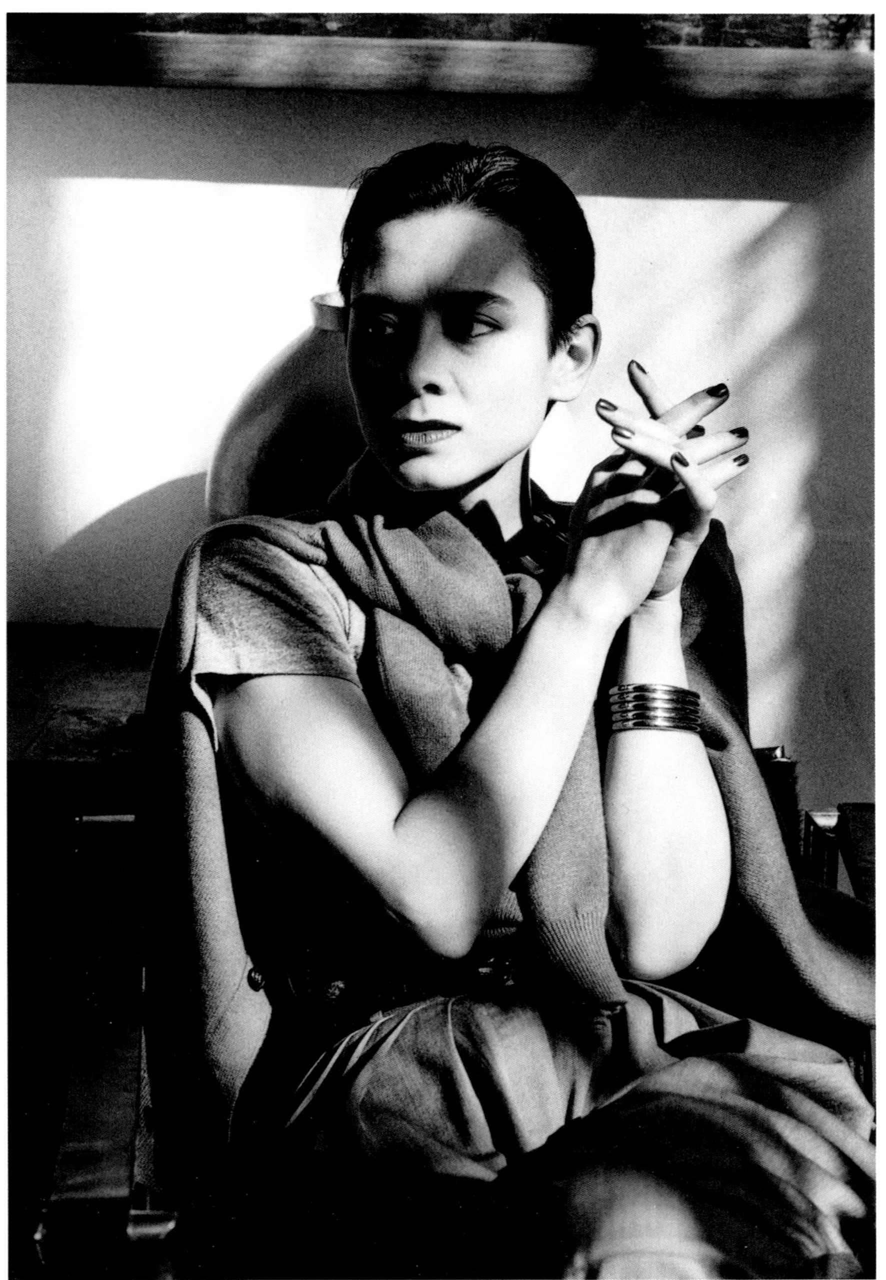

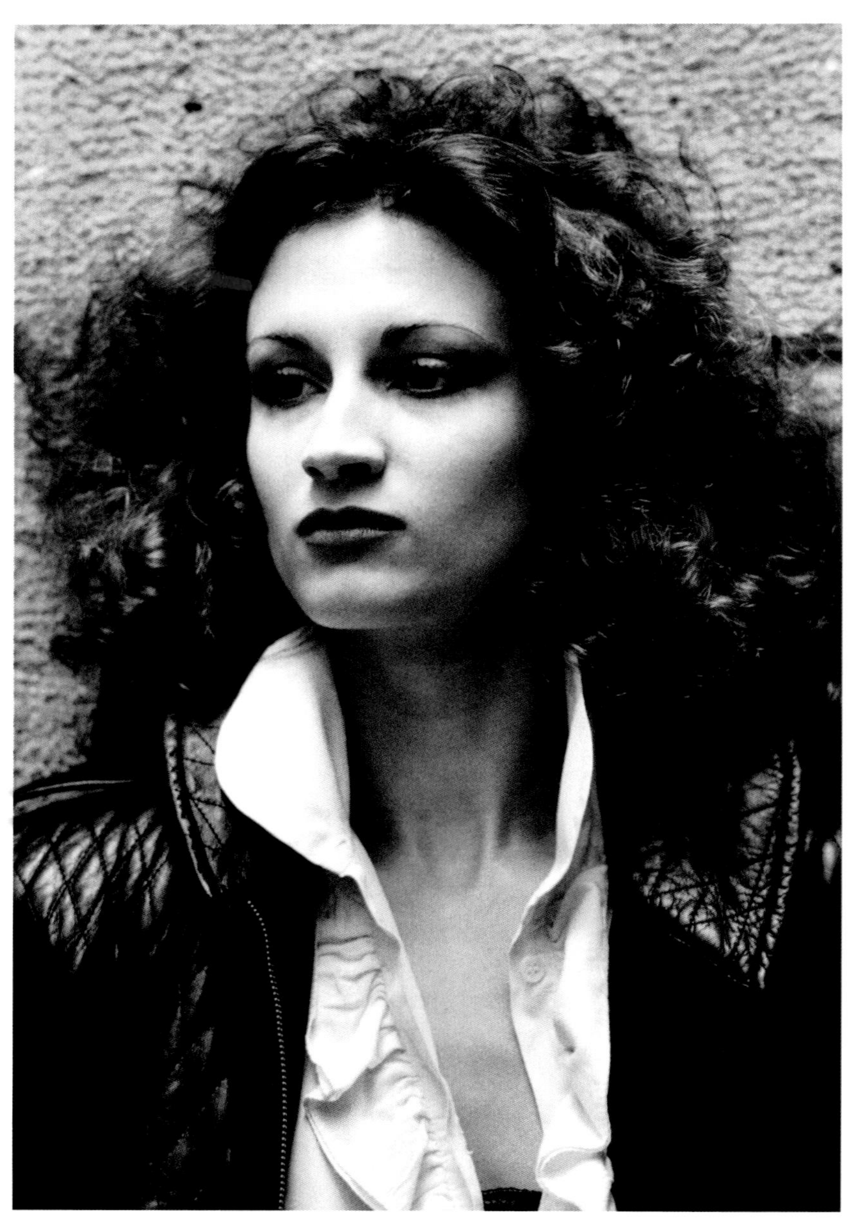

AS: Violetta Sanchez, Paris, 1983

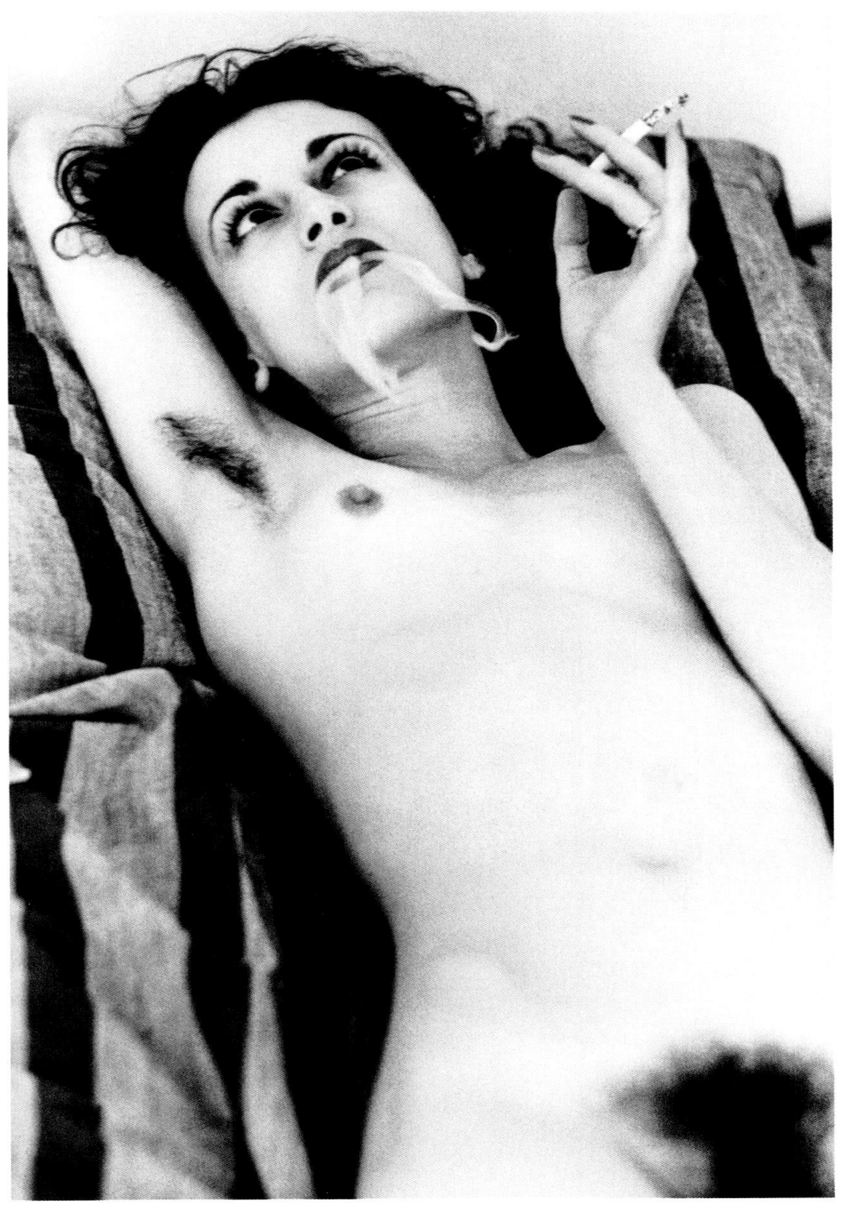

HN: Violetta Sanchez, Paris, 1979

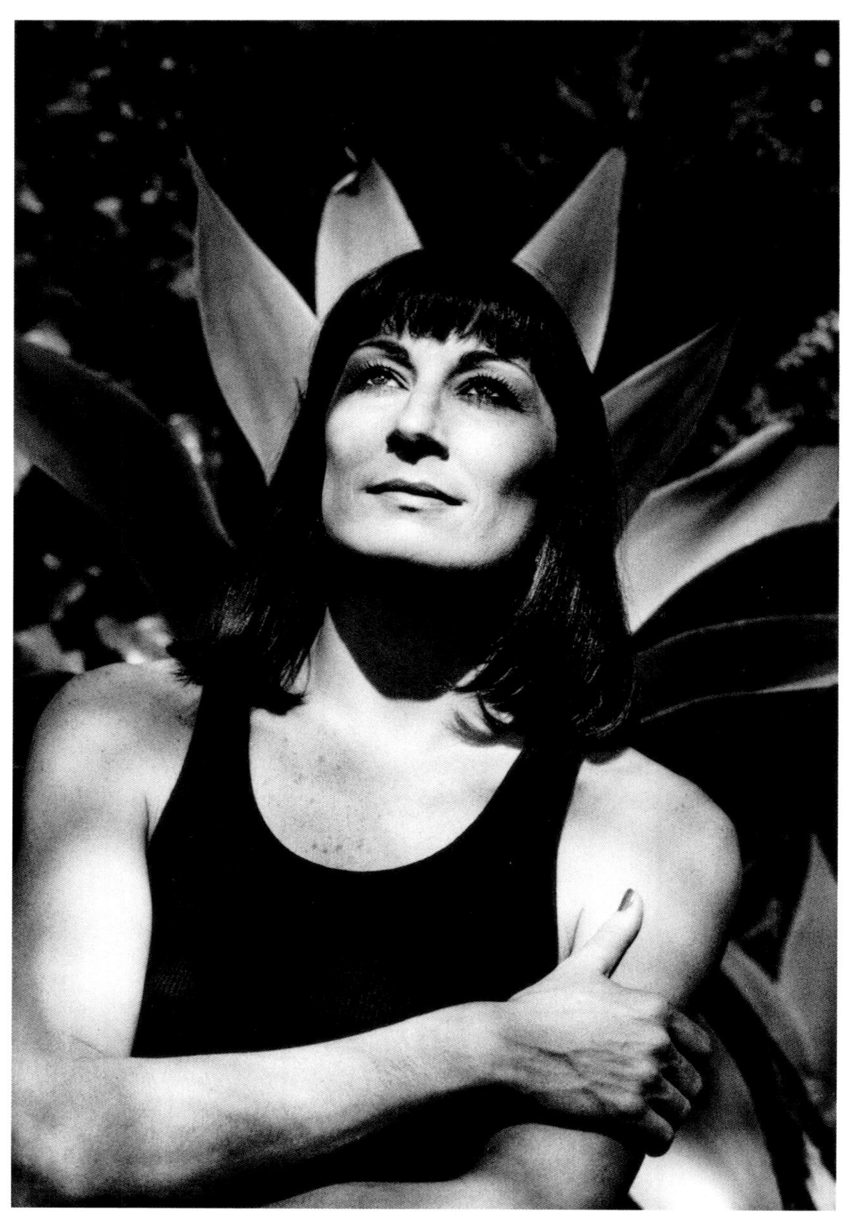

HN: Anjelica Huston, Los Angeles, 1986
AS: Anjelica Huston, Los Angeles, 1983

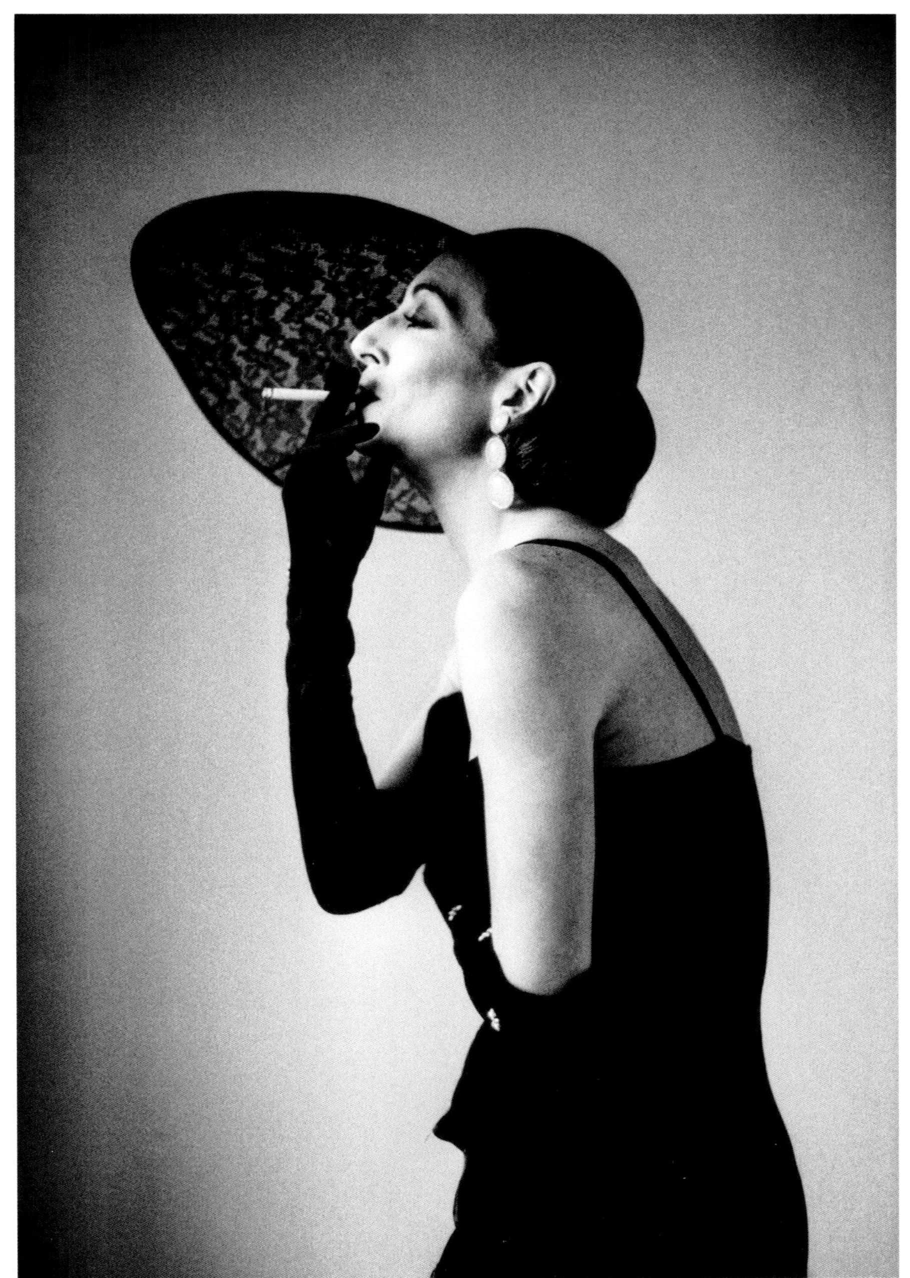

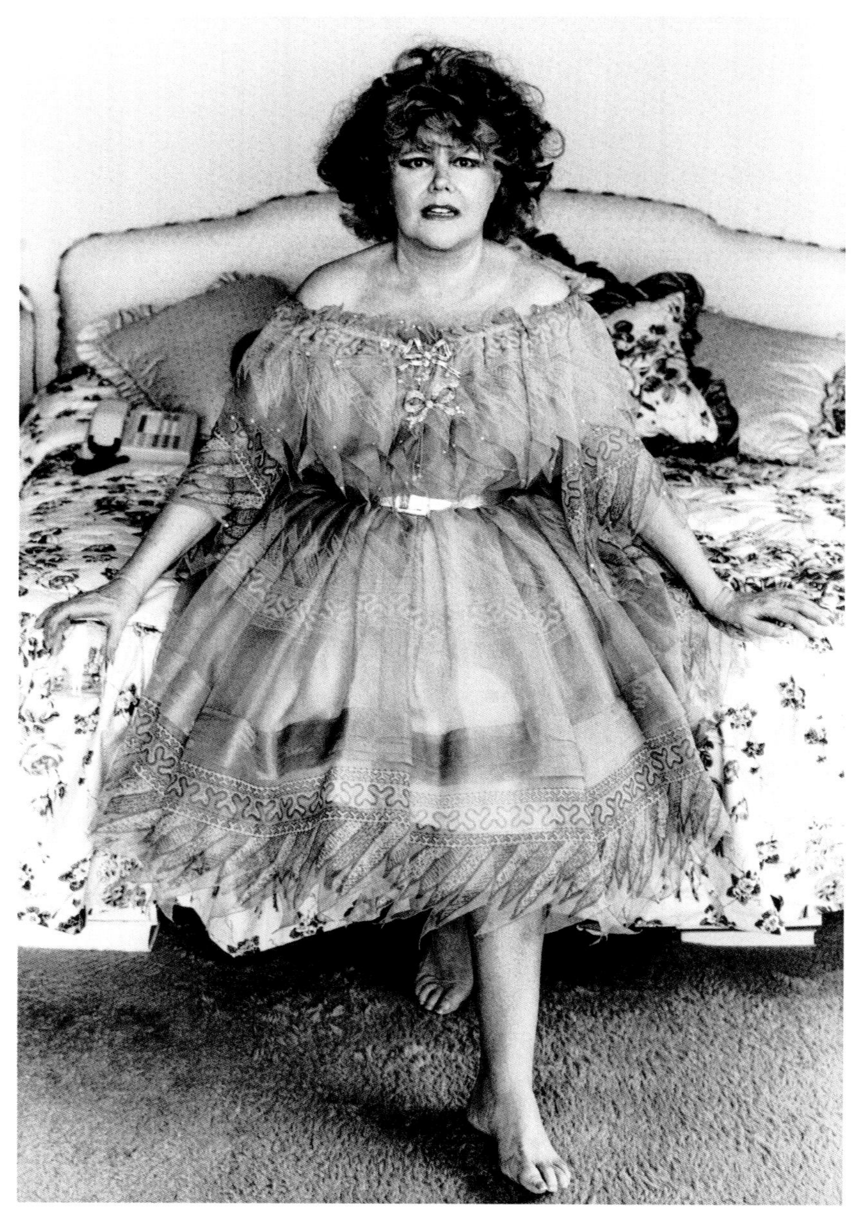

AS: Lady Patricia Rothermere, Cap d'Ail, France, 1989

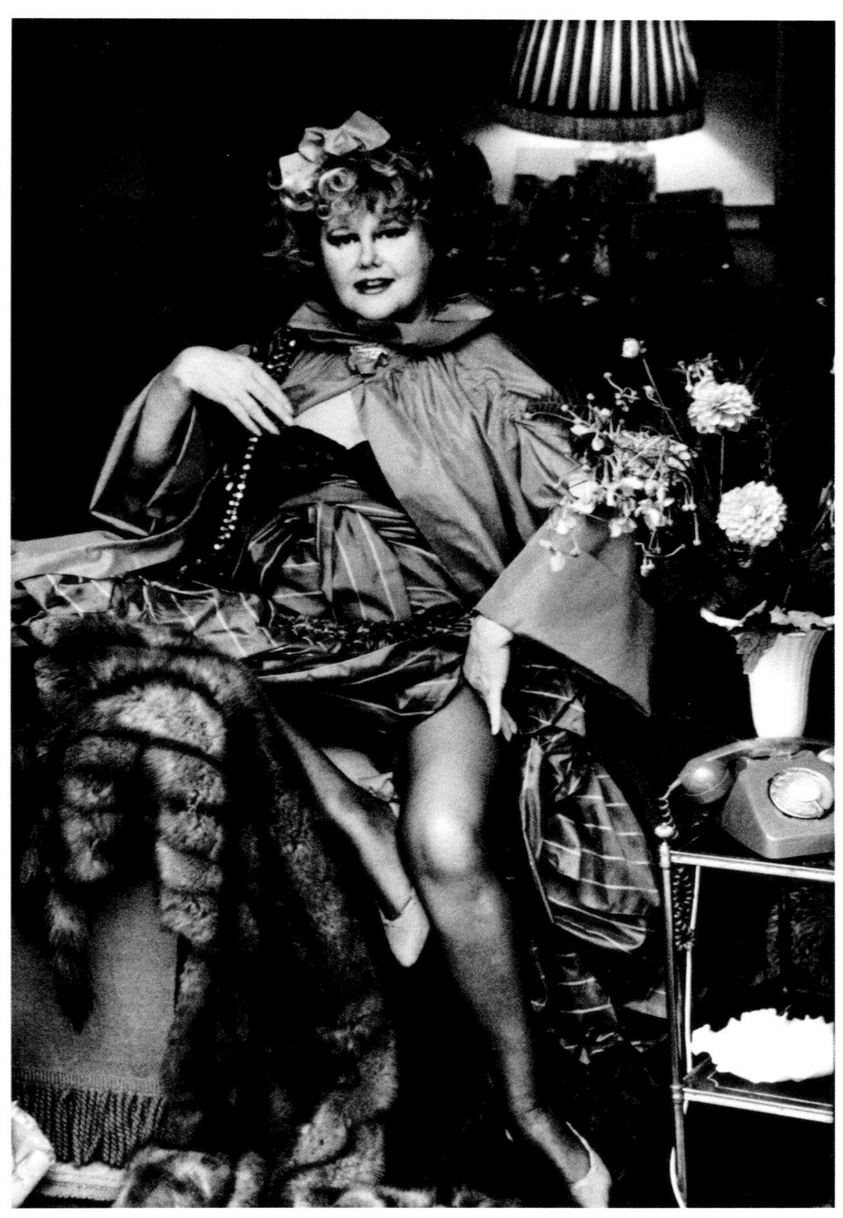

HN: Lady Patricia Rothermere at home, London, 1986

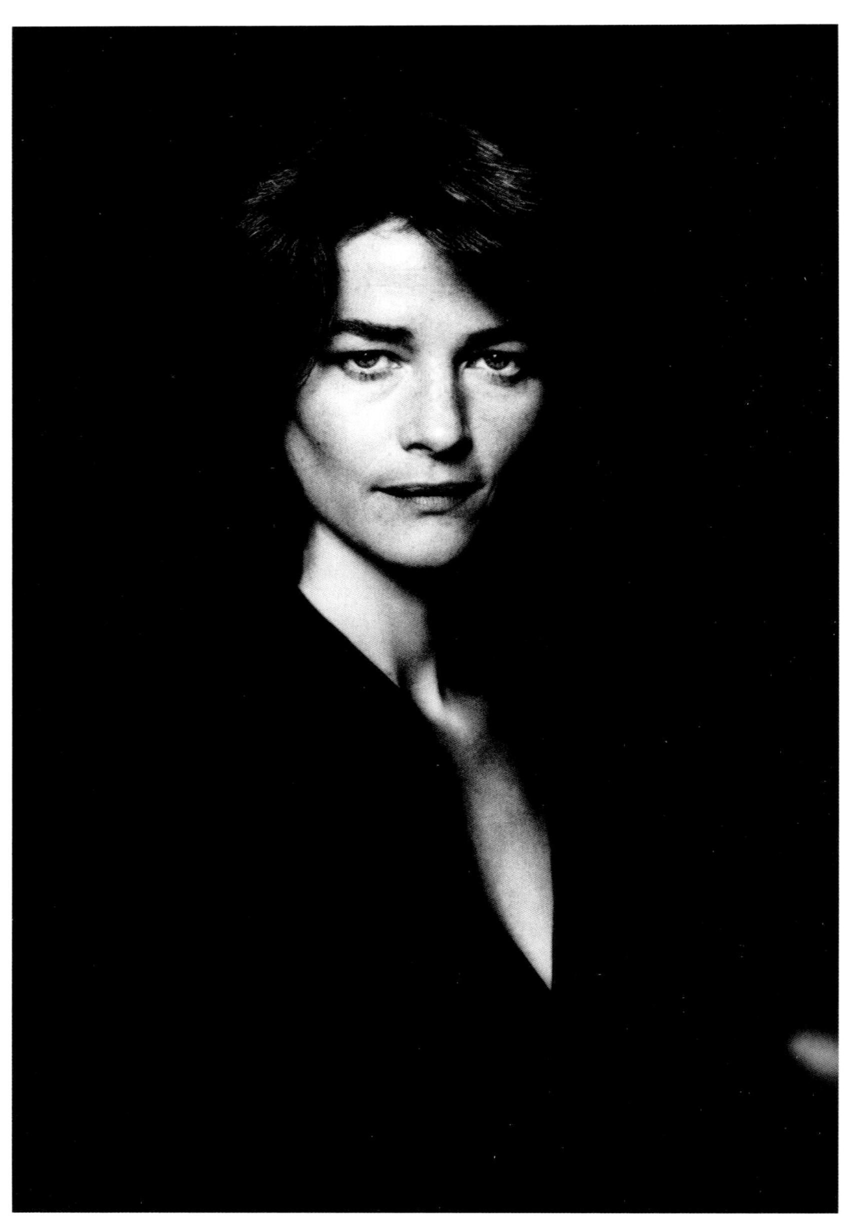

AS: Charlotte Rampling, Paris, 1982
HN: Charlotte Rampling, Paris, 1977

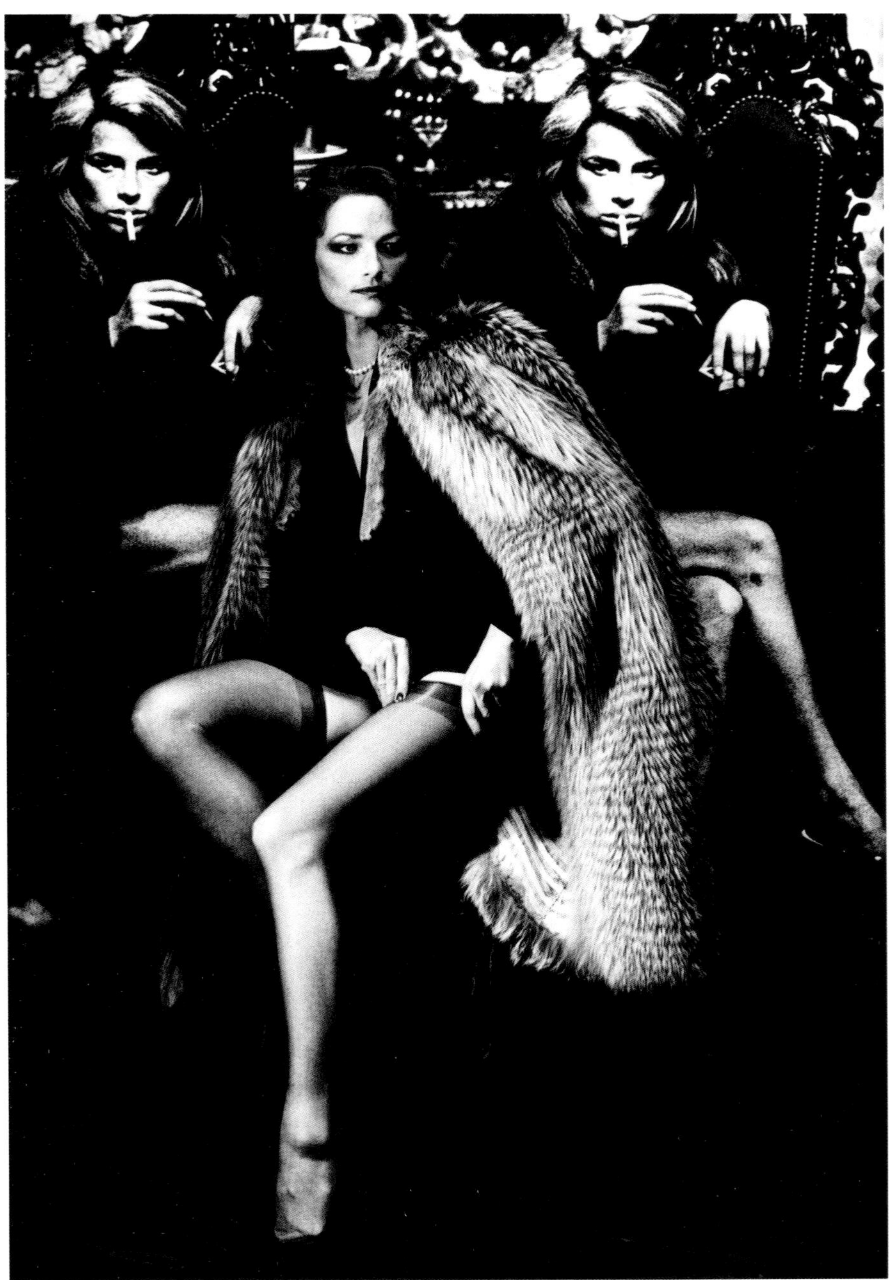

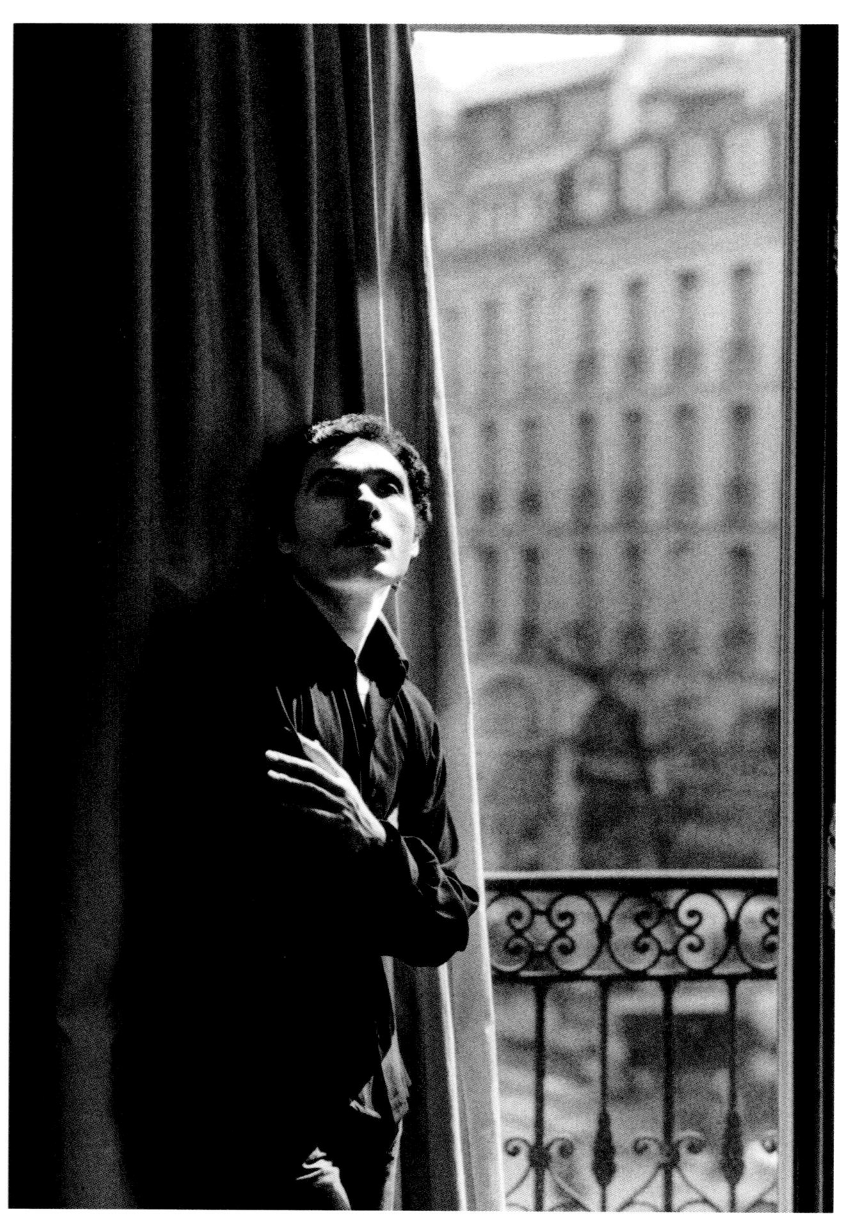

HN: Antonio López, Paris, 1973
AS: Antonio López, Paris, 1977

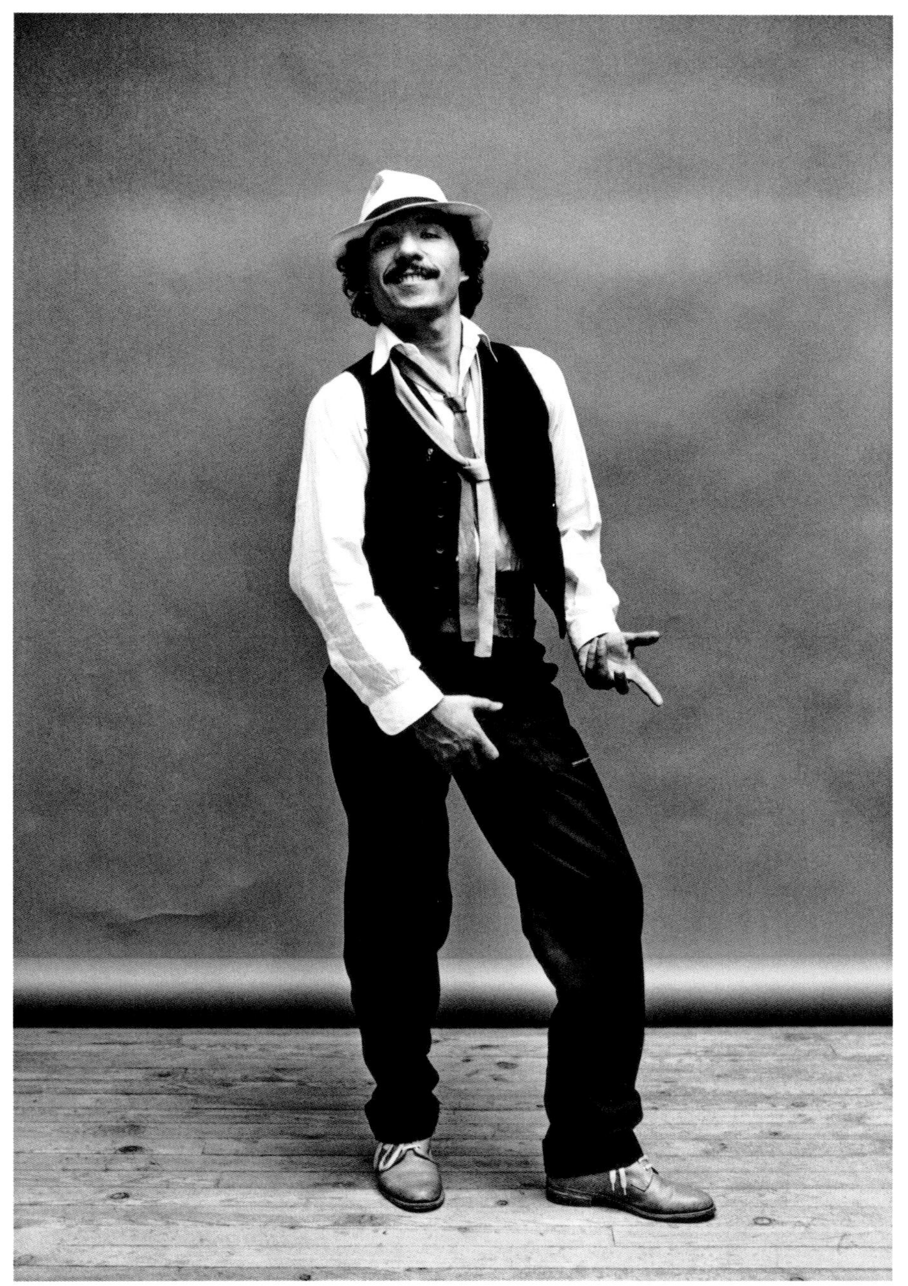

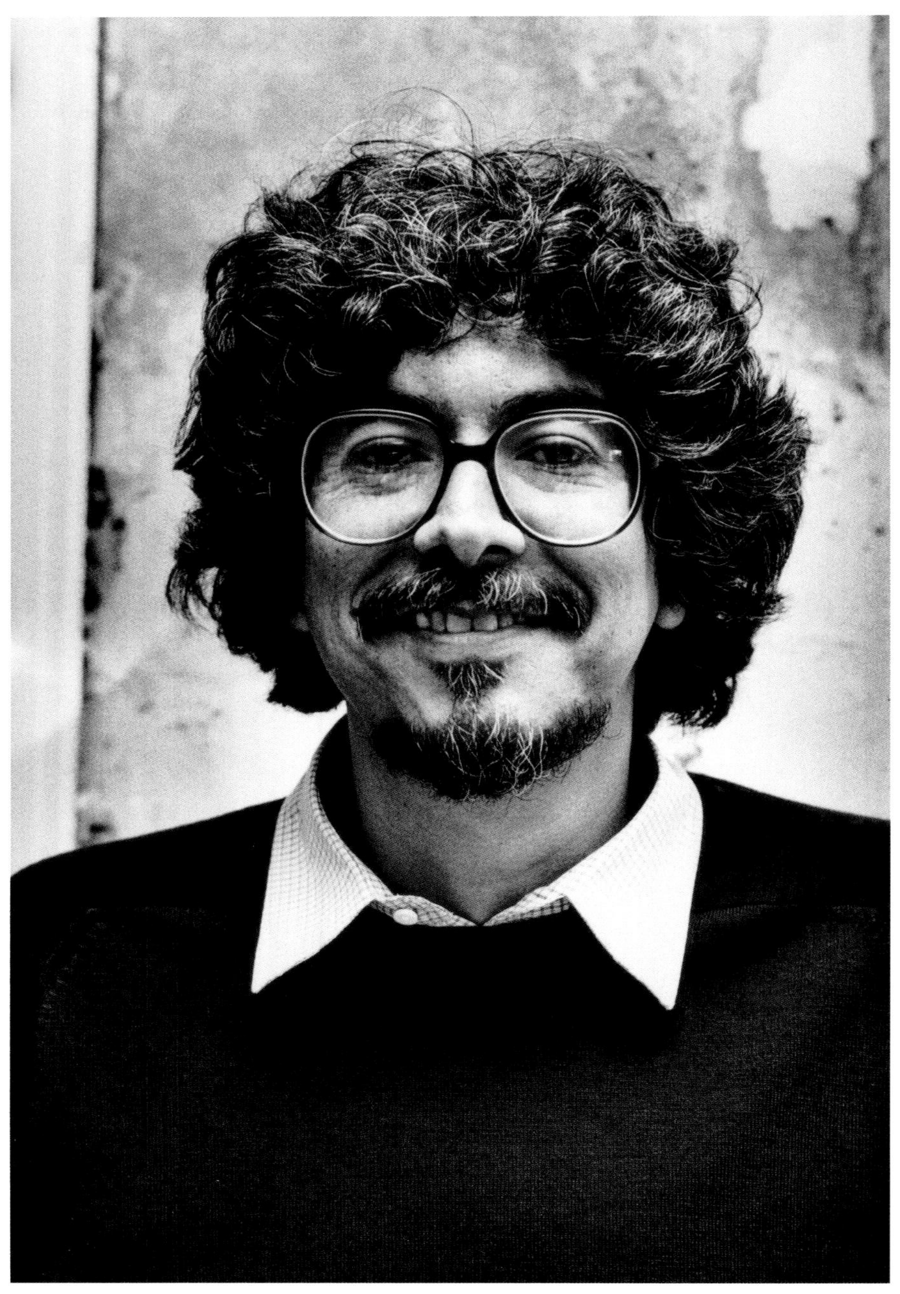

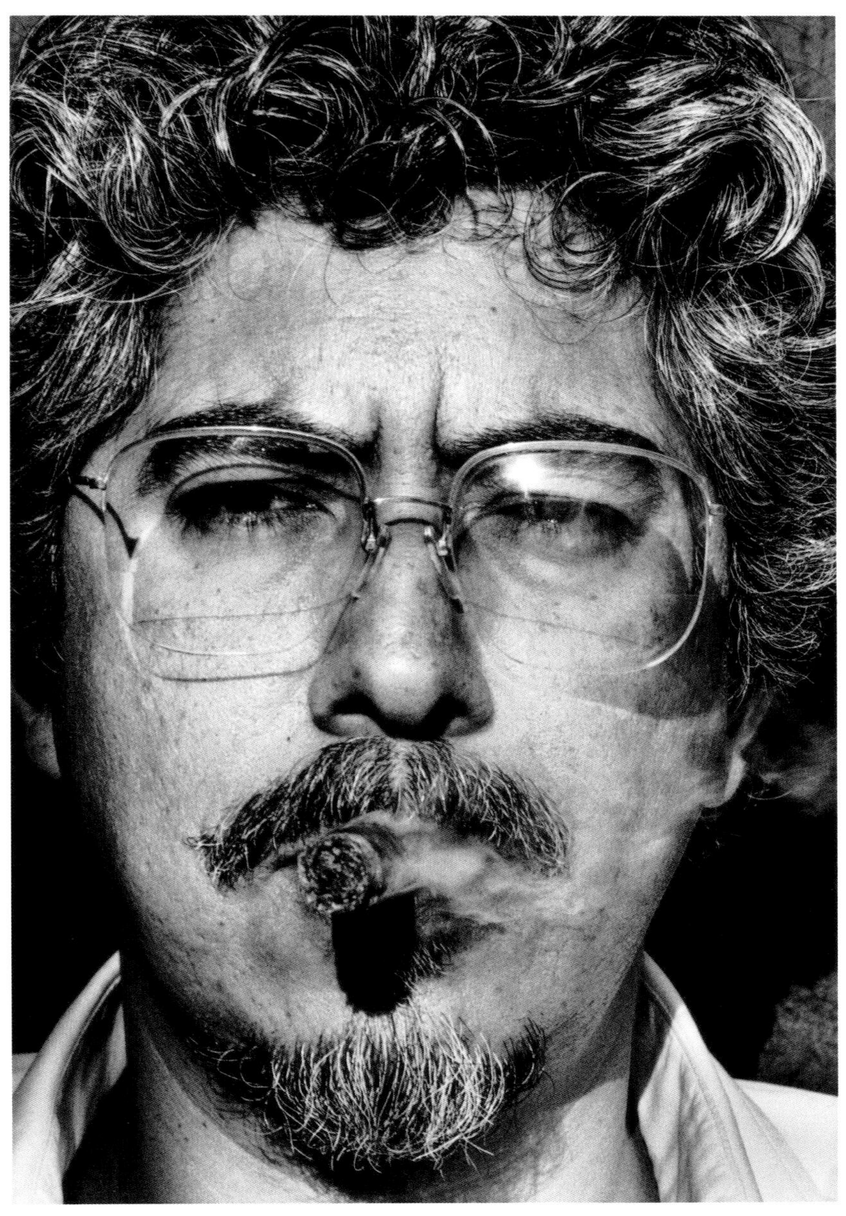

AS: Robert Graham, Venice, California, 1980
HN: Robert Graham, Venice, California, 1984

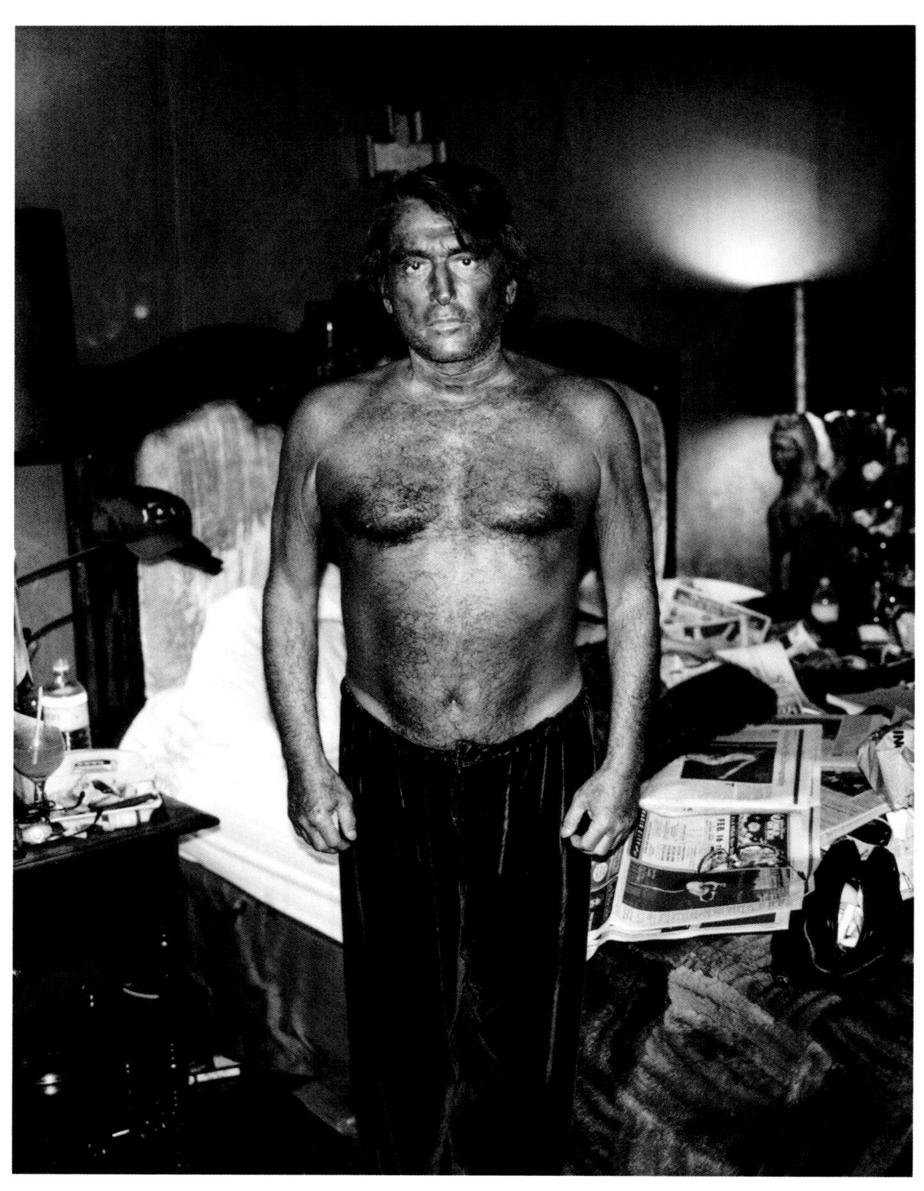

HN: Robert Evans, Beverly Hills, 1996

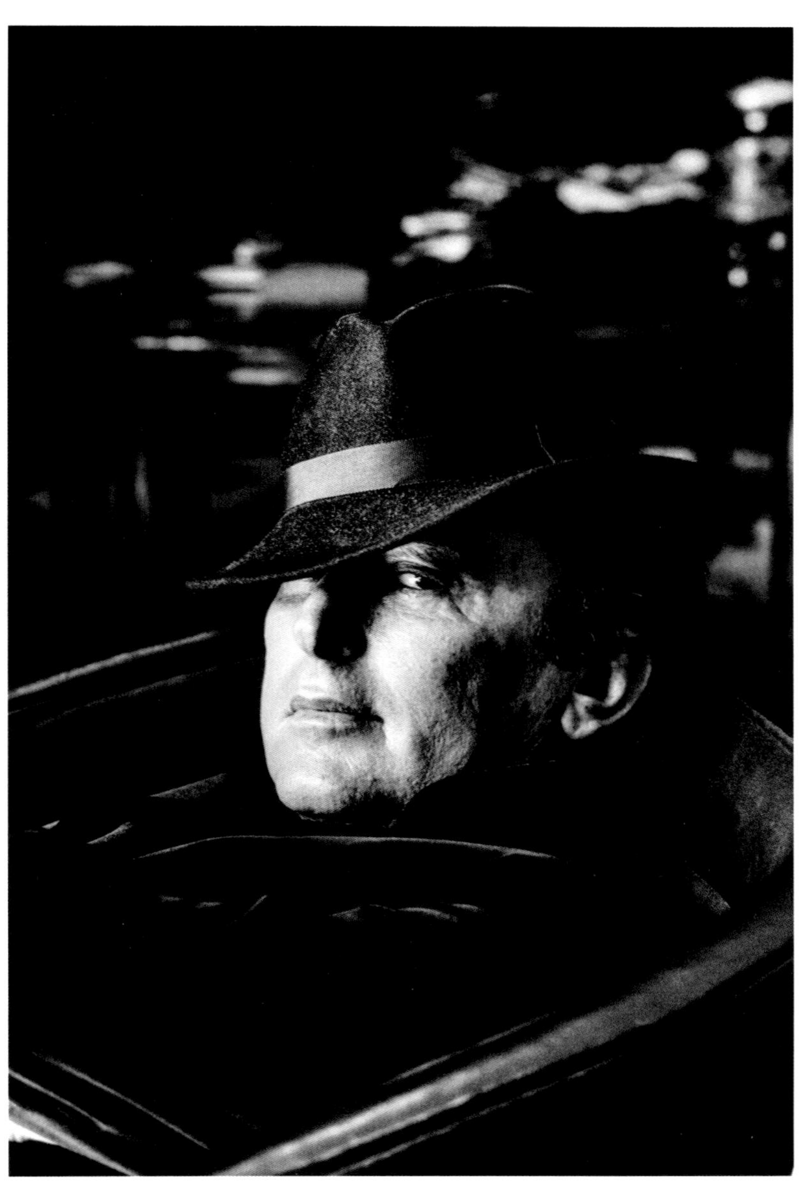

AS: Robert Evans, Los Angeles, 1986

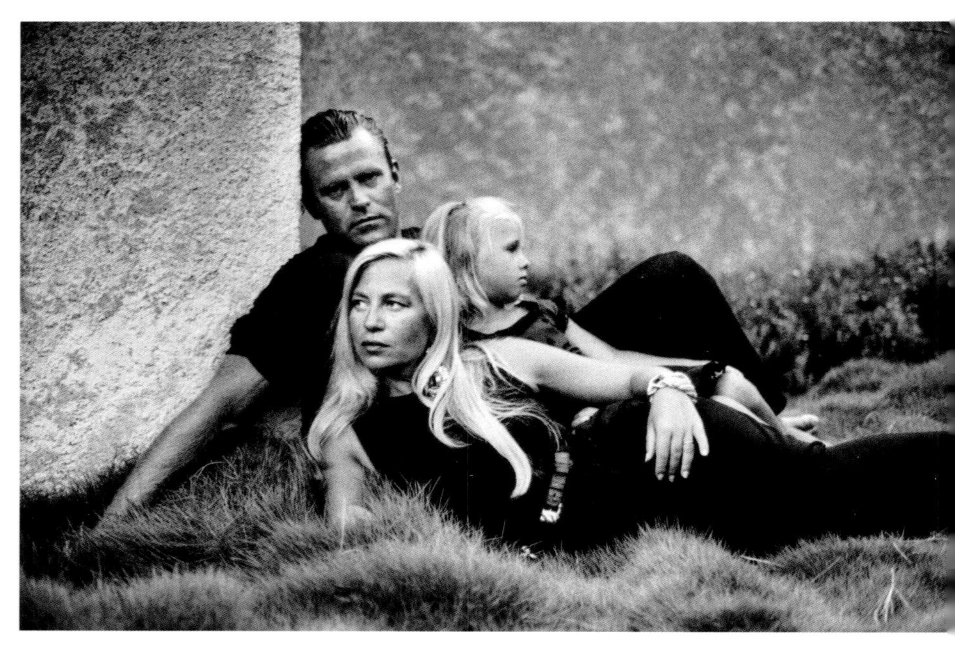

AS: Donatella Versace, Paul Beck and daughter Allegra, Saint-Tropez, 1990

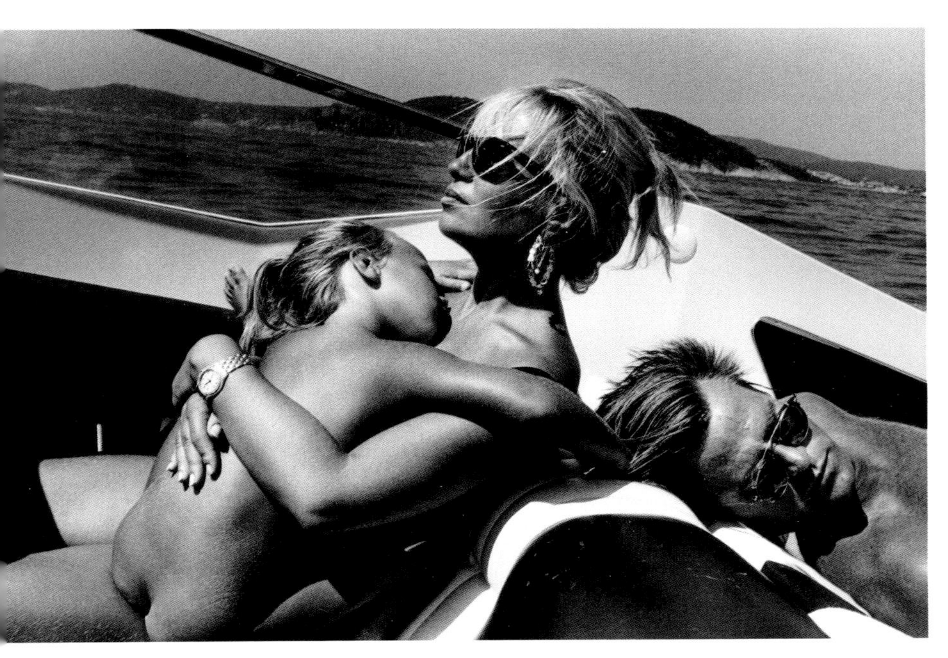

HN: Donatella Versace, off the coast of Antibes, 1990

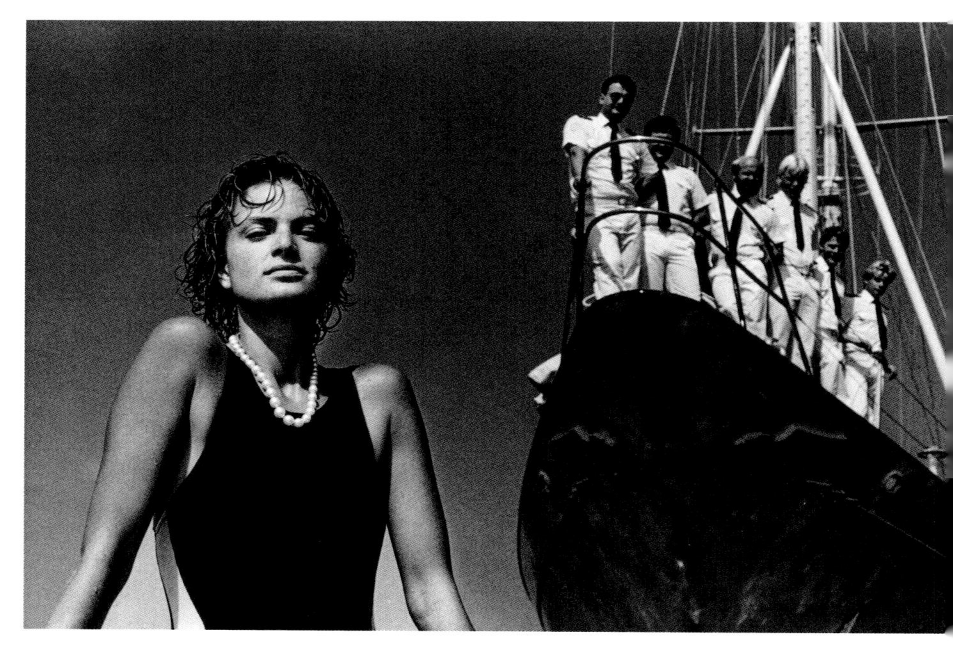

HN: Princess Gloria von Thurn und Taxis, Ibiza, 1985
AS: Princess Gloria von Thurn und Taxis, Regensburg, 1985

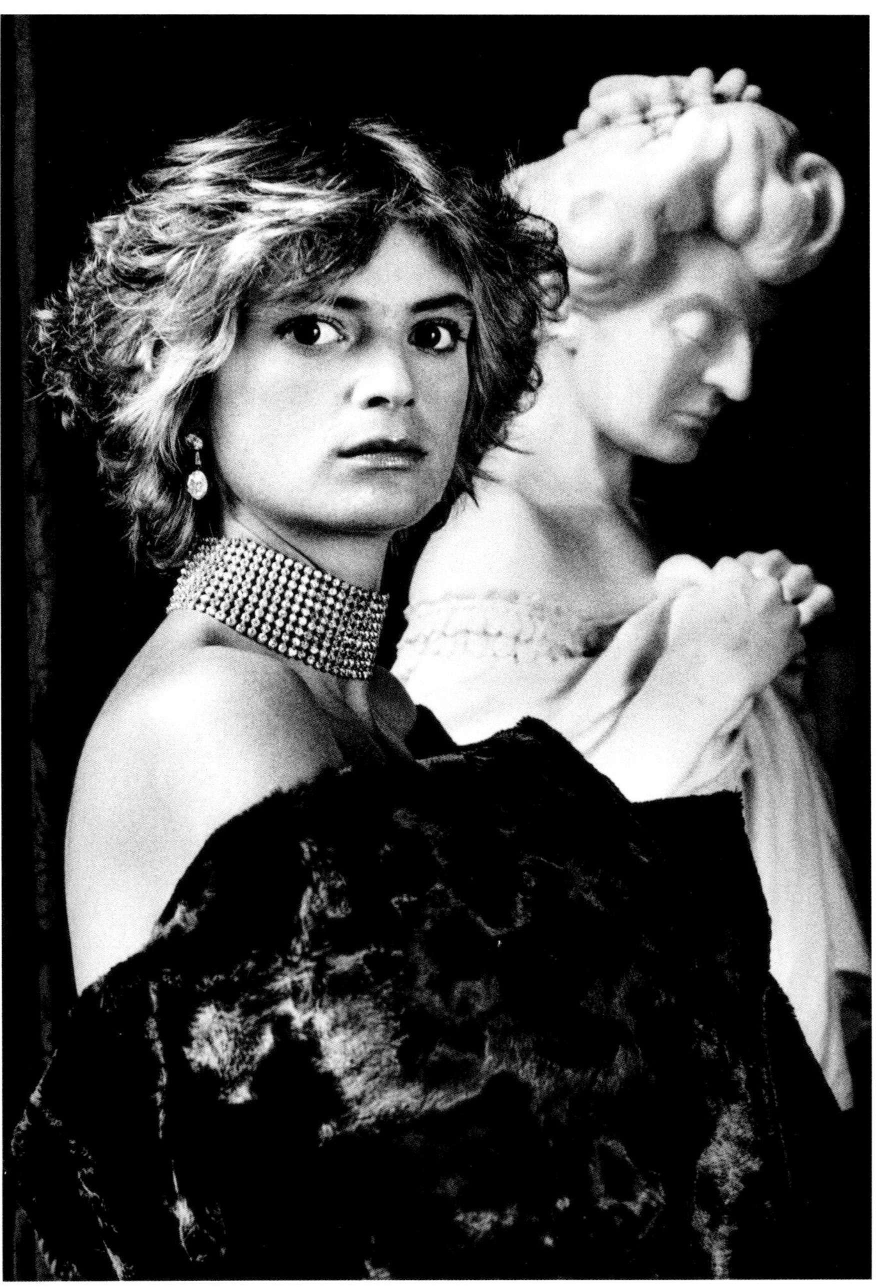

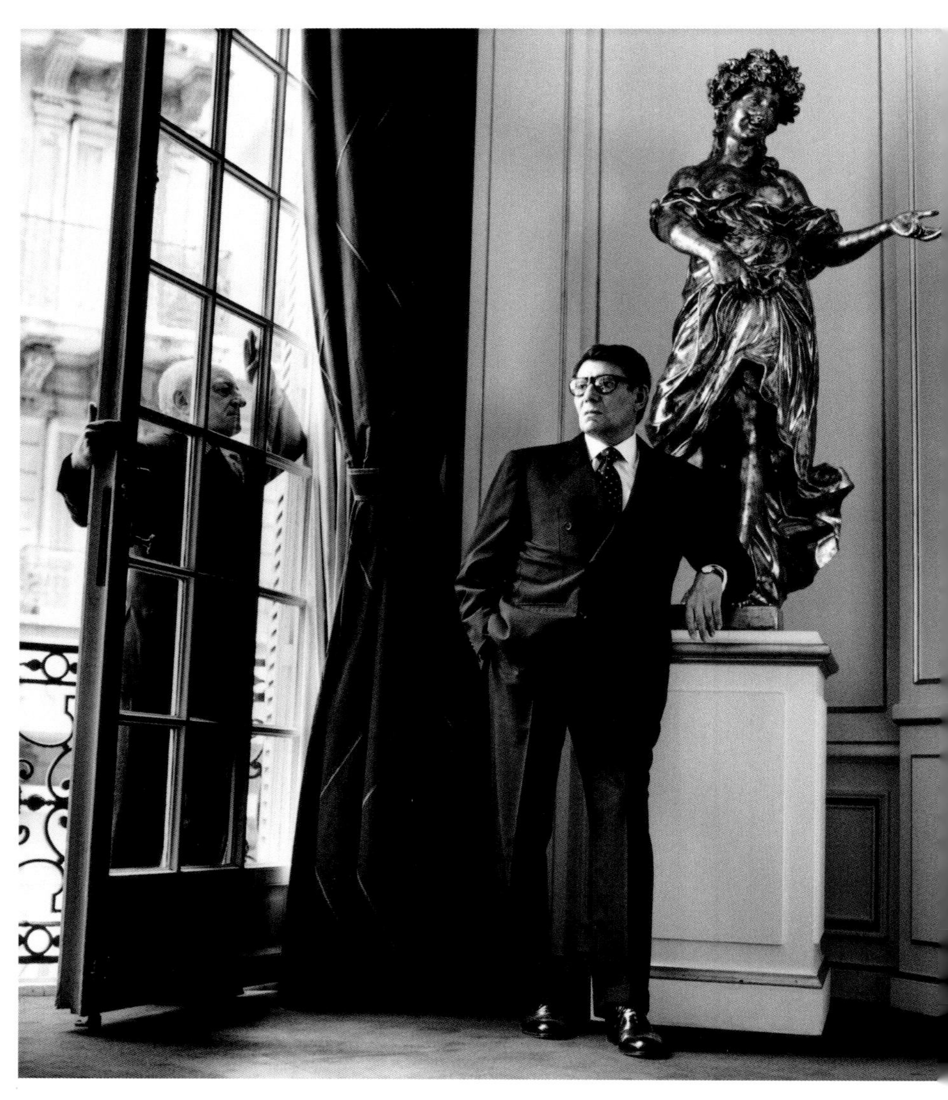

HN: Yves Saint Laurent and Pierre Bergé, Paris, 1996
AS: Yves Saint Laurent and Pierre Bergé, Paris, 1983

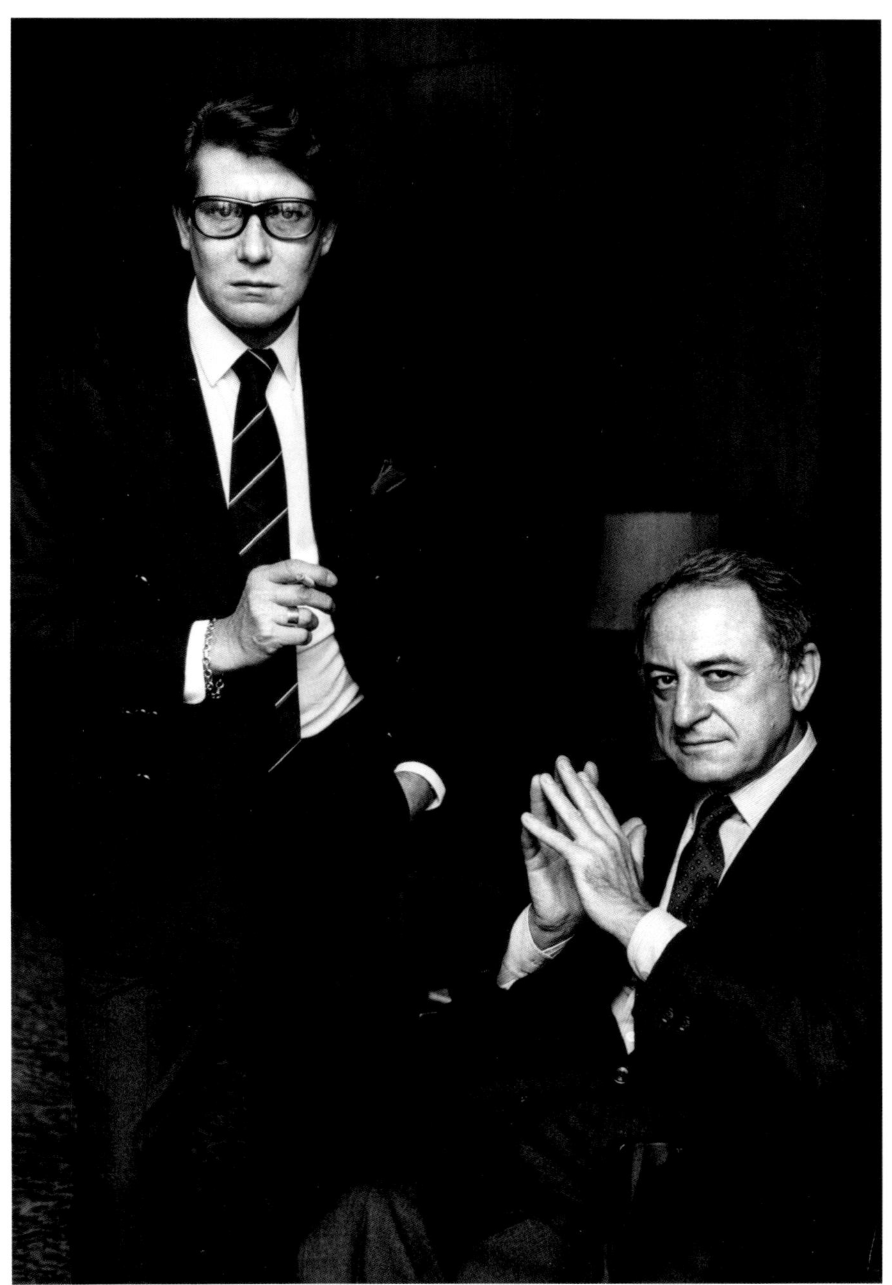

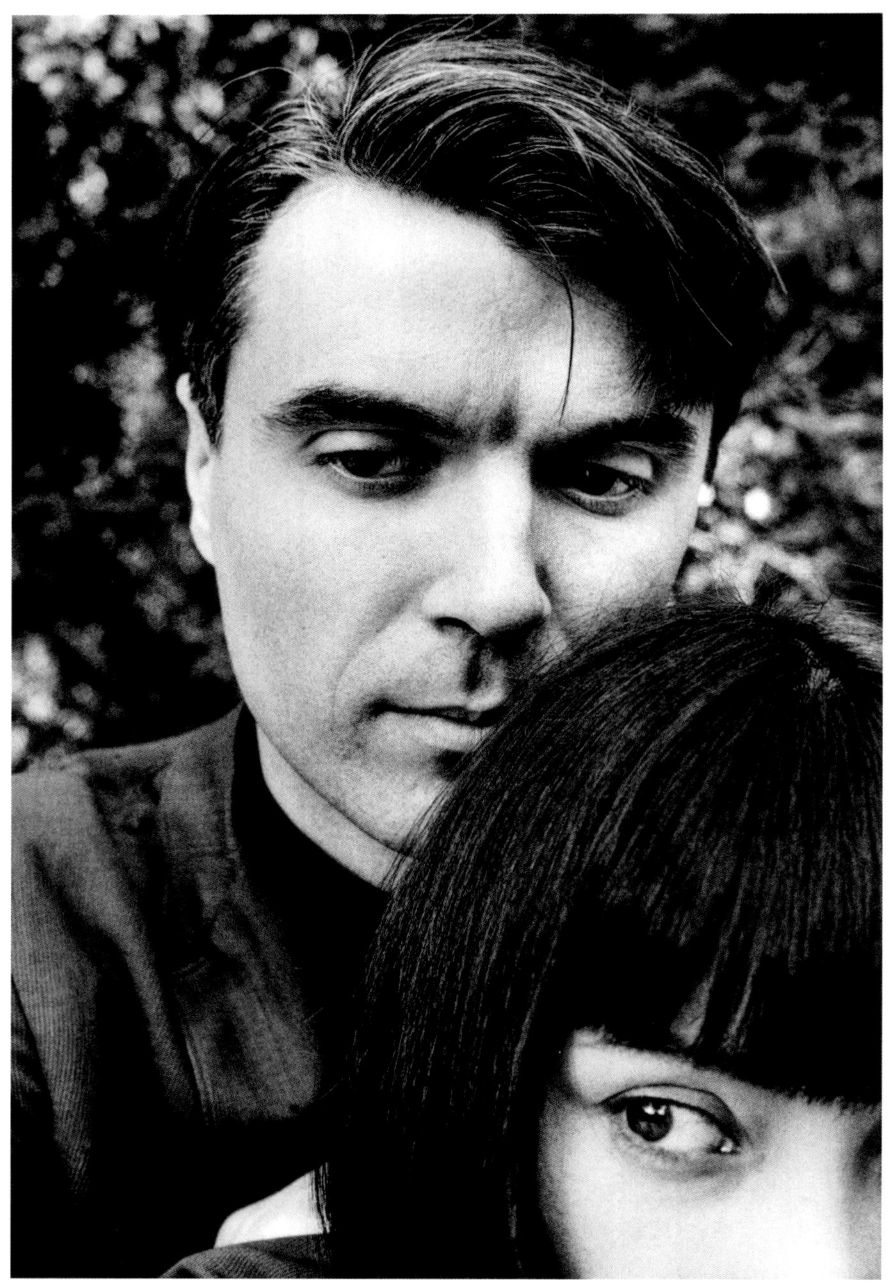

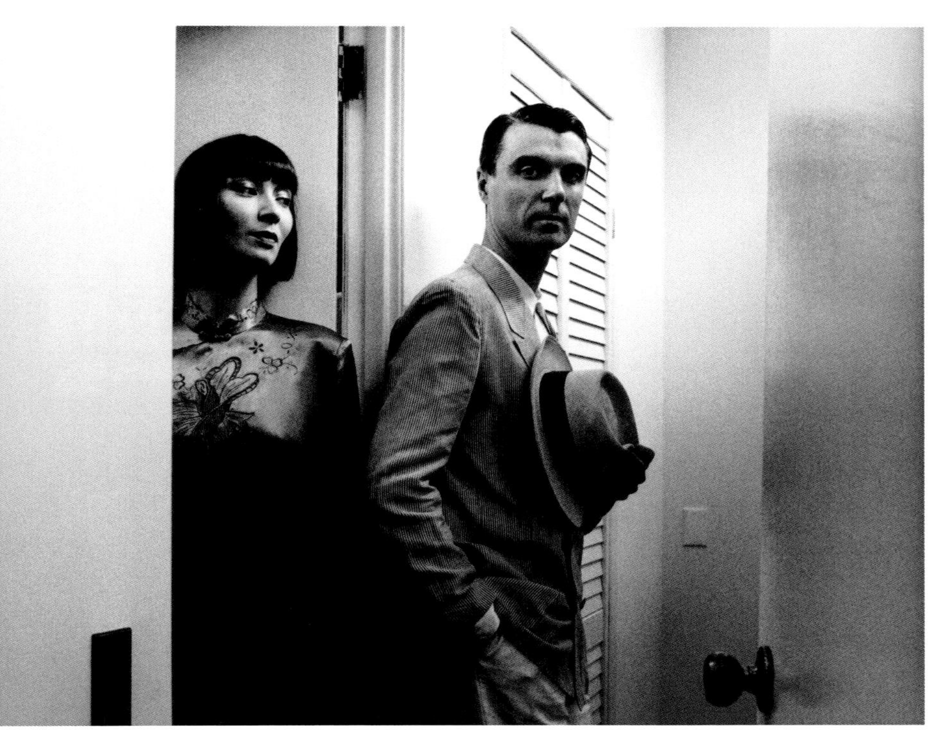

AS: David and Bonnie Byrne, Hollywood, 1986
HN: David Byrne and Bonnie, Los Angeles, 1986

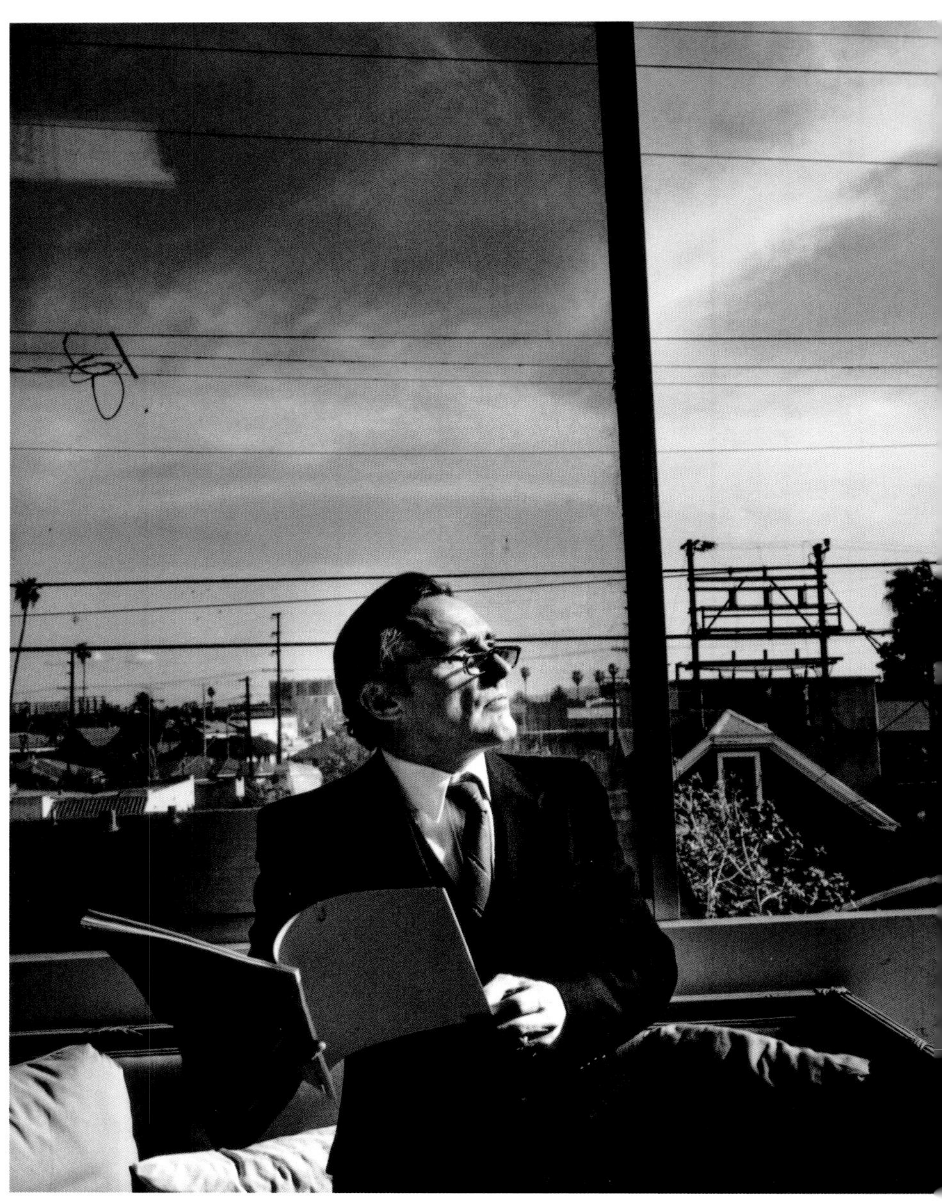

HN: Dennis Hopper, Venice, California, 1985
AS: Dennis Hopper, Santa Monica, California, 1985

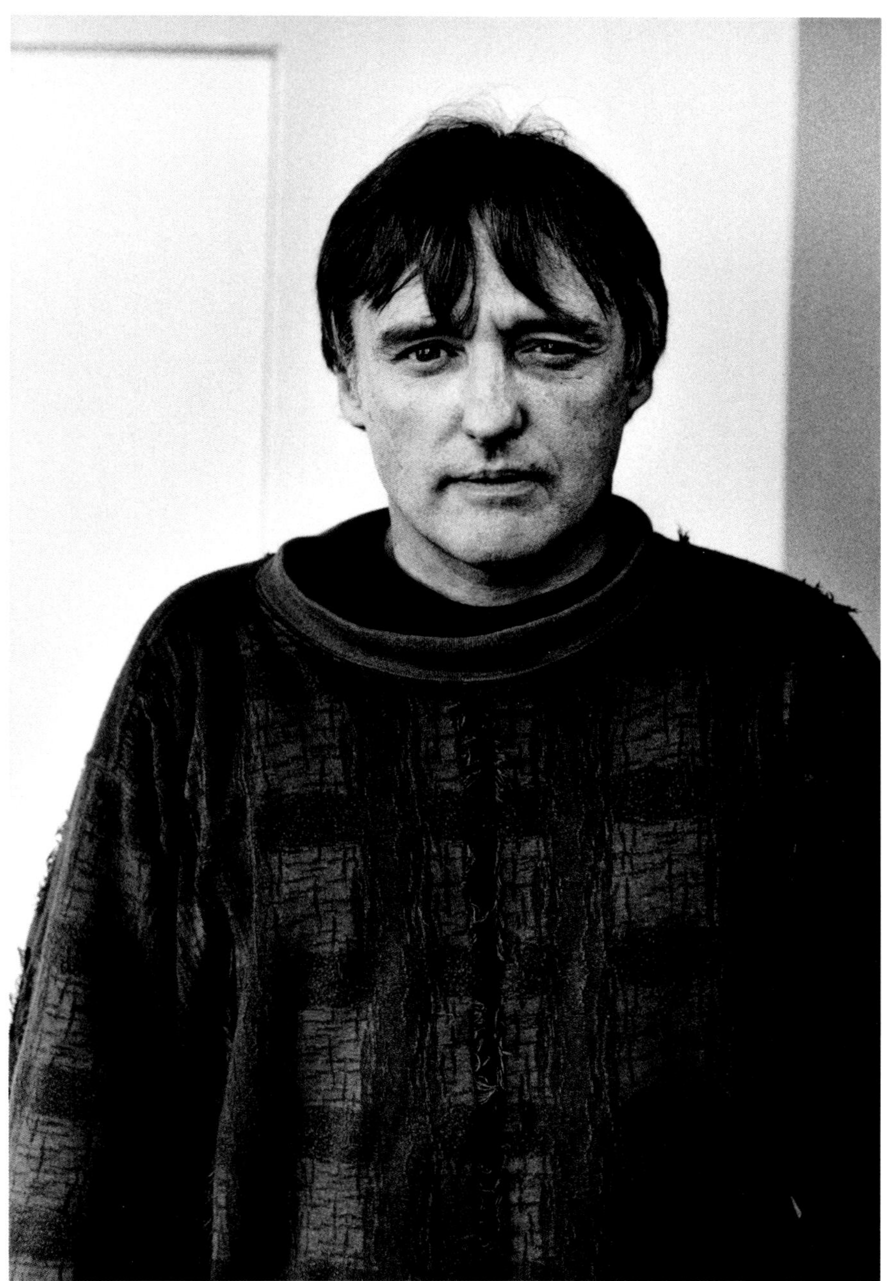

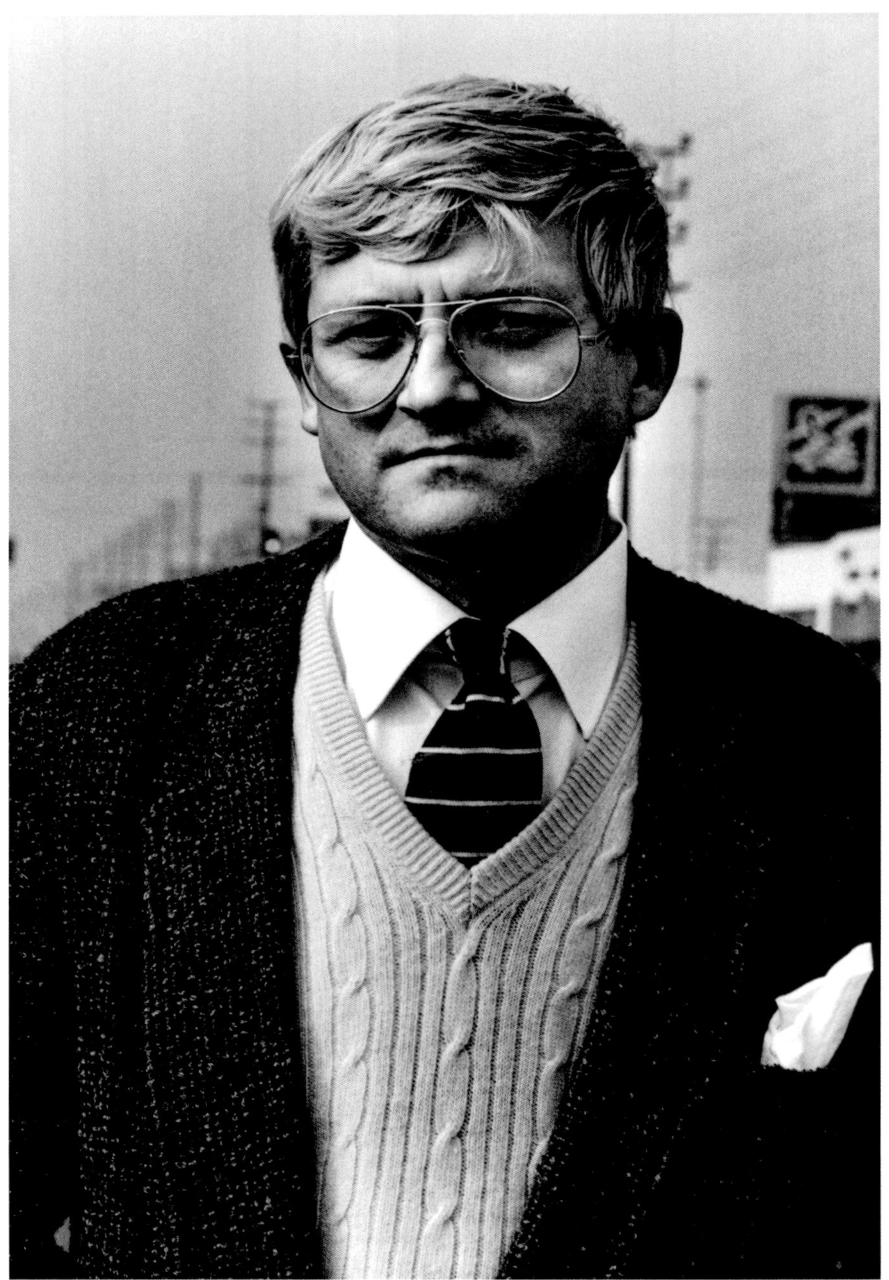

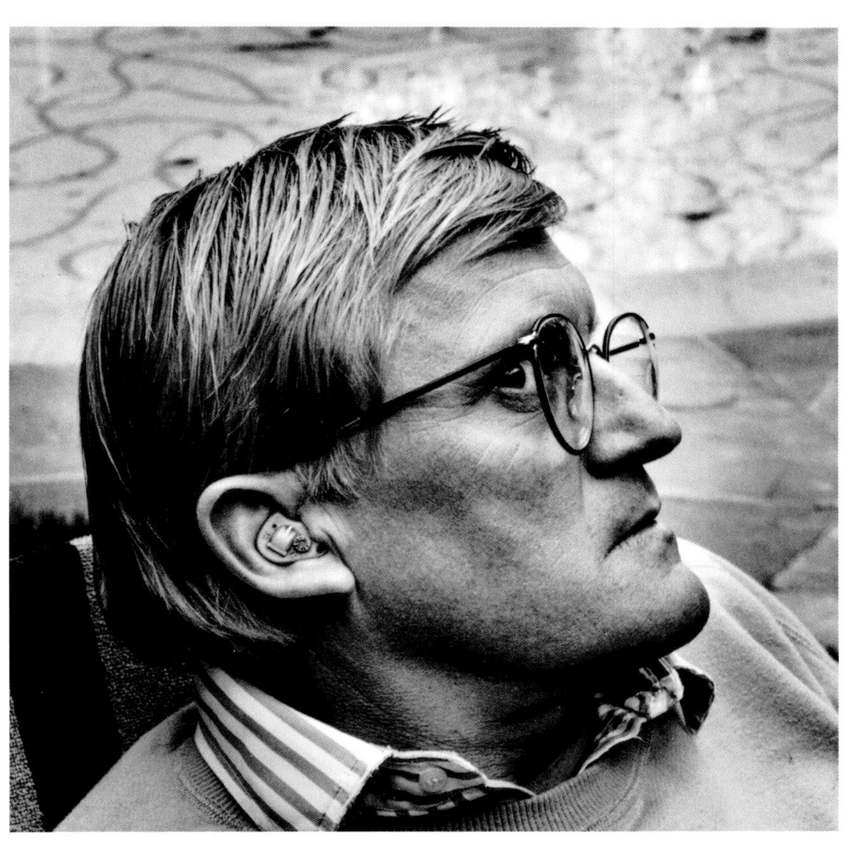

AS: David Hockney, Sunset Boulevard, Hollywood, 1981
HN: David Hockney, Los Angeles, 1988

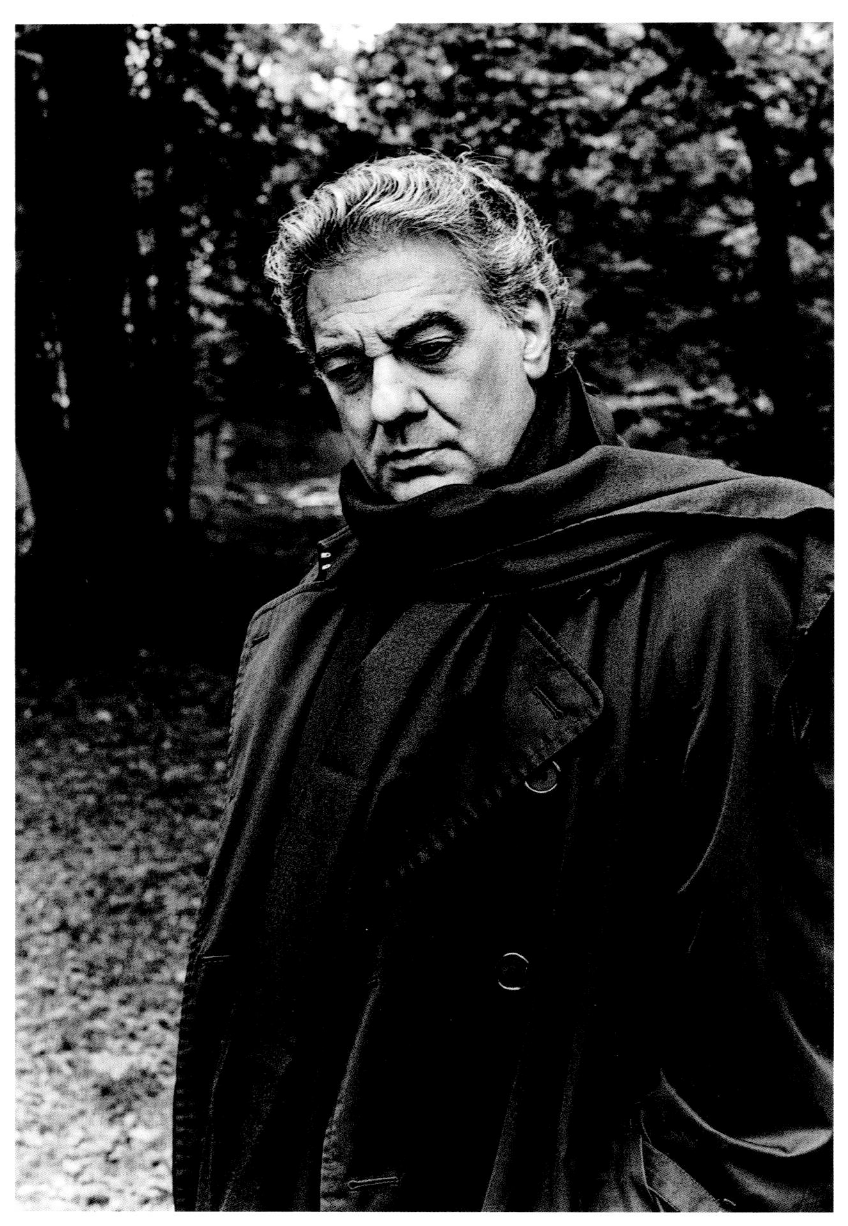

AS: Plácido Domingo, Salzburg, 1998
HN: Plácido Domingo, Schwetzingen, 1993

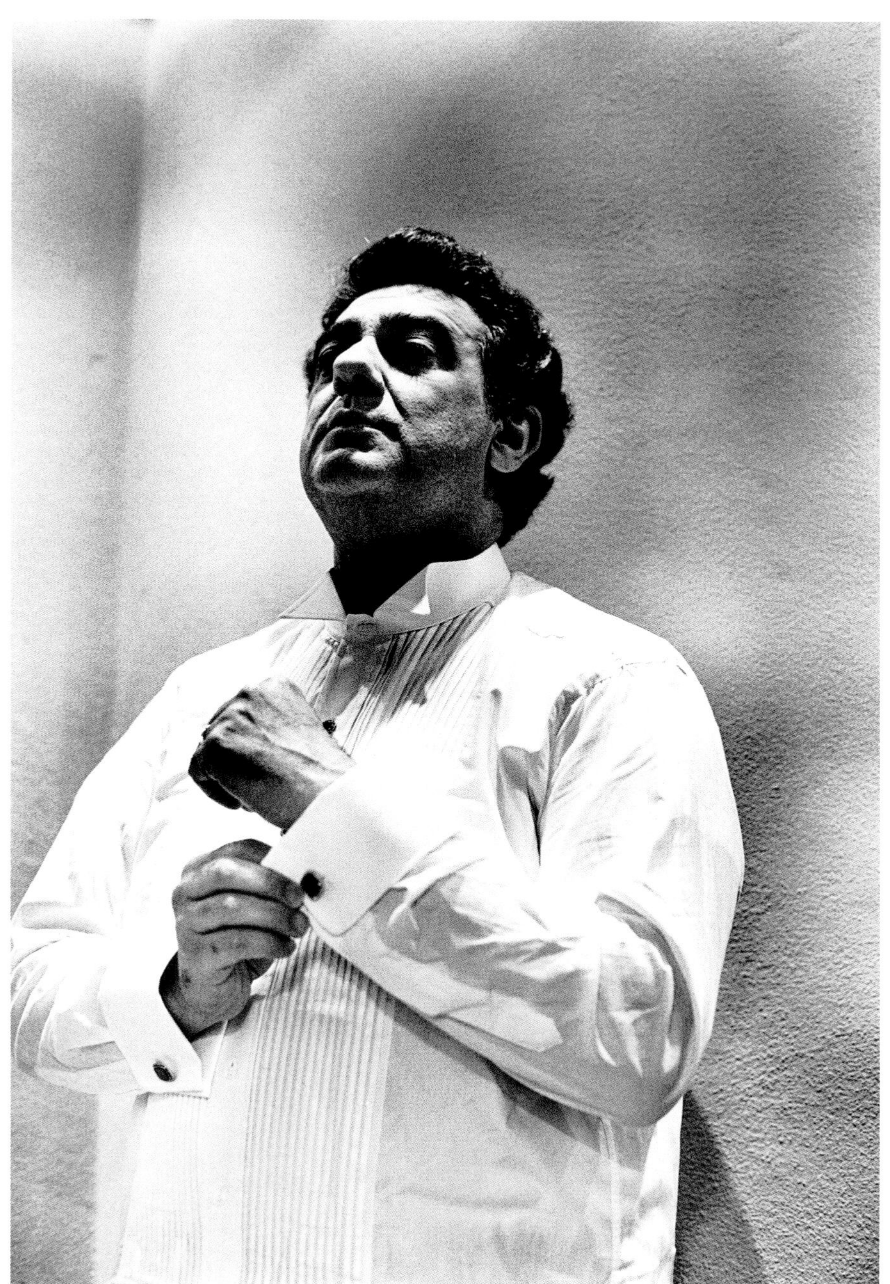

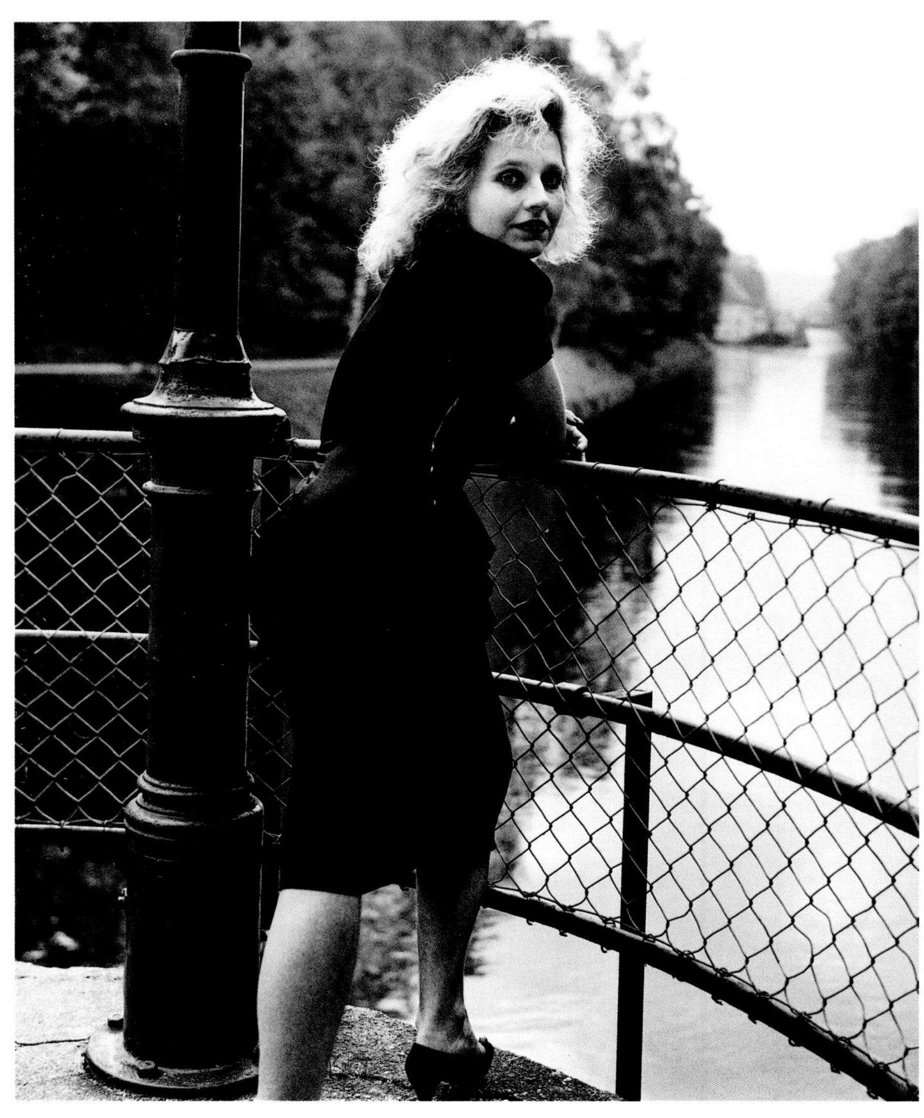

HN: Hanna Schygulla, Munich, 1980
AS: Hanna Schygulla, Hollywood, 1981

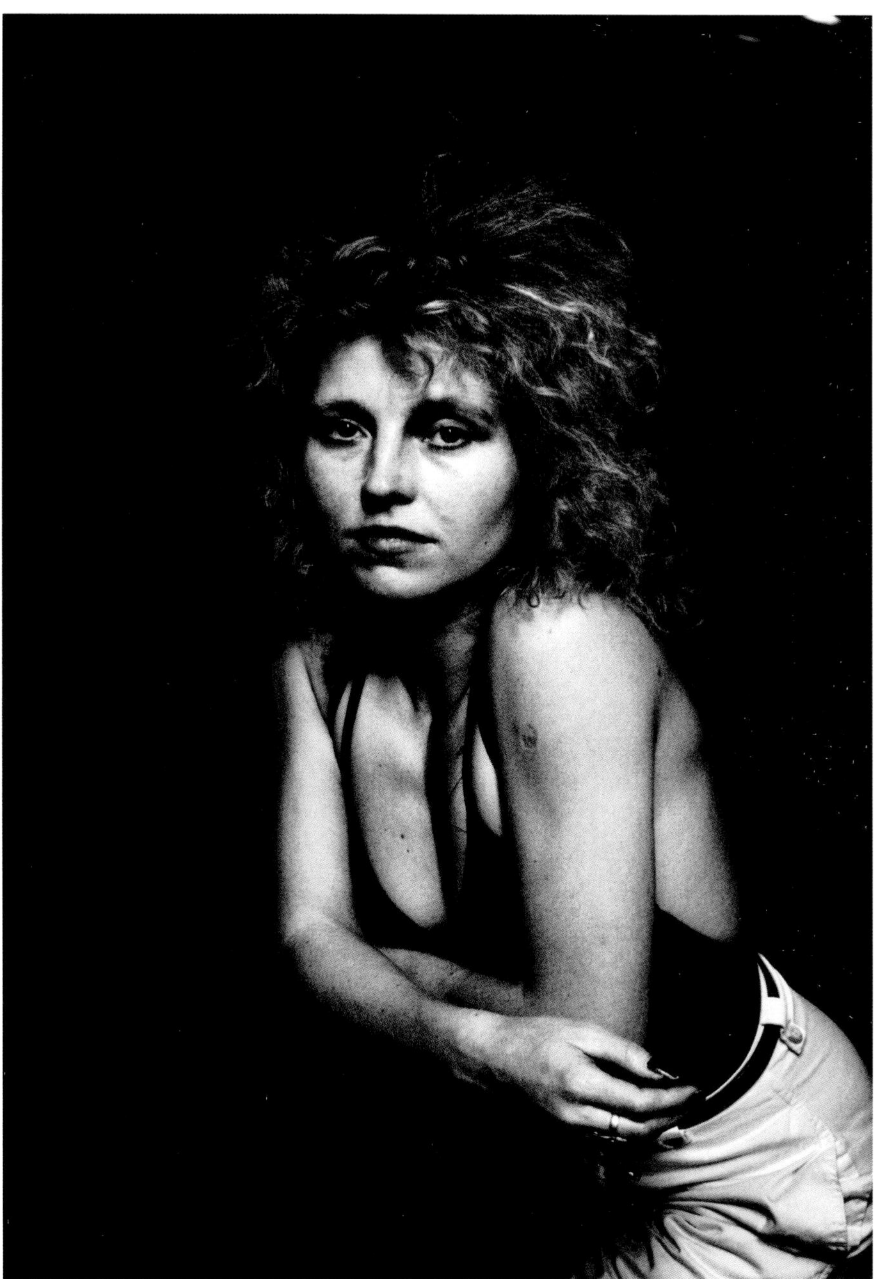

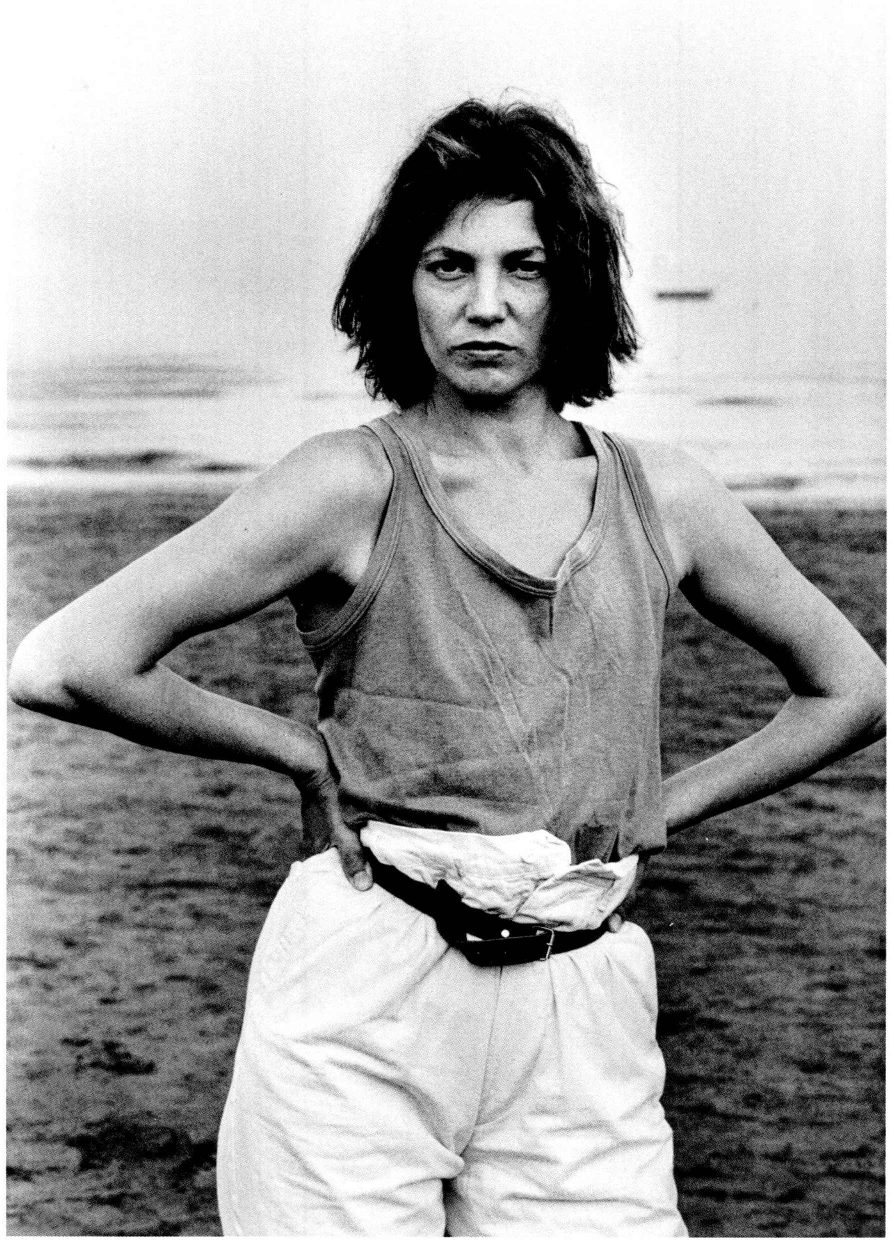

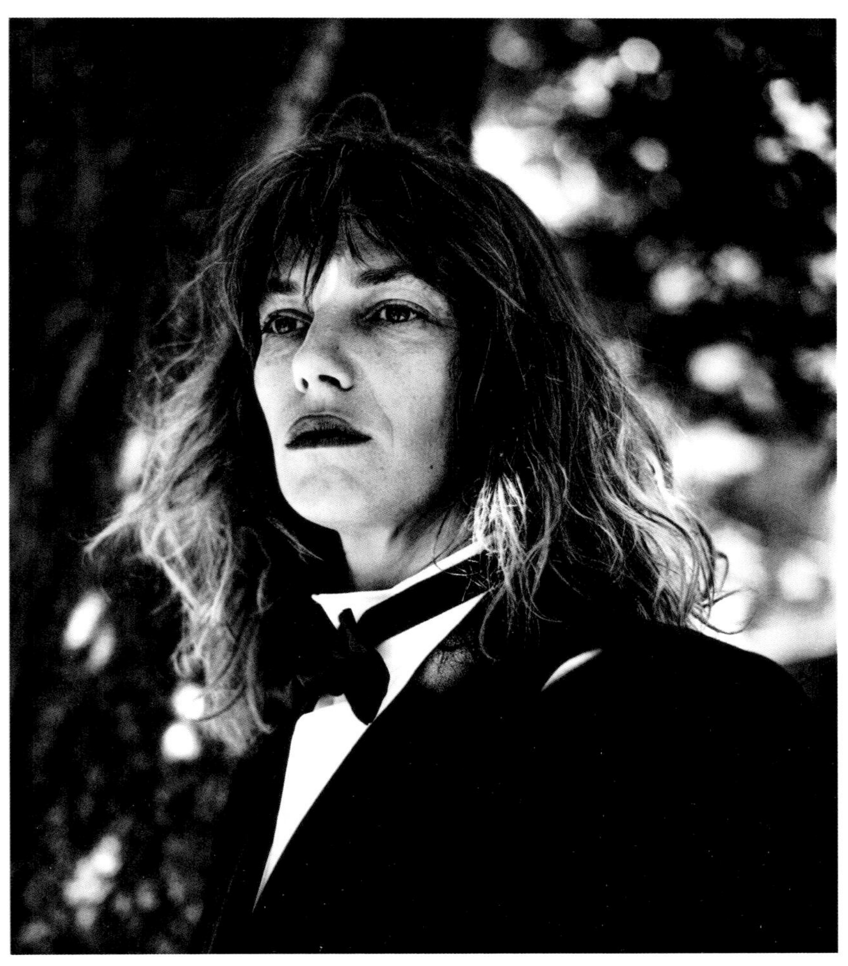

AS: Jane Birkin, Venice, 1984
HN: Jane Birkin, Paris, 1989

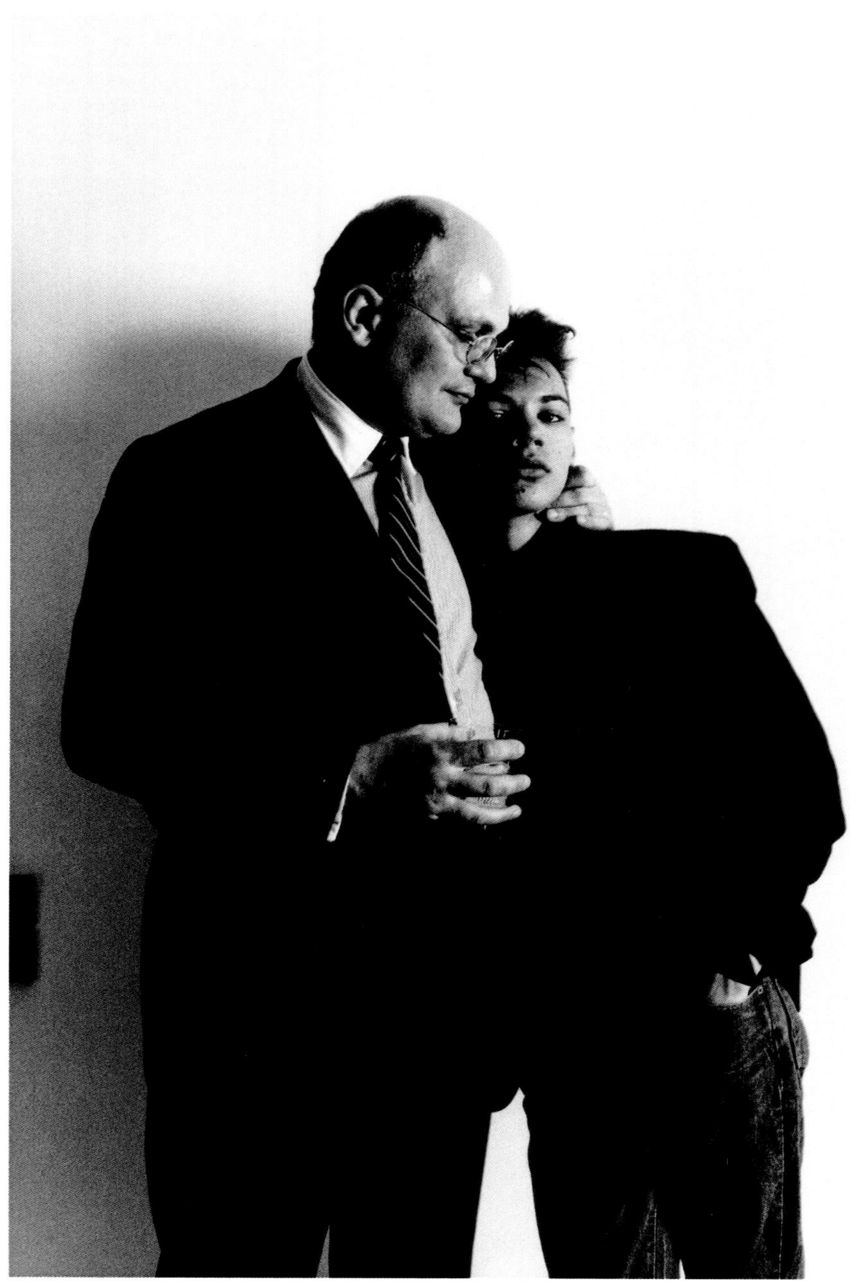

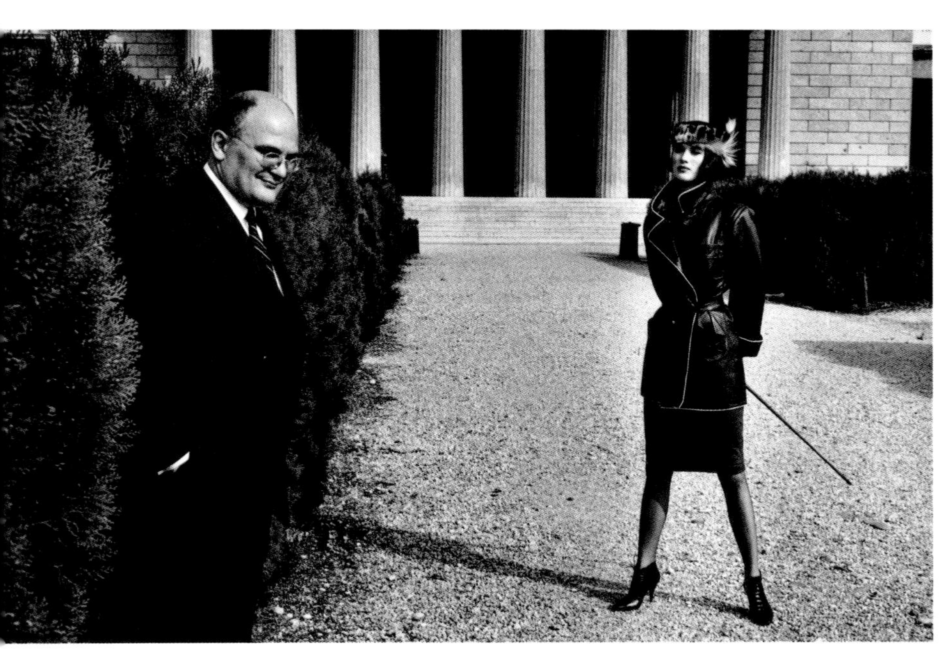

AS: Xavier Moreau and his son Alexis, Monte Carlo, 1984
HN: Xavier Moreau and his wife, Verona, 1984

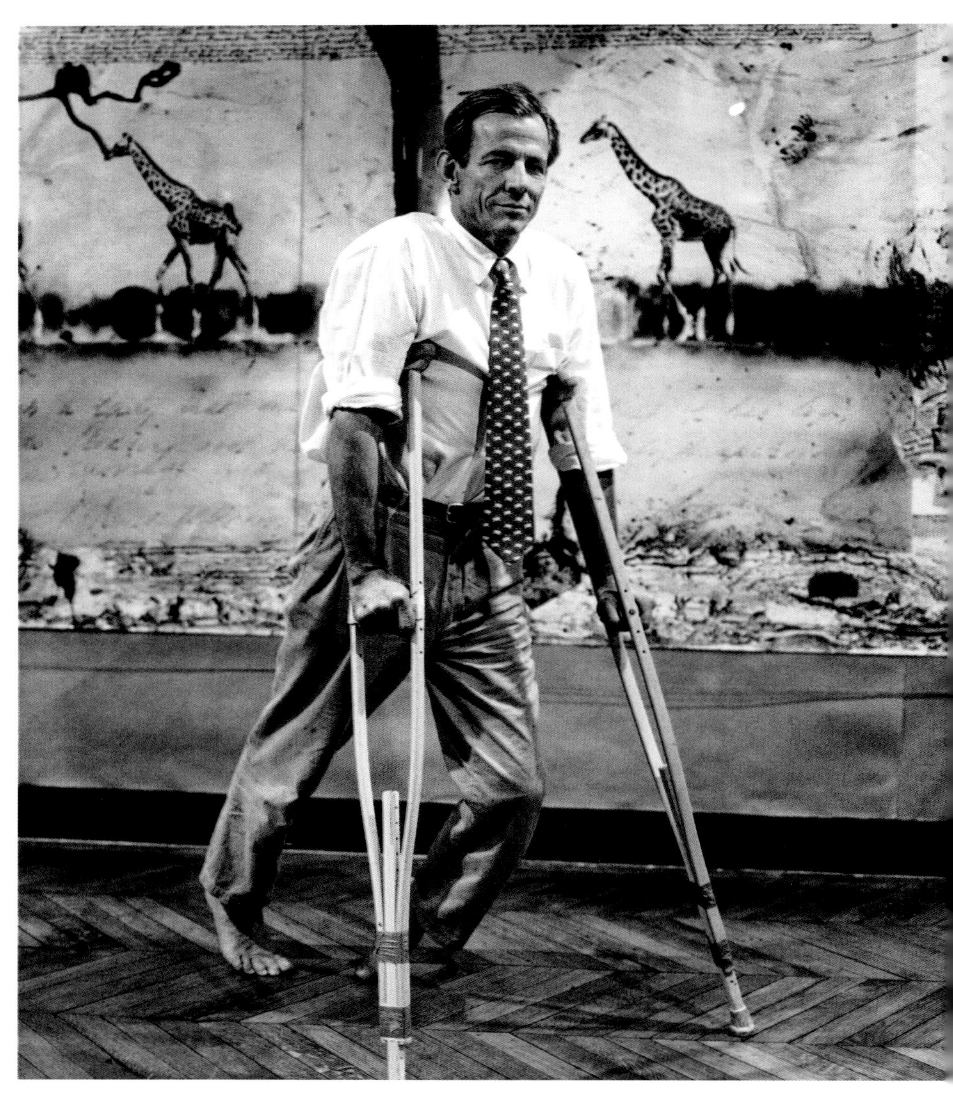

HN: Peter Beard, Paris, 1996

AS: Peter Beard, Venice, 1984

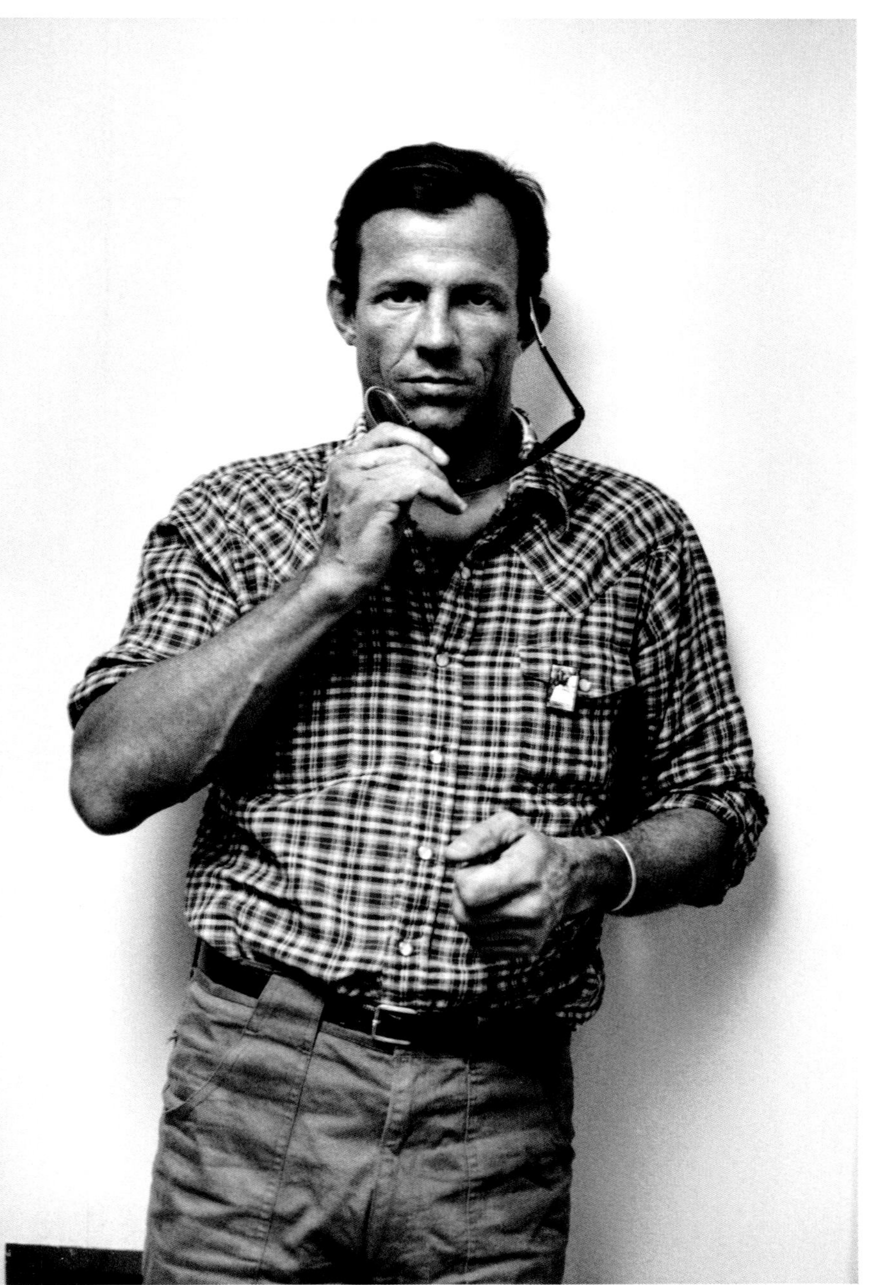

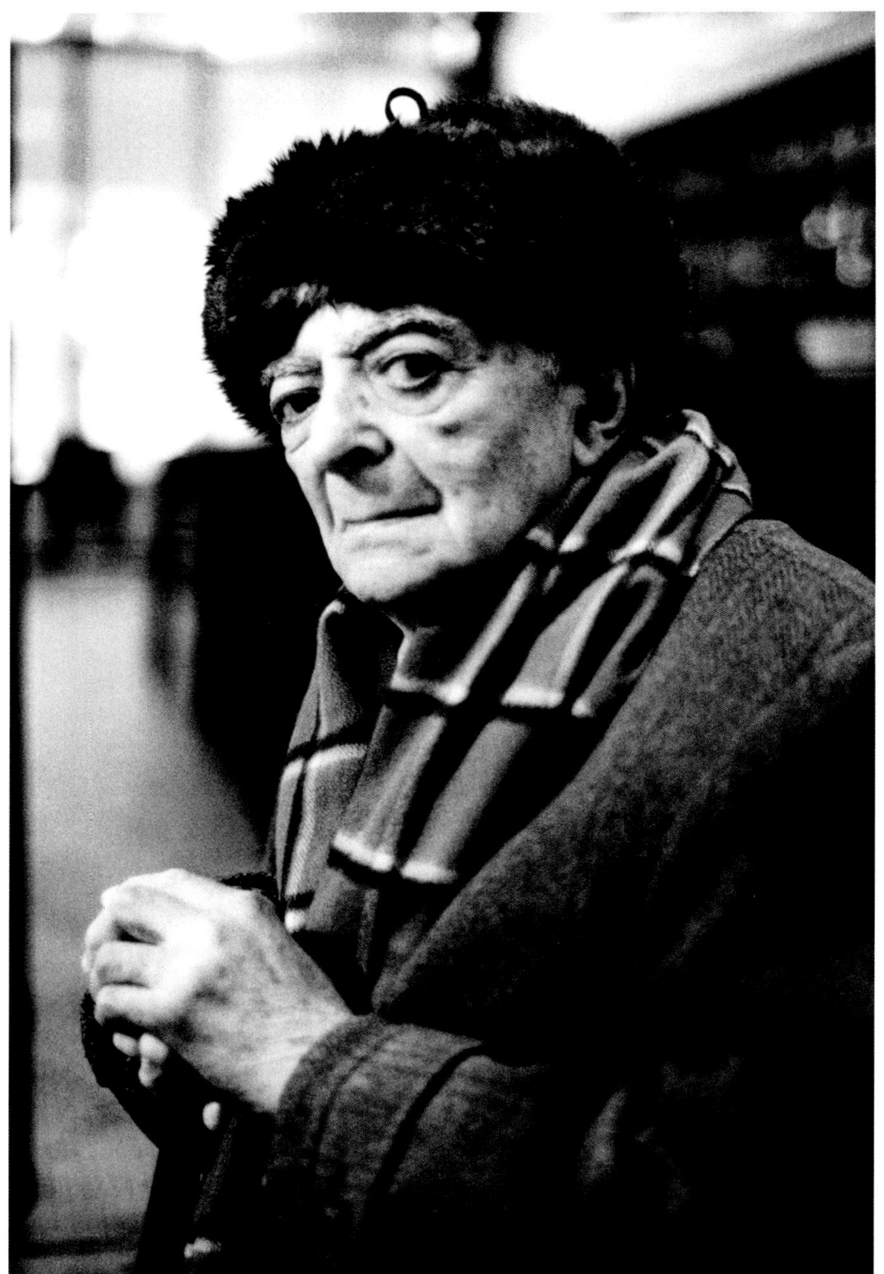

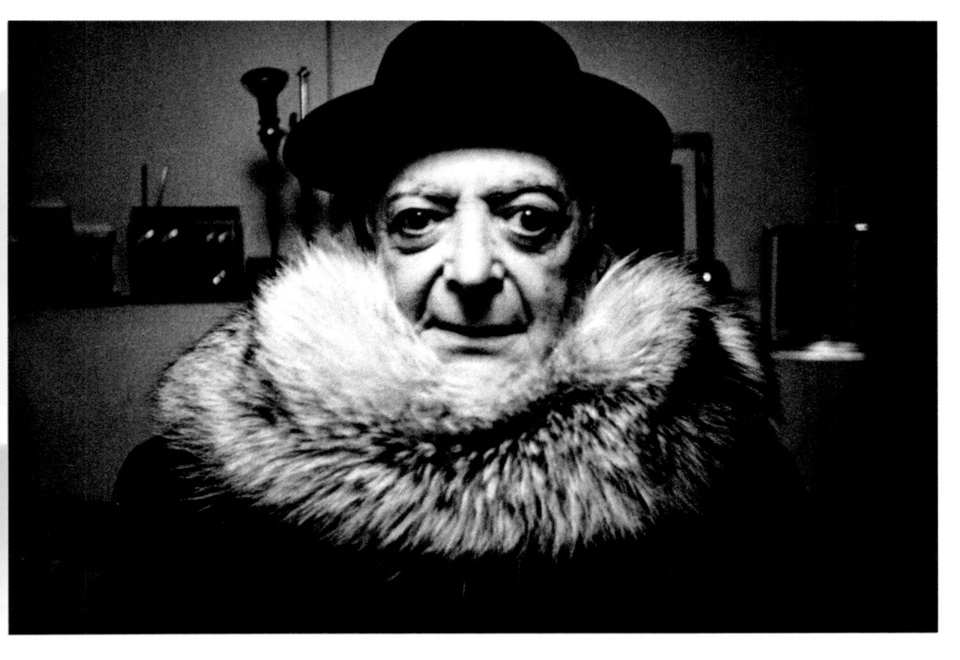

AS: Brassaï, Paris, 1982
HN: Brassaï, Paris, 1973

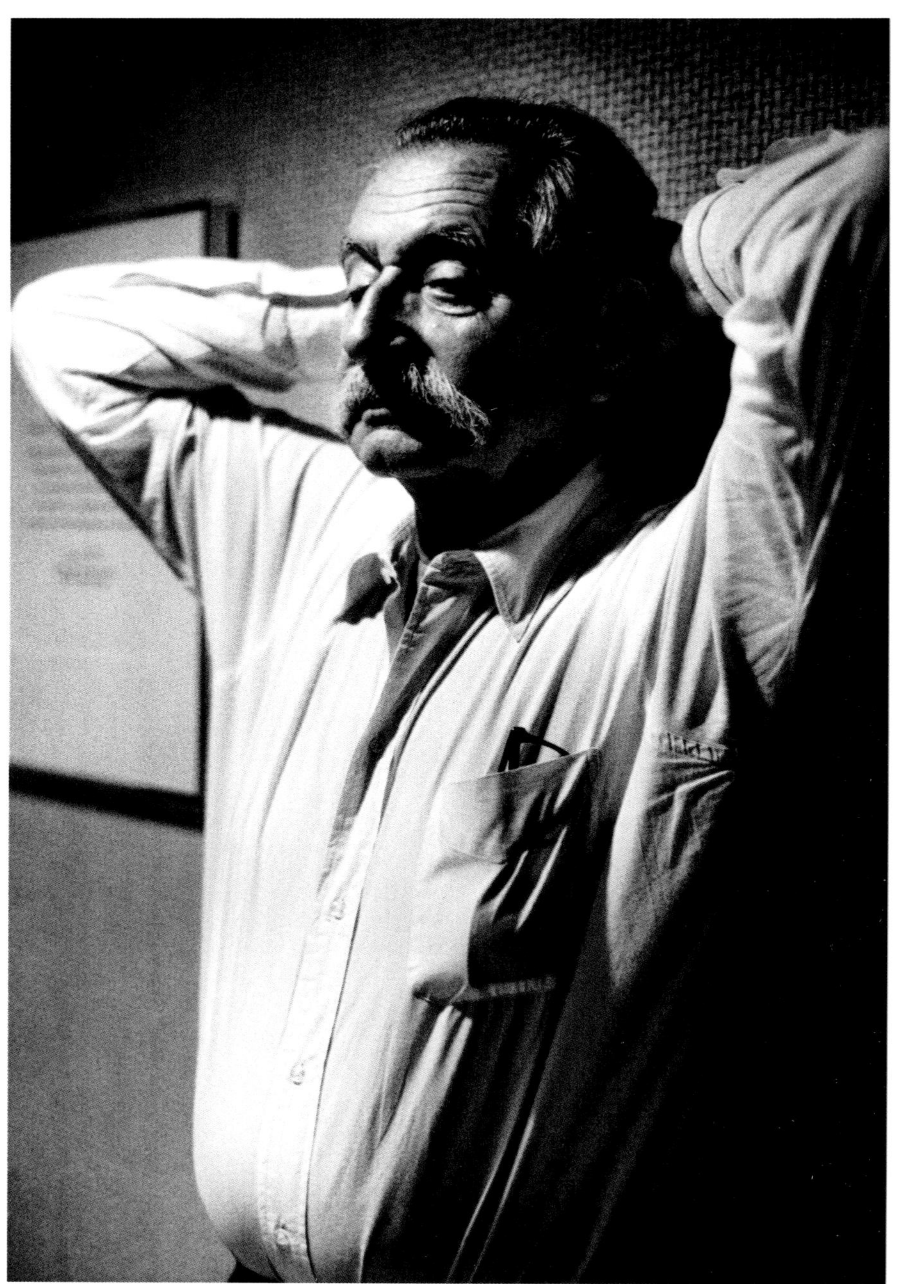

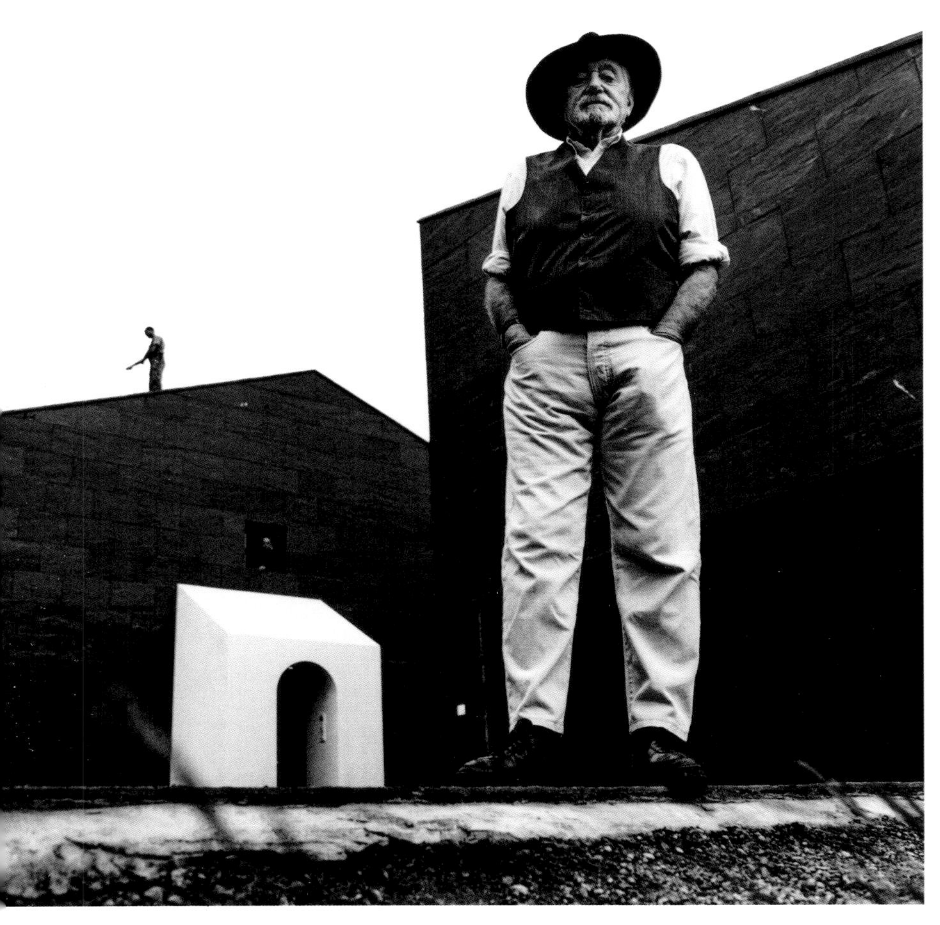

AS: Ettore Sottsass, Monte Carlo, 1990
HN: Ettore Sottsass, Zurich, 1997

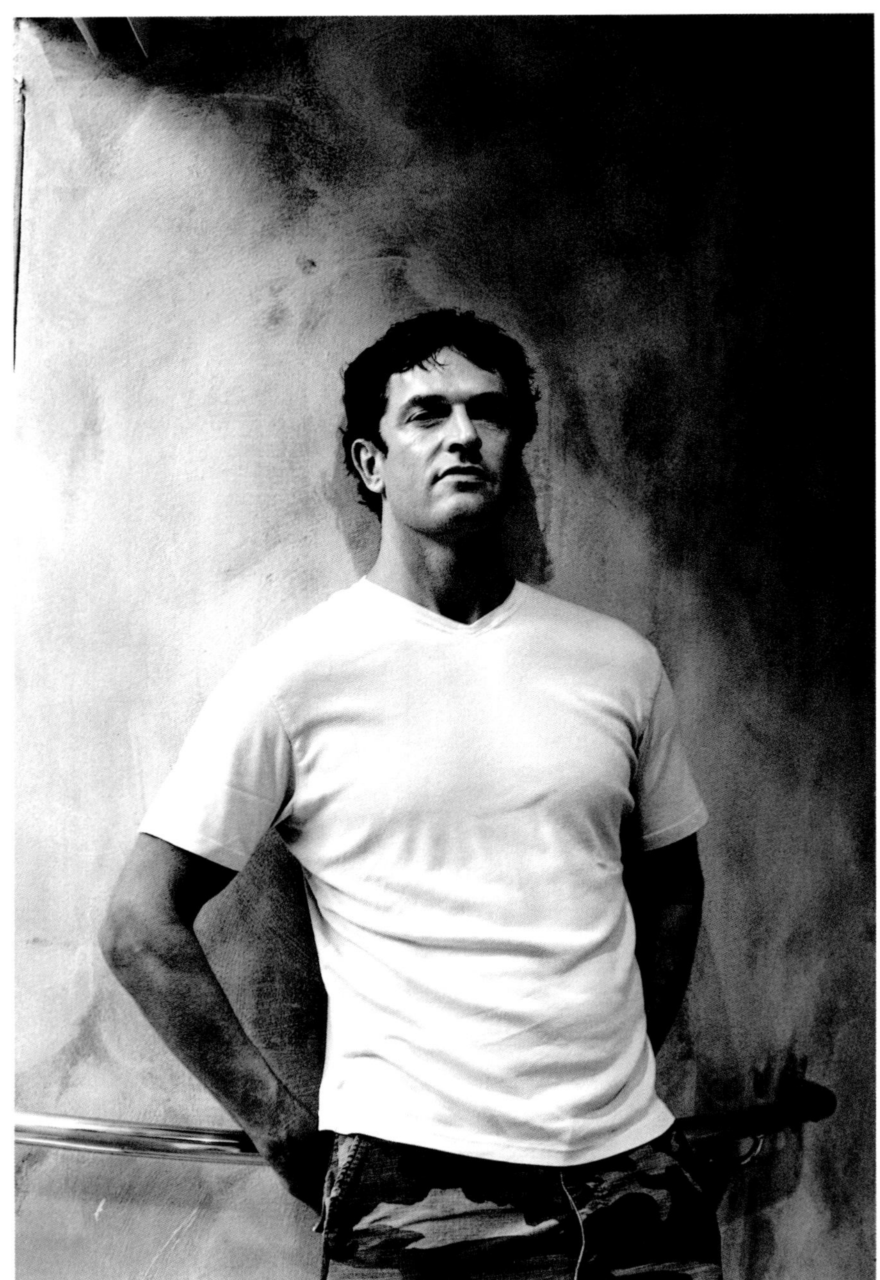

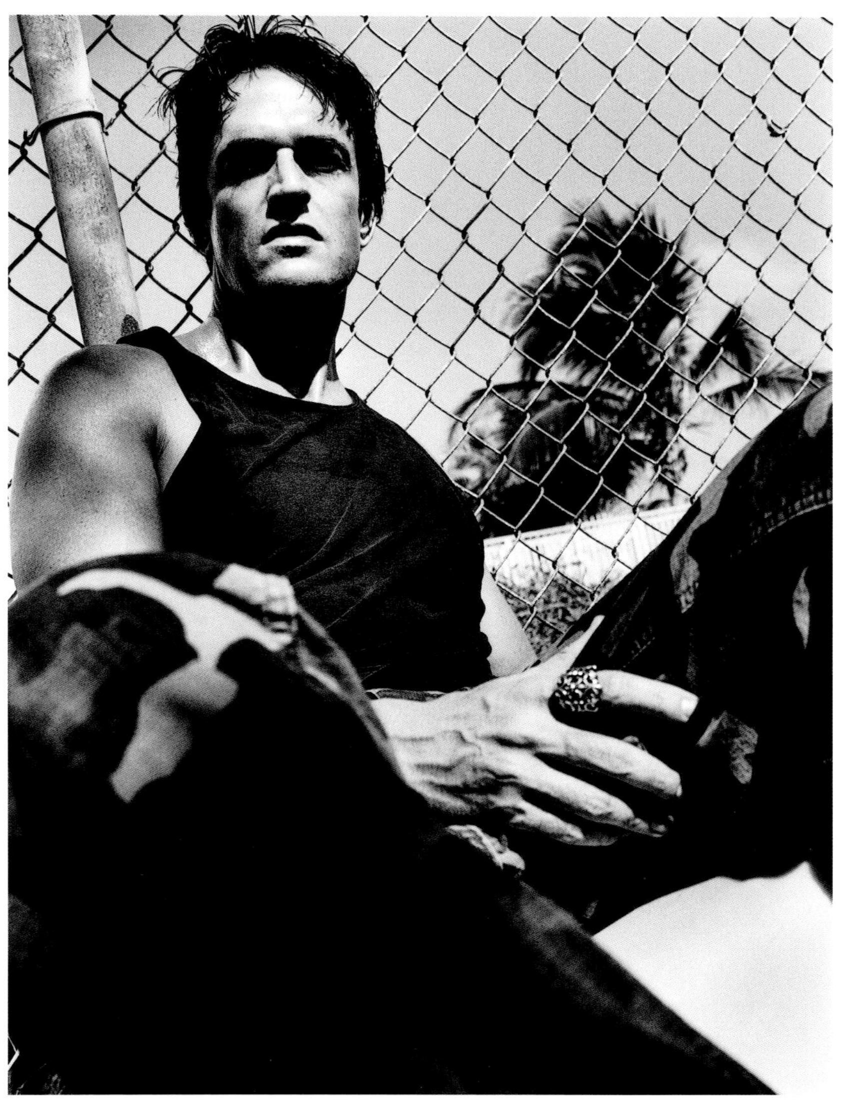

AS: Rupert Everett, Miami, 1999
HN: Rupert Everett, Miami, 1999

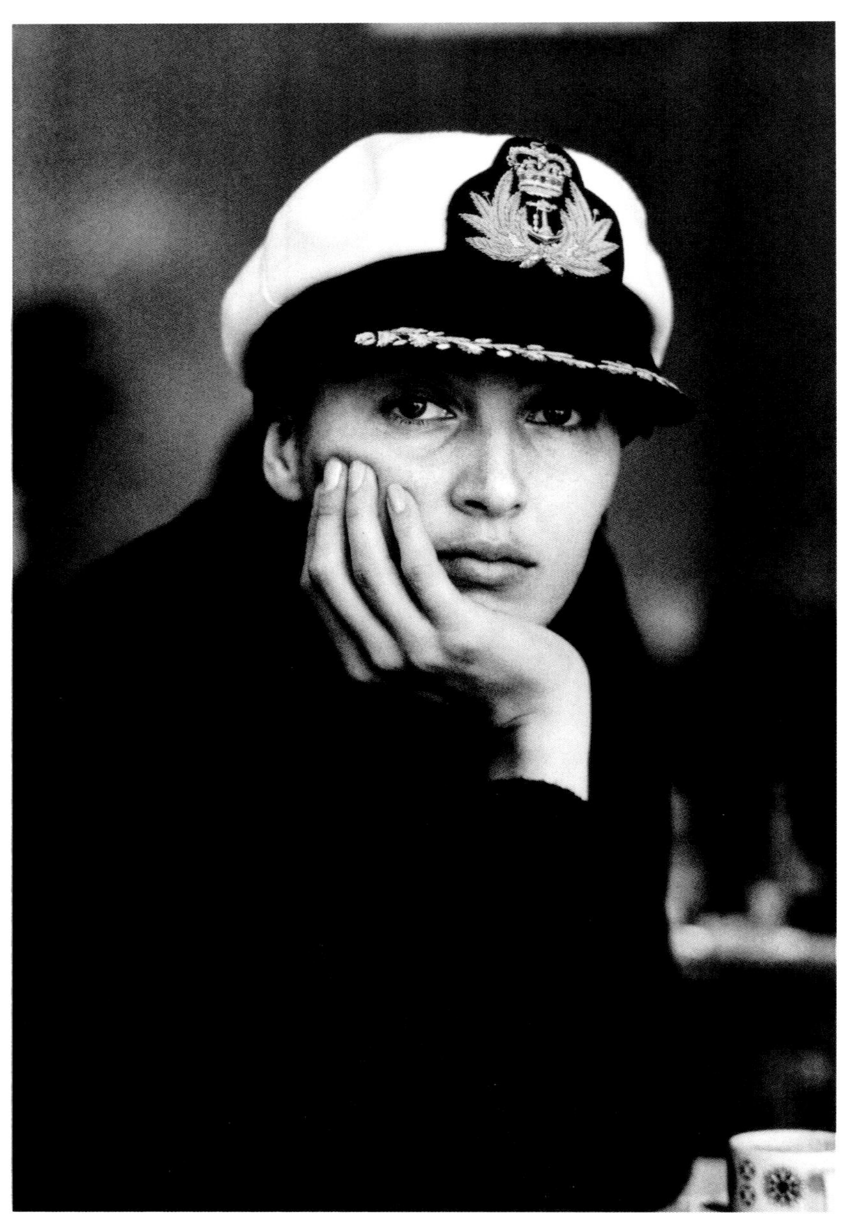

AS: Jenny Capitain, Paris, 1983
HN: Jenny Capitain, Venice, 1984

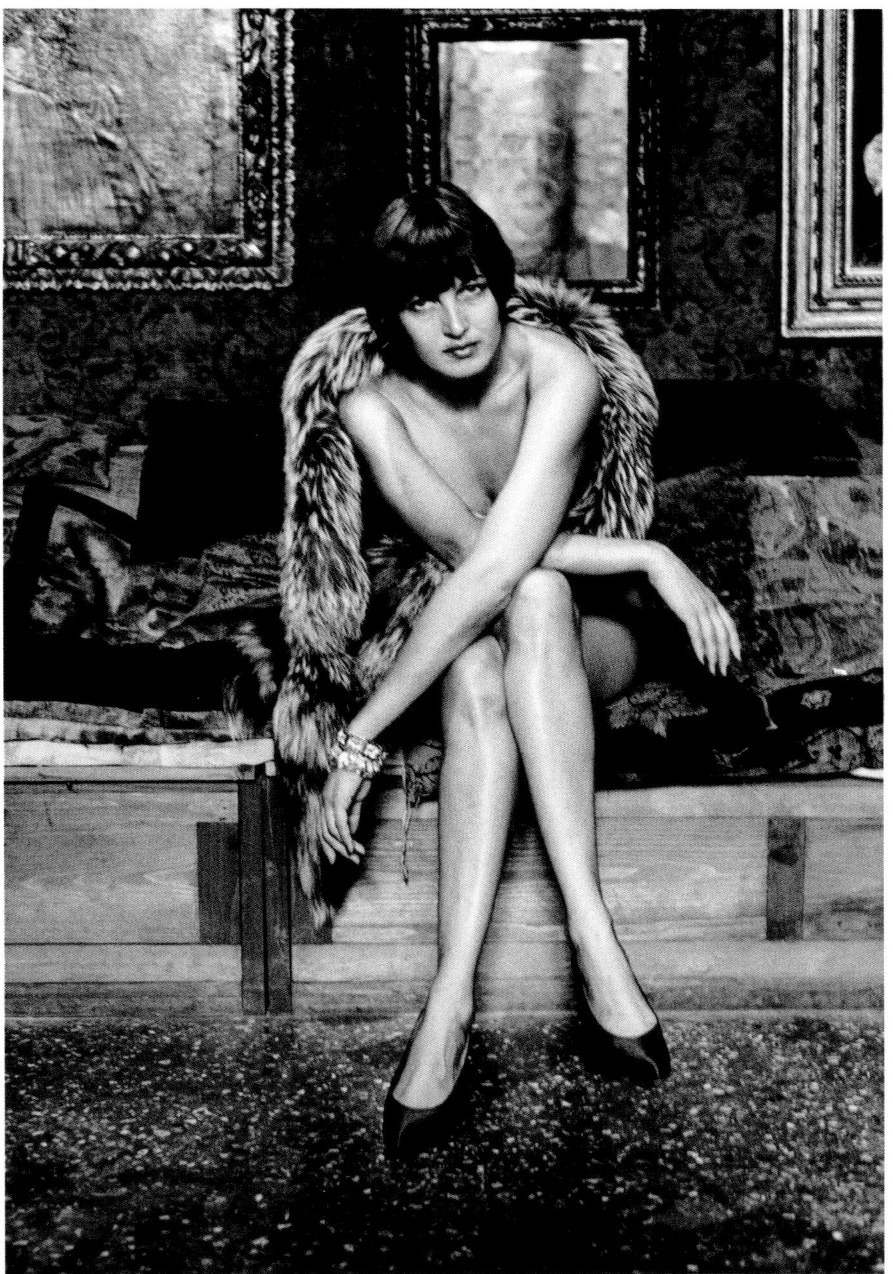

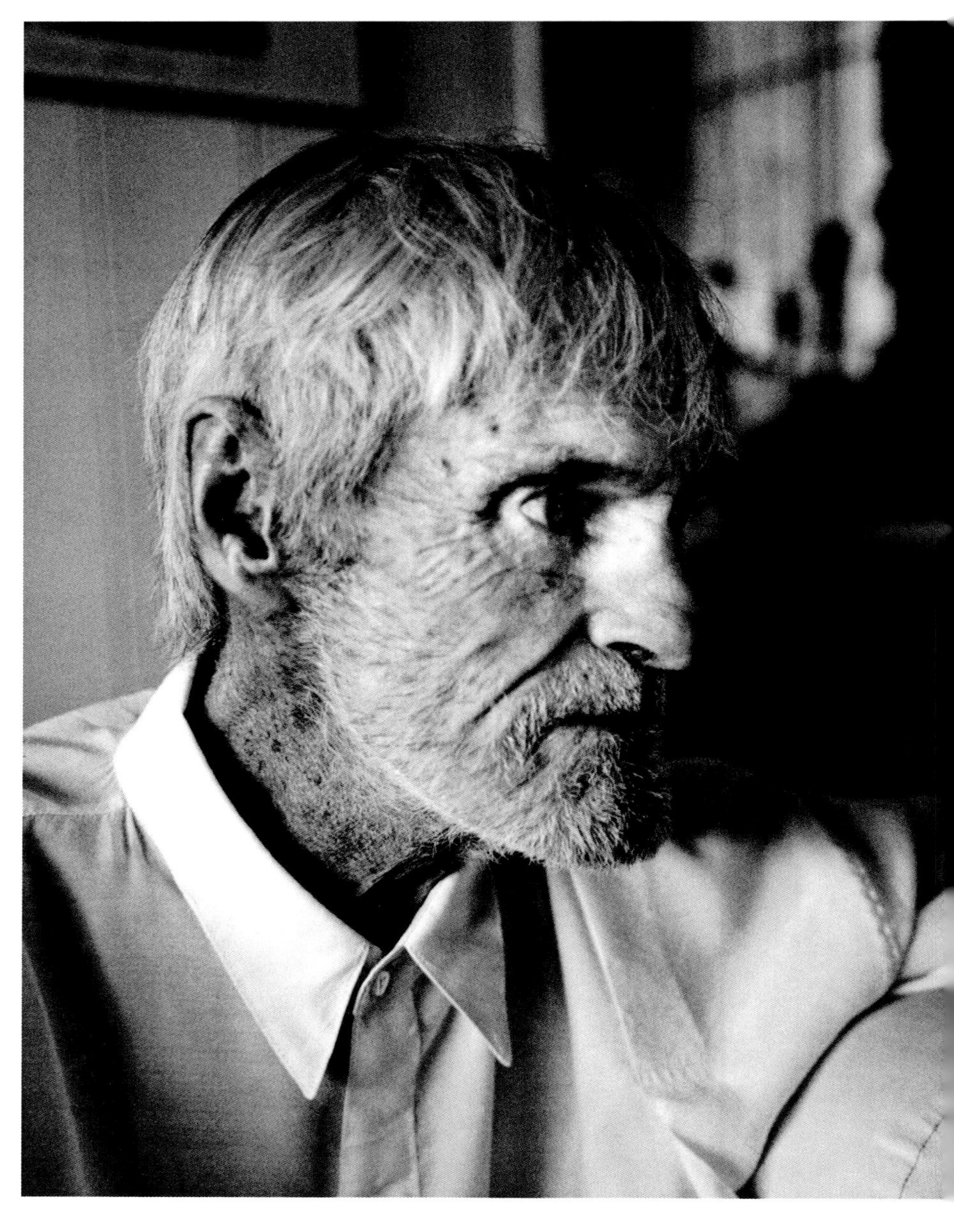

HN: Timothy Leary, Los Angeles, 1996
AS: Timothy Leary, Beverly Hills, 1996

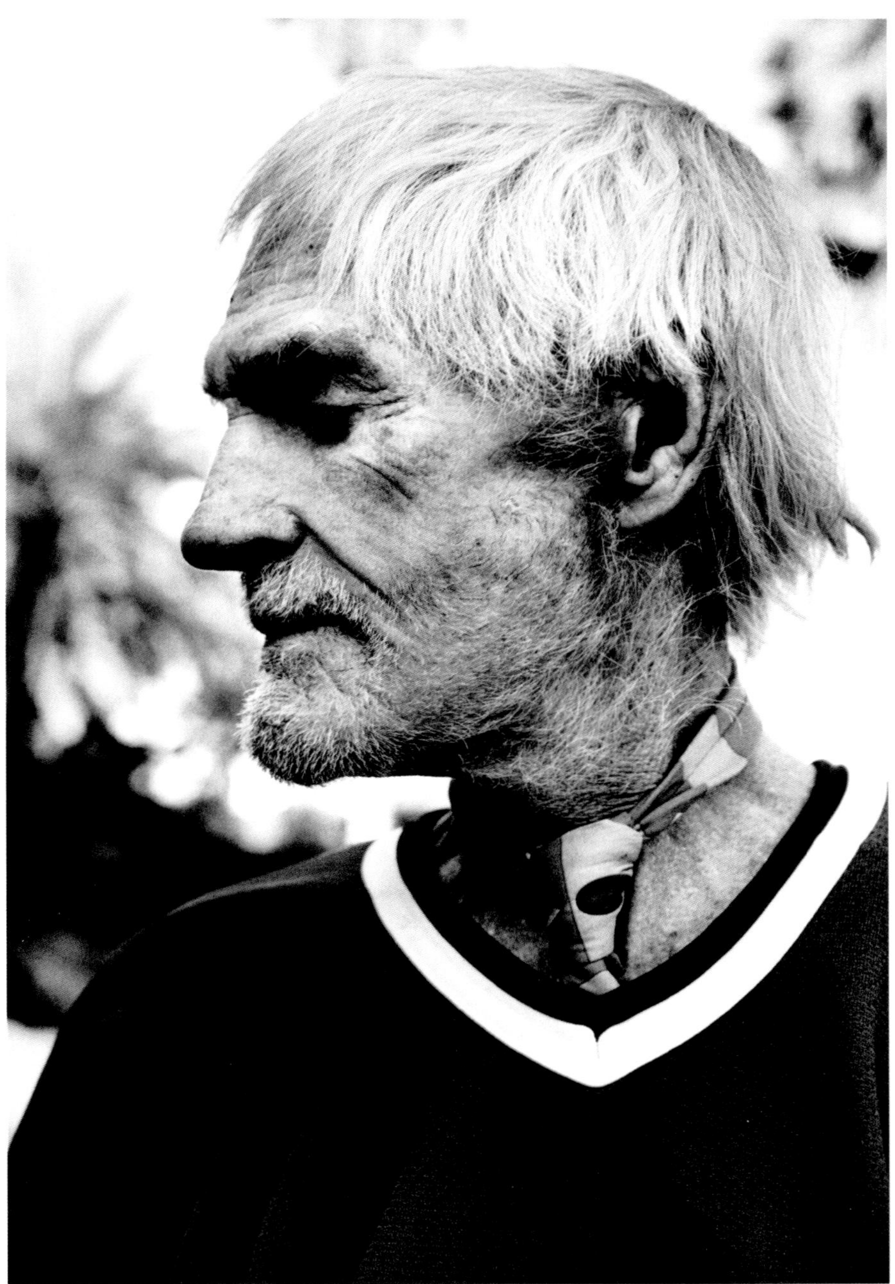

US AND THEM
IMAGES FROM A FIFTY-FIVE-YEAR
HISTORY OF LIFE AND LOVE

There had never been such a project and has not been one since: husband-and-wife photographers published very personal, even intimate, self-portraits and portraits of each other taken over several decades—and supplemented these private photographs with portraits of personalities and celebrities from the jet-set culture. That led to Scalo putting out the legendary publication *Us and Them* in 1998 and to the eponymous exhibition that accompanied it, shown in Copenhagen, Paris, Milan, São Paulo, and Cologne, among other places. Whereas Helmut and June Newton still personally organized those exhibitions in Europe and South America, June had to take over alone for the exhibition in Berlin, with which the Helmut Newton Foundation celebrated its opening in Berlin in June 2004. Helmut Newton had not lived to see it, having died in Los Angeles in January 2004. And so June Newton, who became the driving force behind bringing to a conclusion the Foundation's establishment, continued to develop their joint exhibition for Berlin and added some photographs of her own, including portraits of her husband on his deathbed. They were taken shortly after his fatal heart attack at the Chateau Marmont at Cedars-Sinai Medical Center in Los Angeles and several days later, at his wake at the Chateau Marmont.

Ten years later, *Us and Them* was presented again at the Foundation in Berlin, in a new hanging, accompanied by the reissuing of the eponymous publication by TASCHEN, which is followed now, in turn, by this new, revised edition. *Us and Them* is much more than a joint exhibition and book project. It is a kind of photographic diary that records the life that Helmut and June Newton shared in photographs they took of each other. There are also photographs of actors, artists, and other important cultural figures of the time, including Brassaï and Peter Beard, Yves Saint Laurent and Thierry Mugler, Dennis Hopper and Charlotte Rampling. The portraits taken by Helmut and June Newton in various sittings are presented side by side in pairs in the book and in the exhibition, thus revealing two facets of the same personality.

The eye of June Newton (1923–2021), who, under the pseudonym Alice Springs, created from 1970 a photographic oeuvre that is as autonomous as it is important, seems more private and more intimate than that of her husband, who always staged his subjects like a choreographer, with skillful lighting and selected accessories. Each portrait tells a complex and individual story, and the people in the black-and-white photographs approach us sometimes as private people and sometimes as public ones—with corresponding differences in emotional expression.

Alice Springs worked in three genres, like her husband: the portrait, the nude, and fashion or advertising photography, albeit with differences in emphasis. Her portraits in particular still leave an impression of great authenticity and intensity. Alice Springs first exhibited her portrait photographs in 1978 in Amsterdam; five years later, Editions du Regard in Paris published *Portraits* and followed it with other exhibition catalogues. In her impressive renderings of personalities, Alice Springs managed to capture not only the appearance but also the aura of the person portrayed. The wordless dialogue that led to extraordinary portraits seems to be based on kindred souls. This resulted in numerous photographs of people who are full of empathy, who still convey to their contemporaries a mix of sympathy and curiosity, which is why Alice Springs's work is still so interesting today. They include few studio portraits; the majority were taken in public spaces, usually with natural light, or in front of or in others' apartments. In these elegant portraits, taken quickly, spontaneously, and with simple camera techniques, we encounter both vain posing and natural self-confidence, open or shy facial expressions. The photographs thus become visual commentaries, interpretations of the person portrayed; Alice Springs let every sitter have his or her individuality. Again and again, she managed to add a new, unclichéd, and unusual likeness to a celebrity's already universally valid and famous image. Sometimes her profound knowledge of acting helped her look behind the façade of human expression when she was photographing.

Helmut Newton also began to turn to the genre of portraiture in the 1970s, in parallel with his commissioned work for fashion magazines, at first primarily in Paris. From the 1980s onward, when Helmut and June Newton were traveling regularly to Los Angeles to spend the winter months at the Chateau Marmont, they took numerous portraits of the "famous and infamous" in and around Hollywood, for magazines such as *Egoïste*, *Interview*, *Vanity Fair*, and *The New Yorker*. Helmut Newton had distinct empathy for situations and moods that very few of his colleagues could match. Famously, he avoided working in the studio, instead locating the shoots in the apartments or hotel rooms of those being portrayed. He was thus working on location. His own apartments in Paris and later in Monte Carlo also occasionally served as spartan stages for his subtle dramatizations. Or he used commercial spaces like those of the jeweler Gianni Bulgari, an editing room of the director Francis Ford Coppola, and, again and again, public spaces, including a forest backdrop for the actor Anthony Hopkins. The sitters played themselves or a role they themselves had chosen.

Helmut Newton also showed his portraits, most of which had been commissioned by magazines and were first published there, as photographic enlargements in museums and galleries in the 1980s, including in London, Paris, and Amsterdam, accompanied by exhibition catalogues. In 1987 he published his first book of photographs dedicated exclusively to his portraits, both in black-and-white and in color, with various publishing houses. One year later, he exhibited his portraits—together with those taken by his wife, yet shown independently in two solo exhibitions—at the National Portrait Gallery in London.

Then, in 1998, the joint project *Us and Them* followed, in book form and in accompanying exhibitions. It illustrates an incomparable story of fifty-five years of life and love, with the first part of *Us and Them* offering us a view of the photographers' private life. This publication thus closes the circle in several ways, because the life and work of Helmut and June Newton were linked in diverse ways. One is not possible without the other—and vice versa.

Matthias Harder

US AND THEM
BILDER EINER 55-JÄHRIGEN LEBENS-
UND LIEBESGESCHICHTE

Ein solches Projekt gab es vorher nicht und seitdem ebenso wenig: Ein Fotografen-Paar veröffentlicht sehr persönliche, ja intime Selbstporträts und gegenseitige Porträts, die über mehrere Jahrzehnte entstanden sind – und ergänzt die privaten Aufnahmen durch Bildnisse von Weggefährten und Prominenten aus dem kulturellen Jetset. So entstand 1998 bei Scalo die legendäre Publikation *Us and Them* sowie die gleichnamige begleitende Ausstellung, die u. a. in Kopenhagen, Paris, Mailand, São Paulo und Köln zu sehen war. Während Helmut und June Newton diese Ausstellungen in Europa und Südamerika noch persönlich eingerichtet hatten, musste June dies für die Ausstellung in Berlin, mit der die Helmut Newton Stiftung im Juni 2004 feierlich eröffnet wurde, allein übernehmen. Helmut Newton hatte die Eröffnung seiner Stiftung nicht mehr erleben können, da er im Januar 2004 in Los Angeles verstorben war. Und so hatte June Newton, die zur treibenden Kraft bei der Vollendung der Stiftungsgründung wurde, die gemeinsame Ausstellung in Berlin weiterentwickelt und mit einigen eigenen Fotografien ergänzt, u. a. mit den Porträts ihres Mannes auf dem Totenbett. Sie waren – kurz nach dessen tödlichem Herzinfarkt im Chateau Marmont – im Cedars-Sinai Medical Center in Los Angeles und einige Tage später rund um die Totenfeier im Chateau Marmont entstanden.

Zehn Jahre später wurde *Us and Them* in der Berliner Stiftung erneut präsentiert, in neuer Hängung und begleitet von der Wiederauflage der gleichnamigen Publikation bei TASCHEN, der nun wiederum diese erweiterte Neuauflage folgt. *Us and Them* ist weit mehr als ein gemeinsames Ausstellungs- und Buchprojekt. Es ist eine Art fotografisches Tagebuch, das das Zusammenleben von Helmut und June Newton in gegenseitigen Fotografien festhält; hinzu kommen Aufnahmen von Schauspieler:innen, Künstler:innen und anderen bedeutenden Kulturschaffenden der Zeit. Unter ihnen befinden sich Brassaï und Peter Beard, Yves Saint Laurent und Thierry Mugler, Dennis Hopper und Charlotte Rampling. Die von Helmut und June Newton bei unterschiedlichen Sitzungen aufgenommenen Porträts werden im Buch und in der Ausstellung als Bildpaare unmittelbar nebeneinander präsentiert und offenbaren so zwei Facetten derselben Persönlichkeit.

Der Blick June Newtons (1923–2021), die unter dem Pseudonym Alice Springs seit 1970 ein ebenso eigenständiges wie bedeutendes Bildwerk schuf, erscheint privater und intimer als der ihres Mannes, der die Porträtierten stets wie ein Choreograf mit geschickter Lichtregie und ausgewählten Accessoires inszenierte. Jedes Porträt erzählt eine komplexe und individuelle Geschichte, und die Menschen auf den Schwarz-Weiß-Aufnahmen begegnen uns mal als private und mal als öffentliche Person – mit entsprechend unterschiedlichem emotionalem Ausdruck.

Alice Springs hat wie ihr Ehemann in drei Genres gearbeitet: Porträt, Akt und Mode respektive Werbefotografie, allerdings mit unterschiedlicher Gewichtung. Vor allem ihre Porträts wirken bis heute mit großer Authentizität und Intensität nach. Ihre Porträtfotografien stellte Alice Springs erstmals 1978 in Amsterdam aus, fünf Jahre später folgten die Publikation *Portraits* bei Editions du Regard in Paris und danach weitere Ausstellungskataloge. Mit ihren eindrucksvollen

Persönlichkeitsschilderungen gelang es Alice Springs nicht nur, das Aussehen der Dargestellten einzufangen, sondern auch deren Aura. Der wortlose Dialog, der zu den außergewöhnlichen Porträts führte, scheint auf einer Art Seelenverwandtschaft zu beruhen. So entstanden zahlreiche Menschenbilder voller Empathie, die noch immer die Mischung aus Einfühlung und Neugierde auf ihre Zeitgenossen transportieren, die das Werk von Alice Springs bis heute so interessant macht. Nur wenige Studioporträts sind darunter, die Mehrzahl entstand – meist bei natürlichem Licht – im öffentlichen Raum sowie vor oder in den Wohnungen der Dargestellten. In den eleganten Bildnissen, die schnell, spontan und mit einfacher Kameratechnik entstanden, begegnen uns abwechselnd eitle Posen oder ein natürliches Selbstbewusstsein, ein offenes oder schüchternes Mienenspiel. So werden die Aufnahmen zu visuellen Kommentaren, zu Interpretationen der Dargestellten, jedem und jeder Einzelnen ließ Alice Springs seine respektive ihre Individualität. Dabei gelang es ihr immer wieder, dem allgemeingültigen und bekannten Image der Prominenten ein klischeefreies, neues und ungewöhnliches Abbild hinzuzufügen. Möglicherweise half ihr die tiefe Kenntnis des Schauspiels, beim Fotografieren gleichzeitig auf und hinter die Fassade des menschlichen Ausdrucks zu schauen.

Helmut Newton begann, sich in den 1970er-Jahren ebenfalls dem Genre Porträt zuzuwenden, parallel zu seinen Auftragsarbeiten für die Modemagazine, zunächst vor allem in Paris. Ab 1980, als Helmut und June Newton regelmäßig nach Los Angeles reisten, um im Chateau Marmont die Wintermonate zu verbringen, kamen zahlreiche Porträts der ‚Berühmten und Berüchtigten‘ in und um Hollywood hinzu, entstanden für Zeitschriften wie *Egoïste*, *Interview*, *Vanity Fair* oder *The New Yorker*. Wie nur wenigen seiner Kollegen ist Helmut Newton ein ausgeprägtes Gespür für Situationen und Stimmungen zu eigen.

Dabei vermied er es bekanntlich, im Studio zu arbeiten, stattdessen verlegte er die Aufnahmen in die Wohnungen oder Hotelzimmer der zu Porträtierenden. Er arbeitete also *on location*. Auch die eigenen Wohnungen in Paris oder später in Monte Carlo funktionierte er gelegentlich zu einer spartanischen Bühne für seine subtilen Inszenierungen um. Oder er nutzte Geschäftsräume wie beim Juwelier Gianni Bulgari, einen Schneideraum beim Regisseur Francis Ford Coppola und immer wieder den öffentlichen Raum, inklusive einer Waldkulisse wie für den Schauspieler Anthony Hopkins. Die Porträtierten spielen sich gewissermaßen selbst oder eine selbst gewählte Rolle.

Auch Helmut Newton zeigte seine Porträts, die zumeist im Auftrag der Magazine entstanden und dort erstmals veröffentlicht wurden, in den 1980er-Jahren als fotografische Vergrößerungen in Museen und Galerien, unter anderem in London, Paris und Amsterdam, begleitet von Ausstellungskatalogen. 1987 veröffentlichte er einen ersten Bildband, der allein seinen Porträts in Schwarz-Weiß und Farbe gewidmet war, in unterschiedlichen Verlagen. Und ein Jahr später stellte er seine Bildnisse – gemeinsam mit seiner Frau und zugleich autonom, nämlich in zwei Einzelpräsentationen – in der Londoner National Portrait Gallery aus.

1998 folgte dann das gemeinsame Projekt *Us and Them*, in Buchform und als begleitende Ausstellungen. Es visualisiert eine unvergleichliche 55-jährige Lebens- und Liebesgeschichte, so blicken wir im ersten Teil von *Us and Them* auch in das Privatleben des Fotografenpaars. So schließt sich der Kreis gleich mehrfach in dieser Publikation, denn das Leben und das Werk von Helmut und June Newton waren auf vielfältigste Weise miteinander verknüpft. Die eine ist ohne den anderen nicht denkbar – und umgekehrt.

Matthias Harder

US AND THEM
IMAGES D'UNE HISTOIRE D'AMOUR ET D'UNE VIE COMMUNE DE 55 ANS

Un tel projet n'a jamais existé, ni avant ni depuis. Un couple de photographes publie des auto-portraits et des portraits mutuels, très personnels, voire intimes, réalisés sur plusieurs décennies, et complète ces clichés privés par des portraits de compagnons de route et de célébrités de la jet-set. C'est ainsi qu'ont vu le jour en 1998 l'ouvrage légendaire *Us and Them* paru chez Scalo et l'exposition homonyme qui l'accompagnait et qui fut notamment présentée à Copenhague, Paris, Milan, São Paulo et Cologne. Alors qu'Helmut et June Newton avaient organisé personnellement ces expositions en Europe et en Amérique latine, June a dû assumer seule cette tâche pour l'exposition inaugurale de la Fondation Helmut Newton présentée en juin 2004 à Berlin, Helmut Newton étant décédé en janvier 2004 à Los Angeles. Devenue la force motrice de l'inauguration, June Newton a poursuivi seule la conception de l'exposition commune à Berlin, la complétant de quelques photographies personnelles – notamment les portraits de son mari sur son lit de mort. Ces photos avaient été prises au Cedars-Sinai Medical Center à Los Angeles peu après l'infarctus fatal d'Helmut à l'hôtel Château Marmont, et quelques jours plus tard lors de la cérémonie funéraire dans ce même hôtel.

Dix ans plus tard, *Us and Them* était présenté une deuxième fois à la Fondation à Berlin, dans un nouvel accrochage et accompagné de la réédition de la publication homonyme chez TASCHEN, suivie à son tour par la présente réédition révisée. *Us and Them* est bien plus qu'un projet d'exposition et de livre communs. C'est une sorte de journal photographique qui retrace la vie commune d'Helmut et June Newton à travers des photographies réciproques, auxquelles s'ajoutent des clichés d'actrices et d'acteurs, d'artistes et d'autres figures de la culture de l'époque. L'on y trouve notamment Brassaï et Peter Beard, Yves Saint Laurent et Thierry Mugler, Dennis Hopper et Charlotte Rampling. Les portraits réalisés en sessions séparées sont présentés en regard comme des diptyques, révélant ainsi deux facettes de la même personnalité.

Le regard de June Newton (1923–2021), qui, sous le pseudonyme d'Alice Springs, a créé à partir de 1970 une œuvre picturale aussi autonome qu'importante, présente un côté plus privé, plus intime que celui de son mari qui, tel un chorégraphe doublé d'un habile éclairagiste, a toujours mis en scène ses modèles avec des accessoires soigneusement choisis. Chaque portrait raconte ainsi une histoire complexe et individuelle, et les personnes photographiées en noir et blanc nous apparaissent tantôt en tant que personnes privées, tantôt en tant que personnes publiques – avec des expressions différentes sur le plan émotionnel. Tout comme son mari, Alice Springs a travaillé dans trois genres : portrait, nu et mode ou photographie publicitaire, il est vrai répartis différemment. Ses portraits, en particulier, ont conservé une grande authenticité et intensité. Alice Springs a exposé ses photographies de portraits pour la première fois en 1978 à Amsterdam, qui feront cinq ans plus tard l'objet du livre *Portraits* aux Éditions du Regard à Paris avant de donner, par la suite, d'autres catalogues d'exposition. Avec ses impressionnantes approches de chaque personnalité, Alice Springs n'a pas seulement réussi à capturer ses modèles sur le plan physique, mais aussi leur aura. Le dialogue muet qui a conduit à ses portraits remarquables semble reposer sur une sorte d'affinité d'âme. Ainsi ont vu le jour de nombreuses images pleines d'empathie : elles véhiculent toujours ce mélange particulier de perception intuitive et de curiosité envers les autres qui rend l'œuvre d'Alice Springs si intéressante aujourd'hui encore. Rares sont les portraits faits en studio : la plupart l'ont été dans l'espace public, le plus souvent en lumière naturelle, mais aussi devant ou à l'intérieur du domicile des modèles. Dans ces portraits pleins d'élégance, réalisés rapidement, spontanément, sans sophistication technique, nous trouvons aussi bien des poses vaniteuses qu'une présence naturelle, un jeu d'expression ouvert ou réservé. Les photographies se présentent dès lors comme des commentaires visuels, les interprétations de personnes représentées, dont Alice Springs a, chaque fois, préservé l'individualité. À l'image reçue et connue des célébrités, la photographe a ainsi su ajouter chaque fois une représentation inédite, inattendue et exempte de tout cliché. Il se peut qu'à l'heure de photographier, sa profonde connaissance du jeu d'acteur l'ait aidée à voir simultanément les deux côtés de la façade de l'expression humaine.

Helmut Newton a lui aussi commencé à se tourner vers le portrait dans les années 1970, parallèlement à ses travaux de commande pour des magazines de mode, au début surtout à Paris. À partir de 1980, alors qu'Helmut et June Newton se rendent régulièrement à Los Angeles pour passer l'hiver à Château Marmont, ils réalisent de nombreux portraits de « célébrités » à Hollywood et dans les environs, pour des magazines comme *Égoïste*, *Interview*, *Vanity Fair* ou *The New Yorker*. Comme peu de ses collègues, Helmut Newton avait un sens aigu des situations et des ambiances. On sait qu'il évitait de travailler en studio, préférant les séances dans les appartements ou les chambres d'hôtel de ses modèles. Il travaillait donc in situ. Il lui arrivait aussi de transformer ses appartements – à Paris ou plus tard à Monte-Carlo – en cadre spartiate de mises en scène raffinées. Ou bien il exploitait des espaces de vente, comme celui du joaillier Gianni Bulgari, une salle de montage chez le réalisateur Francis Ford Coppola, et régulièrement l'espace public, notamment un décor de forêt comme pour l'acteur Anthony Hopkins. Les modèles jouent en quelque sorte leur propre rôle, ou celui qu'ils se sont choisi. Dans les années 1980, Helmut Newton a exposé ses portraits – pour la plupart commandés par des magazines et publiés pour la première fois dans ces derniers – sous forme d'agrandissements photographiques dans des musées et des galeries, notamment à Londres, Paris et Amsterdam, accompagnés de catalogues d'exposition. En 1987, Newton a publié chez différents éditeurs internationaux son premier livre entièrement consacré à ses portraits en noir et blanc et en couleurs. Un an plus tard, ses portraits figureraient à la National Portrait Gallery à Londres – avec ceux de sa femme et séparément, c'est-à-dire dans deux présentations spécifiques.

En 1998, le projet commun *Us and Them* verra le jour – sous forme de livre et d'expositions. Il dévoile 55 ans d'une incomparable histoire d'amour et de vie commune – la première partie d'*Us and Them* nous fait découvrir la vie privée du couple de photographes. Avec la présente publication, la boucle est donc bouclée à plus d'un titre, car la vie et l'œuvre d'Helmut et June Newton ont été liées de multiples façons. L'une est impensable sans l'autre – et inversement.

Matthias Harder

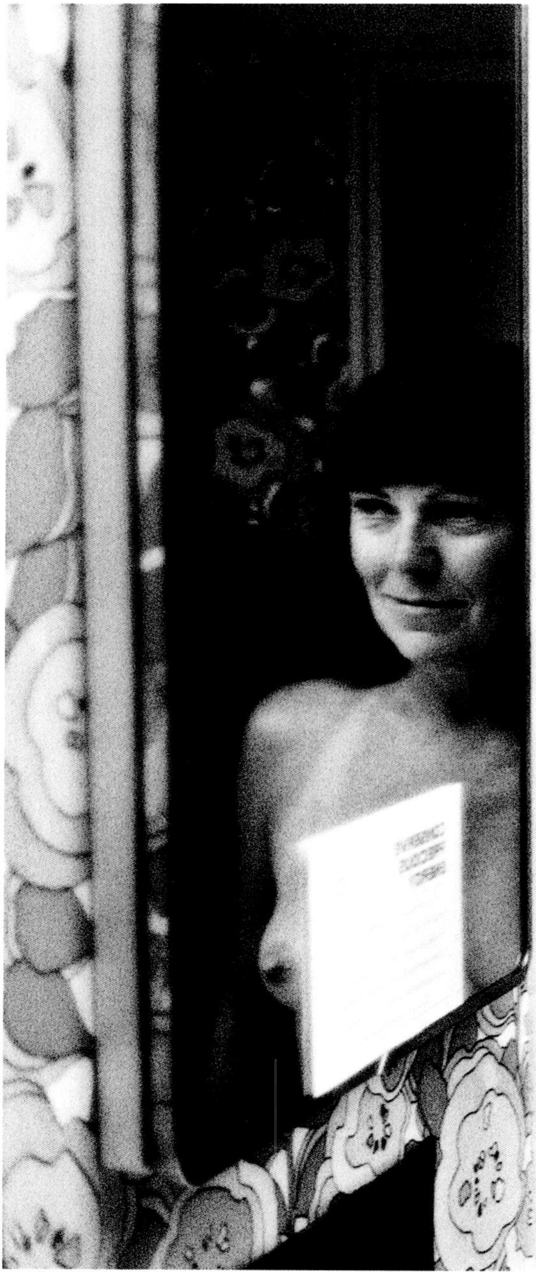

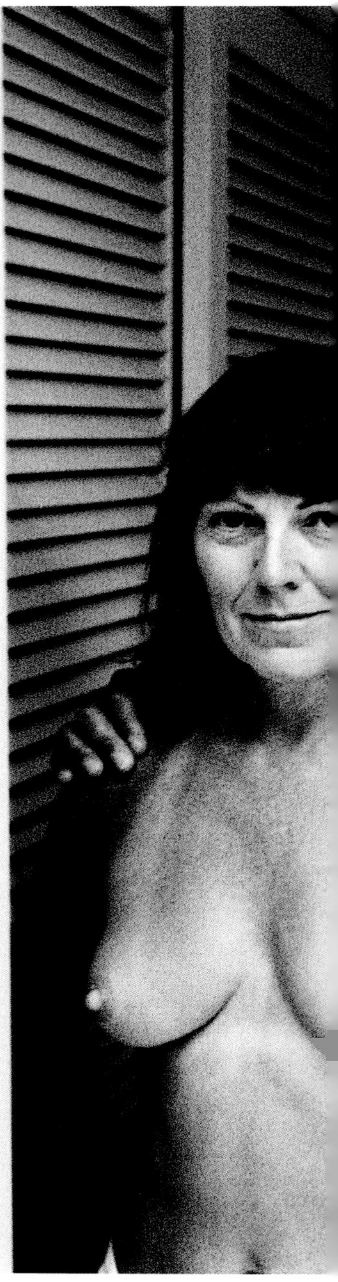

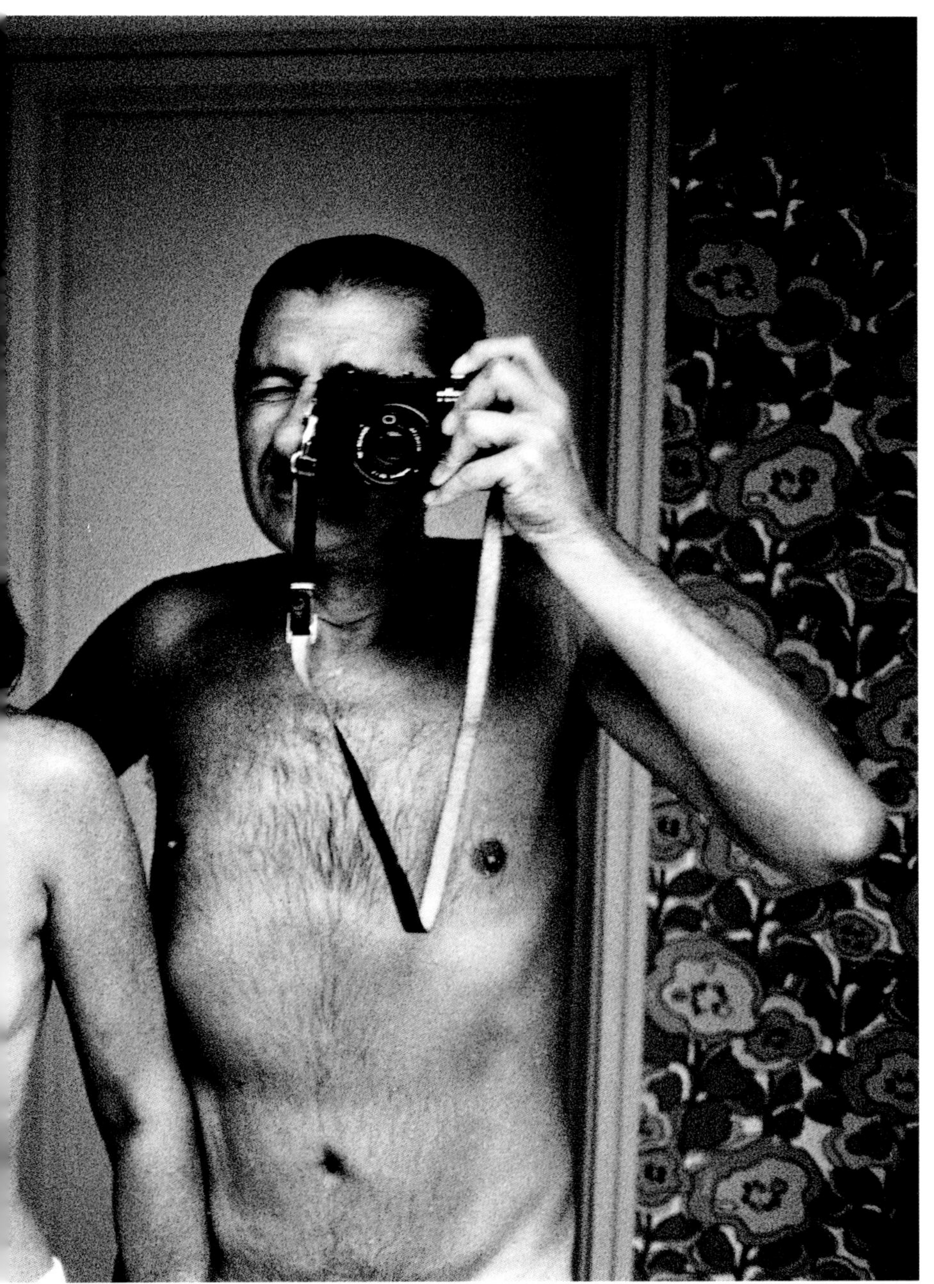

FRONT COVER AS: Helmut with models Myka,
Nina, and Annie, Monte Carlo, August 1997
PAGE 2 AS: Chateau Marmont, Hollywood, 1991
PAGE 4 HN: Ramatuelle, 1976
PAGES 190/191 HN: Paris, 1974
BACK COVER HN: In our kitchen, Rue Aubriot,
Paris, 1972

**EACH AND EVERY TASCHEN BOOK
PLANTS A SEED!**
TASCHEN is a carbon neutral publisher. Each
year, we offset our annual carbon emissions
with carbon credits at the Instituto Terra, a
reforestation program in Minas Gerais, Brazil,
founded by Lélia and Sebastião Salgado. To
find out more about this ecological partnership,
please check: www.taschen.com/zerocarbon.
Inspiration: unlimited. Carbon footprint: zero.

To stay informed about TASCHEN and our
upcoming titles, please subscribe to our free
magazine at www.taschen.com/magazine, follow
us on Instagram and Facebook, or e-mail your
questions to contact@taschen.com.

© 2023 TASCHEN GmbH
Hohenzollernring 53, D–50672 Köln
www.taschen.com

© 2023 Helmut Newton Foundation, Berlin

EDITOR June Newton, Monte Carlo
ENGLISH TRANSLATION Steven Lindberg, Berlin
GERMAN TRANSLATION Harald Hellmann, Cologne
FRENCH TRANSLATION Alice Petillot, Paris;
Wolf Fruhtrunk, Villeneuve-Saint-Georges

Printed in Italy
ISBN 978–3–8365–9691–6